DATE DUE

AFFECT AND ATTACHMENT IN THE FAMILY

Jeri A. Doane, Ph.D., is a Clinical Professor of Psychiatry at the UCLA School of Medicine and the West Los Angeles VA Medical Center, and is in private practice in West Los Angeles. Diana Diamond, Ph.D., is an Associate Professor in the doctoral program in clinical psychology at the City University of New York and an Adjunct Clinical Professor at the New York Hospital–Cornell Medical Center. Dr. Diamond is also in private practice in New York City.

AFFECT AND ATTACHMENT IN THE FAMILY

A FAMILY-BASED TREATMENT OF MAJOR PSYCHIATRIC DISORDER

Jeri A. Doane, Ph.D.,
AND
Diana Diamond, Ph.D.

BasicBooks
A Division of HarperCollins*Publishers*

The authors gratefully acknowledge the *British Journal of Psychiatry* for permission to reproduce figure 4.5, "Disturbed (High Risk) Intergenerational Attachment as a Predictor of Parental Negative Affective Style After Three Months of Treatment."

Designed by Ellen Levine

Library of Congress Cataloging-in-Publication Data

Affect and attachment in the family : a family-based
    treatment of major psychiatric disorder / Jeri A. Doane
    and Diana Diamond.
        p.   cm.
    Includes bibliographical references and index.
    ISBN 0-465-00536-5
    1. Mentally ill—Family relationships—Longitudinal
studies.   2. Family psychotherapy.   3. Family—Mental
health.   4. Intergenerational relations—Longitudinal
studies.   5. Attachment behavior.   6. Parent and child.
I. Doane, Jeri A., 1946–   .   II. Diamond, Diana, 1948–   .
RC455.4.F3A39   1994
616.89—dc20   93–40018
                                                                    CIP

94 95 96 97 ◆ /HC 9 8 7 6 5 4 3 2 1

This book is dedicated to Dorothy Sheldon Doane,
to Olga Senuk Diamond,
and to the memory of Stanley Roman Diamond

Our minds are like vast, neglected historical museums—here barely lit, there flooded with radiance—filled for the most part with figures of our selves and our important "others" from every period of our past.

—Leonard Shengold, *Soul Murder: The*
Effects of Childhood Abuse and Deprivation

A thing which has not been understood inevitably reappears; like an unlaid ghost, it cannot rest until the mystery has been resolved and the spell broken.

—Sigmund Freud, *Analysis of a Phobia in a*
Five-Year-Old Boy

Contents

Acknowledgments

WE ARE GRATEFUL to many people who made this work possible. First, we express gratitude to Drs. Ira Levine and Gary Tischler, whose clinical and administrative support for this research was indispensable in implementing the research project on the inpatient wards of the Yale Psychiatric Institute (YPI) in New Haven, Connecticut. In the same vein, we feel fortunate to have been able to work and study in the intellectually and clinically challenging atmosphere that Drs. Ira Levine, Charles Gardner, and Gary Tischler created for their faculty. Their leadership at YPI spawned an extraordinary combination of scholarly pursuit in an atmosphere of rich clinical practice, which fostered the kind of research and clinical thinking reflected in this book.

A special debt is owed to Drs. Ted Lidz and Stephen Fleck for their pioneering research on family dynamics of severely disturbed YPI patients, which set the tone for the scholarly work in the area of family factors in severe psychopathology for a whole generation.

Special appreciation is due to Drs. Daniel Becker and Rebecca Johnston, who worked on the project tirelessly and provided us with helpful insights along the way. We especially want to acknowledge Dr. Rebecca Johnston, who brought her remarkable clinical acumen to designing and carrying out the followup interviews. We are also grateful to Leonard Hill for his conceptual contributions to the project. The YPI clinical staff provided us with many hours of their time during the data collection phases of the project.

Without the cooperation of our patients and their families this book would never have been written. The families in our study generously and courageously opened their souls to us in ways that allowed us to learn about the most essential and often difficult aspects of their family histories. Their commitment to advancing knowledge for the treatment of severe psychiatric disorders made possible this type of deep exploration into family life. Without exception, our families provided us with many hours of their time and with an extraordinarily candid portrait of their thoughts and feelings about what they were experiencing as the study unfolded.

We want to thank our gifted clinical mentors and teachers who have shaped the way we think and practice: Drs. Ann Appelbaum, Sidney Blatt, Stephen Fleck, Charles Gardner, Christoph Heinicke, Ira Levine, Ted Lidz, Harold Raush, Herb Schlesinger, Rodney J. Shapiro, and Lyman Wynne. Dr. Doane would like to give special thanks to Dr. Michael Goldstein, who is not only a gifted researcher but also a gifted teacher of research. Dr. Diamond, in turn, would like to give special thanks to Drs. Doane and Blatt for providing her with superb research mentorship and training when Dr. Diamond was a postdoctoral fellow at Yale. Thanks to Dr. Doane for her generative encouragement of the intergenerational work. The passing on of research mentorship creates an intergenerational aspect of our work that mirrors the study itself.

We are deeply indebted to Martha Loukides Walker, who was the project coordinator on the study. Her extraordinary abilities in managing the day-to-day operations of the project made working on the project a pleasure. Her intelligence, professionalism, and consistent, steady hand were indispensable for managing such a complex study.

Thanks are due to Linda Schwartz, our administrative assistant and secretary, who typed hundreds of documents for us. Thanks also to Nina Huza and Lillian Conklin, who typed the manuscript for this book.

We are grateful to our editors at Basic Books, Jo Ann Miller and Stephen Francoeur, for their appreciation of the complexities of treating major mental disorder and writing about sensitive clinical material. We thank them also for their comprehension of and patience with the difficulties inherent in bicoastal authorship.

We thank our special friends and family who have sustained us with their solace, humor, and moral support over the years of this project: Rebecca Behrends, Nicole Gilbert, Ralph Hoffman, Julie Holmes, Leslie Hyman, Melanie Katzman, Gretchen Law, Martha Lewis, Christine McGill, Catherine Portuges, Tanya Priber, Valerie Rubinstein Von Raffay, Roger Weisburg, and Frank Yeomans.

Dr. Doane is especially grateful to her mother, Dorothy Sheldon Doane, who died while the book was nearing completion. A warm and strong attachment with her inspired a passion for going out in the world and exploring life and people.

Dr. Diamond would like to express her gratitude to her father, Dr. Stanley Diamond, who gave her a love for critical inquiry into the most fundamental aspects of the human condition, and a commitment to human and social justice, which were major sources of inspiration for this book, as was his own work on schizophrenia and the family.

Dr. Diamond is most indebted to the loving support and unflagging nurturance provided by her husband, John Alschuler, whose wisdom has always inspired and sustained her work. Thanks also to their daughter, Julia Rose, who spent many hours working alongside her mother on her own Geosafari junior computer, her dolls lined up on the desk. We hope that our work will inspire her to combine work and family gracefully and sensibly as she grows into womanhood.

This work was supported by a research grant from the National Institute of Mental Health—MH44991, Principal Investigator, J. A. Doane, Ph.D.

CHAPTER 1

Introduction:
Attachment and Family Emotional Climate—An Epigenetic Approach to Studying the Family

The Limitations of the Family Systems Model

THE PERSISTENT POWER of the parent-child attachment or affectional bond has been largely ignored by investigators who study the family's role in the course of major psychiatric disorders. Although the reasons for this oversight are not entirely clear, several trends have been evident in the field of family therapy and research during the last 30 years that may have contributed to this tendency to bypass the role of parent-child attachment in family dynamics. Family therapists during this period tended to emphasize, if not idealize, a systemic, whole family approach to understanding what goes on in families, and family therapy literature has influenced many researchers. Many family therapists still focus on the complexity of the constantly moving, interconnecting family system as the most useful way of understanding a family's dynamics in the consulting room. The term *identified patient* suggests this philosophy in that the patient is often seen as reflecting the pathology of the entire family system and thus as mirroring the problems in the system as a whole. Family therapy programs still train therapists to work primarily with the whole family in conjoint sessions. Typically, the siblings are included as a vital part of the family work, and therapists do not generally split up parents and work with dyadic pairs of one parent and the identified patient-child.

Intergenerational Family Therapy

Intergenerational family therapy has been a somewhat specialized type of family treatment practiced by a minority of family therapists such as Ivan Boszormenyi-Nagy and Geraldine Spark (1973), James Framo (1992), Helm Stierlin (1974, 1977), and Murray Bowen (1978). Bowen (1978) developed concepts such as the "undifferentiated family ego mass," which refers to the emotional vortex that characterizes family systems under stress; "triangulation," which refers to the tendency of dyads to involve a third person in their dynamics due to the powerful forces of love and aggression in dyadic relationships; and "differentiation of self within the family of origin," which refers to the importance of developing a unique identity within a matrix of family relationships. Based on the foregoing concepts, Bowen (1978) developed methods for working with families that often involved several generations. For example, when investigating marital difficulties, Bowen advocated an exploration of the interlocking system of triangles that develop in family systems, as opposed to an investigation of the dyadic attachment issues in the couple dynamics. Bowen (1978) believed that the individual's primary developmental task was to develop person-to-person relationships with significant family members while remaining embedded in a matrix of family relationships, and he developed methods based on this goal for working with families.

Similarly, Boszormenyi-Nagy and Spark (1973) developed a contextual theory of family therapy that emphasized issues surrounding the often-invisible system of family-of-origin loyalties, which can damage relationships in the family of procreation; family members' accountability for past unfair or destructive behavior patterns; and rebalancing of family emotional ledgers when negative behaviors have predominated in the family system through therapeutic work with multiple generations, as they exist both in actuality and in fantasy for current family members. Framo (1992) similarly hypothesized that dysfunctions in individual family members and in dyadic relationships have their roots in maladaptive relational patterns that are transmitted from one generation to the next. He speculated that in many disturbed families, loyalties to the family of origin remain primary, if covert. Thus, he maintained, the need to preserve positive images of parents, regardless of how abusive or inadequate they may have been, involves displacement of negative feelings vis-à-vis the primary objects onto members of the family of procreation (for example, a spouse and/or children).

The intergenerational perspective that contributed most to our approach was that of Helm Stierlin (1974, 1977), who not only understood the power of unresolved intrapsychic issues of parents and the ways in which they were unconsciously enacted in both marital and parent-child relationships but who also developed a family typology and form of therapy based on intergenerational understandings. Stierlin (1974, 1977; Simon, Stierlin, & Wynne, 1985) identified three modes of intergenerationally driven interaction between separating parents and adolescents: binding processes through which family members, who are not well differentiated from their own parents, perpetuate the idea that satisfaction of the adolescent's instinctual, relational, and/or ethical/cognitive needs can only be met within the nuclear family system; expulsion processes through which family members, who themselves might have prematurely separated from their own parents who may have failed to meet their age-appropriate dependency needs, extrude the adolescent by overt neglect or abandonment, or more covertly by pushing the adolescent into premature autonomy; and delegating processes through which family members project onto their adolescent children their own thwarted ambitions and goals, and their own often disowned or unconscious desires and wishes, thereby jeopardizing the adolescent's individuation. Stierlin (1974, 1977; Simon, Stierlin, & Wynne, 1985) maintains that change of such entrenched homeostatic family patterns necessitates a multigenerational approach involving processes of demystification, belated mourning, balancing of accounts, and reconciliation across generations. Stierlin's comprehensive, multigenerational family therapy is unique in that it encompassed not only the relational dynamics, but also the internal representational worlds of each family member. Indeed, Stierlin (1974) points out that "in the actual practice of family therapy, it was difficult, if not impossible, to disregard individual members who had their own wishes and needs, who had benefitted or suffered from the actions of other members, who blamed or absorbed blame, who felt guilty or made others feel guilty, and whose interests clashed or agreed" (p. 323). In sum, Stierlin's identification of such binding, delegating, and expelling modes in the families of separating adolescents as interpersonal variations on the intrapsychic themes of their parents' own aborted or curtailed separation processes foreshadowed some of the findings of the current study that link disturbed intergenerational representations with negative forms of affective interactions in the current family.

In recent years a number of more systemically oriented family theorists and therapists have begun to focus on the contribution of intergenerational attachment bonds in understanding current family dynamics. Mara Selvini Palazzoli (1922), for example, in her most recent writings underscores the role of intergenerational disappointments and injuries in perpetuating powerful maladaptive patterns of interaction in families with severely disturbed adolescents and young adults.

Although all of the aforementioned family theorists and therapists adhere to a multigenerational perspective, their focus tends to be on the complexities of the multigenerational contributions to difficulties with unbinding or separation processes, as opposed to the ways in which past relational legacies disrupt attachments and hinder attempts at reconnection—which is the focus of our work. In addition, very few intergenerational family therapists or theorists have been able to use empirical research to further develop their clinically derived hypotheses about the significance of multigenerational family history for the current interactional climate.

Yale Psychiatric Institute Family Study: An Intergenerational Family Research Project

The Yale Psychiatric Institute Family Study (YPIFS), on which this book is based, is one of first research studies with solid longitudinal research data to back up an intergenerational approach to family treatment. From 1984 to 1991, the YPIFS researchers investigated multigenerational patterns of attachment in over 50 families with a severely disturbed family member. The researchers then studied the impact of such patterns on current family functioning, particularly on the affective exchanges among family members. The study is also one of the few empirical studies that has explored the *mechanisms* of transmission of multigenerational attachment patterns, especially the way in which affective exchanges may convey and perpetuate the prototypical attachment patterns as they are represented internally in individual family members in particular family types. In this regard the study deviates from most other empirical family research, which follows the predominant systems model among family theorists and therapists, and which emphasizes overt behavior rather than the internal world of family members.

The emphasis on systems characteristics influenced empirical researchers to study attributes of the family such as communication styles, the role of power in the family, levels of disruptiveness, measures of verbal fluency, and forms of deviant communication (Doane, 1978). During the 1960s and 1970s, numerous studies involved different ways of measuring communication patterns in families, and most of the researchers sought diagnostic specificity through the identification of deviance (Singer & Wynne, 1963, 1965; Wynne, Singer, Bartko, & Toohey, 1977). In particular, schizophrenics' families were studied to determine whether something uniquely pathological about the system dynamics in these families existed and might help explain the development of a schizophrenic disorder in one of the children. Interest in such studies has waned in recent years, although researchers have not ruled out a contributory role of family factors in the etiology of serious illness. The increasing hegemony of biological psychiatry and a political climate that emphasizes self-help converged to create a research atmosphere that discourages studies that might implicate aspects of the parents' personalities or histories in the onset or maintenance of severe psychopathology.

Research on Expressed Emotion

In the 1970s a shift in thinking in family research occurred when British research on expressed emotion (EE) showed, for the first time, a powerful, predictable, empirical relationship between aspects of the patient's familial environment and clinical relapse in patients suffering from schizophrenia (Brown, Birley, & Wing, 1972; Vaughn & Leff, 1976a). As replication studies began to proliferate, other investigators began to study the effects of family therapy on reducing the parental hostility, criticism, and emotional overinvolvement that was associated with an increased risk of relapse for the patient (Falloon et al., 1982; Hogarty et al., 1986; Leff & Vaughn, 1981). These treatment studies demonstrated that a combination of psychoeducation and behaviorally oriented family management techniques, plus maintenance doses of neuroleptic medication, dramatically reduced relapse in schizophrenics during the first nine months after discharge from hospitalization for an acute episode of schizophrenia.

Enthusiasm for such behaviorally oriented psychoeducation treatment models for families with major psychiatric disorders such as schizophrenia peaked in the 1980s as clinicians became aware of the efficacy of these approaches. Grassroots organizations such as the National Alliance for the Mentally Ill (NAMI) also began to grow rapidly during this period. NAMI has adamantly opposed research that measures parental EE or similar indicators of parental behaviors that may contribute to children's relapses.

In NAMI's view, EE studies and the treatment forms they have spawned represent parent bashing. NAMI contends that phenomena such as EE reflect the cumulative effects of the frustration, associated with the burdens of care, that the relatives of patients with severe psychiatric disorders feel. The powerful political impact of organizations such as NAMI has strengthened the arguments of those who have advocated an educational, consultative, and skills-training approach to treating the families of severely disturbed patients. These approaches typically ignore such fundamental issues as why parents might be so persistently angry and critical, and they do not delve into the quality of the dyadic or triadic family attachment relationships. Instead, the clinician must find the right way to provide the parents with the education and skills necessary to help the patient manage the symptoms of the illness.

Limitations of Treatment Methods Spawned by EE Research

During the 1970s and 1980s, questions about *how* parental characteristics such as criticism or emotional overinvolvement affect the severely disturbed patient were bypassed. Family treatment studies of patients with severe psychopathology showed dramatic decreases in their relapse rates following family therapy. These findings contributed to the untested assumption that the reductions had occurred because family treatment had decreased the parents' tendency to criticize or intrude on the patient's inner life in overstimulating and unhelpful ways.

Many clinicians who worked with severely disturbed patients from chaotic families, however, began to notice that these direct, education-oriented approaches (Wynne, 1984) were often not especially well suited to many of the families they treated. The structured tasks that made up the bulk of the treatment often were difficult to implement because families often did not learn to generalize the skills they learned during treatment sessions. More specifically, affect storms in the family continued to occur or resumed after family therapy ceased, resulting in clinical crises or the severely disturbed family member's relapse.

As clinicians, we became increasingly aware of the limitations of the strict consultation model, behavior management strategies, and purely systemic approaches of family therapy for work with severely disturbed families. Although some families seemed to grasp a straightforward, consultation approach readily, others showed little change in the underlying family dynamics or expressed a desire to address relational issues, including aspects of the dyadic attachment relationships in the family. We often had the sense that psychoeducation, skills-training, and behavioral problem-solving techniques were appropriate, but premature. In other words, many of our severely disturbed patients, in both inpatient and outpatient settings, had families who were not ready for psychoeducational models of treatment, because the basic affectional ties that might ensure the families' cooperation in addressing and changing maladaptive or pathogenic behaviors were lacking. Families with impaired attachment relationships seemed to have particular difficulty in refraining from critical or overinvolved behaviors. Family members often reverted to overemotional ways of reacting and relating to the patient, despite psychoeducation about how such behaviors contribute to relapses and despite behavioral techniques to limit parental criticism and overinvolvement.

Furthermore, we found ourselves relying on object relations theory—which emphasizes not so much the interplay of drive and defense in individual personality development as the configurations of self in emotionally charged interactions with significant others that constitute the internal representational world (Greenberg & Mitchell, 1983; Kernberg, 1976, 1980, in press)—to guide our conceptualization of cases and our design of family interventions. In other words, like others in the field (e.g., Stierlin, 1974, 1977; Framo, 1992; Lidz, 1992; Reiss, 1989), we found that paying attention to the representational world of individual family members enhanced our family work. We observed that in the family arena, past experiences and relationships that have crystallized into internalized images of self and others are continually reprojected and externalized in current family transactions, which can be mystifying and recalcitrant to change unless one understands their intrapsychic roots.

A Return to a Focus on Attachment in Family Research

The clinical observations outlined thus far led to the development of the Yale Psychiatric Institute Family Study, whose research findings suggest that parent-child attachments are powerful mediators of how parents relate to their children and construct their children's emotional worlds. Our study suggests that parental communication styles make an important contribution to parent-child relational dynamics, but they are often only the tip of the relational iceberg. Hostility, criticism, and intrusion are often difficult to eliminate, perhaps because existing models for understanding these pathogenic characteristics are inadequate.

The YPIFS research findings support a renewed emphasis on dyadic relationships within the family. An understanding of family members' attachment histories and of current attachment relationships allows the therapist to design thoughtful *epigenetic* interventions—that is, ones focused at the developmental level, where they are likely to have the most impact. By learning about patients' parental emotional injuries that stem from childhood attachment experiences, therapists can interrupt the inter-generational transmission of these attitudes and frustrations, and break the cycle of transmitting risk factors across the generations. Therapists can use hypotheses about the parent's internal world, derived from represen-tations of attachment to parent figures, to help identify and transform mal-adaptive or pathogenic relational patterns between a parent and his or her child.

If the individual attachment history and dyadic attachment bonds are indeed so important, then why engage in family treatment? In working with severely disturbed adolescents and young adults who are struggling with major psychiatric disorders, a well-planned combination of individ-ual and family-based interventions is often the treatment of choice. Some-times, when treatment efforts are especially well coordinated, the inter-laced efforts of the individual therapist and the family therapist create significant changes that probably would not occur with either treatment modality on its own. Especially in major psychotic disorders such as schiz-ophrenia or severe personality disorders, family treatment is often essen-tial to the patient's ability to stay out of the hospital or out of danger. In addition, when medication compliance is an important part of survival, family involvement can spell the difference between success and failure. Finally, as Theodore Lidz (1992) astutely points out, the family milieu and transactions continue to exert a formative influence throughout the life cycle, reshaping the individual's life course, ego functioning, and object relations in crucial ways. Along with Lidz and others, we believe that fam-ily and individual approaches to both treatment and theory are mutually enhancing, rather than mutually exclusive, and that indeed, an integration of the two can lead to a richer and more complex depth psychology, "in the sense of carrying the origins of psychopathology into prior genera-tions" (Lidz, 1992). Thus, clinicians should always consider not only the impact of multigenerational family factors on individual development but also a blend of individual and family modalities of treatment where appropriate.

Why Is Family Therapy Important?

In today's climate of brief treatment, it becomes increasingly important to intervene with patients in ways that are focused, relevant to the patients' and families' unique needs and resources, and as brief as possible. Pro-grams that offer one treatment modality or one technique for all patients and families with a given disorder overlook the heterogeneity of family types and problems, and the program staff thus may miss crucial aspects of individuals' and families' pathology. At the same time, treatment programs that offer broad-based assessment and treatment plans, regardless of how comprehensive or in-depth they may be, are not very effective when the clinicians have only days or weeks to provide treatment.

The approach offered in this book is a focused, semistructured way for clinicians to create treatment hierarchies, make treatment choices, and organize clinical interventions, using crucial data about family attachment and relational patterns. Such an approach has proven very effective for working with patients who have a variety of serious psychiatric disorders, including severe personality disorders, acute psychoses, schizophrenia, and bipolar disorders, as well as with substance-abusing adolescents and young adults.

Our dual focus on the quality of parent-child attachment and the ways that family members express affect rests on the belief that these dimensions are as important as issues of individual diagnosis and family communication. As clinicians, we are constantly struck by the tendency of severely disturbed patients and their families not only to re-create their attachment histories but also to reenact these histories in their day-to-day interactions. A patient's pervasive sense of being an outsider, of not fitting in, of not being normal, of not having a sense of connectedness to others often has dual roots in the primary attachments to parental figures and in the ostracism that severe psychopathology entails. Helping our patients come to terms with both their severe disturbance and their problematic attachment histories is one of our primary therapeutic tasks. Working with a patient's family members both in the extended and nuclear family in an intergenerational fashion can create opportunities for understanding, change, and reintegration of aspects of the self for the patient and for his or her parents.

Brief Outline of the Book

The book begins with a discussion of the relevant research literature and theoretical ideas in the realms of both attachment and EE that formed the basis for designing the YPIFS (chapter 2). In chapter 3, we present an overview of the YPIFS research design and of selected methods and procedures used to address key research questions. Chapter 4 contains the results of several key statistical analyses of the YPIFS data. Readers who are more clinically oriented may choose to skip this section.

In chapter 5, the focus shifts to treatment issues, and a family typology based on the research study findings is presented. Chapters 6, 7, and 8 are devoted to detailed descriptions of the clinical issues and treatment strategies that characterize each of the three family types: disconnected, high-intensity, and low-intensity families. Finally, chapter 9 contains a discussion of some of the clinical techniques and sequencing strategies for the therapist. In this chapter we also discuss our own theoretical model for understanding how change occurs when this treatment model is applied.

The case material presented in the book is based on a synthesis of clinical vignettes from many different families in the study. Details have been altered to protect the identities of the patients and their families: excerpts from the speech samples have been altered, composite cases are presented, and all other quoted material has been disguised. Such alterations in no way compromise or distort the validity of our observations. Our concern in making these alterations is to protect the patients and families who so openly and generously shared their experiences with us.

We want to describe for other clinicians our research data and our attempts to distill these findings into a model that can be used to guide *treatment*. Thus, we have chosen not to focus on the many positive attributes and strengths that we observed in our study families. Although the unique strengths of each family are obviously important when working with the family, we want to convey information about how risk factors might be transmitted, often inadvertently, and about how these processes can be repaired. We hope that readers will not assume that our approach emphasizes pathology to the exclusion of the positive aspects of family life.

CHAPTER 2

A Review of Previous Studies on Expressed Emotion, Affective Style, and Attachment

---

I N THE Yale Psychiatric Institute Family Study (YPIFS) we have explored whether disturbances in the parents' early attachment relationships in their families of origin are associated with enduring tendencies to relate in negative ways to their adolescent and young adult offspring, and particularly to revert to negative affective exchanges in stressful face-to-face interactions. In focusing on the implications of parents' attachment with their own parents for the type of emotional climate that parents create in the family of procreation, our study has been influenced by recent developments in both attachment research and research in expressed emotion (EE) and affective style (AS). This chapter involves a selective review of the research literature in both attachment and expressed emotion, or affective style, and a synthesis of the findings into a model that has guided our family typology and associated treatment methodology. The more clinically oriented reader may wish to skip the in-depth theoretical discussion in this chapter and move on to chapter 5.

The Genesis of Expressed Emotion

The EE concept originated in the research of George Brown and his colleagues in Great Britain, who observed higher rates of relapse among schizophrenic patients whose parents, in individual interviews, had been rated high on critical and hostile attitudes and emotional overinvolvement

(Brown, Birley, & Wing, 1972; Brown, Carstairs, & Topping, 1958). The concern with links between the emotion expressed by families and patients' relapses arose from the growing interest in, first, the treatment and fate of patients with chronic psychiatric disorders and, second, the types of family and treatment conditions that might ameliorate the course of such disorders. Subsequently, measures of emotional overinvolvement were refined in empirical investigations of those aspects of family functioning and of parental attitudes that correlated significantly with clinical relapse in a schizophrenic population. Ultimately, ratings of parents' critical, overinvolved, and hostile attitudes proved to be the most effective predictors of patients' posthospitalization functioning.

The criticism score, which is derived from a frequency count of the number of critical comments made by a relative about the patient in the course of the interview, involves comments that reflect dislike or disapproval of the behavior or characteristics of the person. The hostility rating, which is measured on a 4-point scale, measures the extent to which the family member attacks the patient or expresses intense, unremitting dislike or hatred for him or her. Emotional overinvolvement, which is rated on a 6-point scale, measures overprotectiveness, self-sacrificing behaviors, and exaggerated or dramatic emotional reactions. The three measures are combined into a composite rating of high or low expressed emotion, with the cutoff points for each scale being derived empirically by the scale's efficacy in predicting schizophrenic relapse.

Replication studies in London (Vaughn & Leff, 1976a) and Los Angeles (Vaughn, Snyder, Jones, Freeman, & Falloon, 1984) reconfirmed the original findings of the strong association between EE and schizophrenic relapse, defined as symptom exacerbation as well as rehospitalization, with relapse rates three to four times higher for patients in high versus low EE families. Further, other studies indicated that this significant association tended to persist at 2 years after discharge (Falloon et al., 1985; Leff & Vaughn, 1981). Julian Leff and Christine Vaughn (1981) reported that maintenance dose neuroleptic treatment and reduced contact with relatives somewhat ameliorated the pathogenic influence of high EE relatives on the patient in the posthospitalization period.

In a recent study, Gordon Parker and his colleagues (Parker, Johnston, & Hayward, 1988) reported an association between EE and the course of schizophrenia, but they found that relapse rates were also linked to standard prognostic indicators such as the number of previous hospitalizations. Most investigators of EE or affective style and relapse have not reported an association between family factors and patient variables such as the severity or type of symptoms measured at the same cross-sectional point in time. This lack of association between EE and symptomatic state, as measured cross-sectionally, has often been offered as evidence for the proposition that parental EE is a freestanding parental attribute that negatively affects the patient's recovery in ways that have little to do with any particular aspect of the psychiatric disorder itself, such as the severity or duration of the psychotic symptoms.

The Relationship between Parental Attitudes and Family Interactions

Although measures of EE were found to predict relapse in a schizophrenic population, the question remained whether EE ratings, which are based on family attitudes as expressed during individual interviews, in fact reflect the nature of prototypical family transactions. How the high EE attitudes of relatives are related to their behavior with the patient, and how such attitudes are conveyed to the patient, were issues investigated by Jeri Doane and colleagues at UCLA. In 1978, Doane developed a measure called Affective Style (AS), which was designed to capture the clinically meaningful affective attitudes and behaviors that were verbally expressed toward a patient during a face-to-face family discussion task. AS can be considered a transactional measure of family emotional climate that is designed to measure the degree of criticism, intrusiveness, and or guilt-inducing remarks parents make during an emotionally charged family discussion. Statements that are supportive in nature, such as empathy, praise, and acknowledgment of progress, are also coded.

Despite similarities between the AS and EE measures, important differences exist. The AS measure, in contrast to the EE one, does not directly measure emotional overinvolvement but does differentiate between types of criticism. Several studies have supported the validity of the EE and AS measures. Keith Valone (Valone, Norton, Goldstein, & Doane, 1983) found that parents who were rated high EE on an individual interview also tended to express an excessive number of critical comments toward their offspring in actual family transactions, as indicated by the AS measure. This finding was replicated in a British study of schizophrenic patients (Strachan, Leff, Goldstein, Doane, & Burtt, 1986), as well in another American sample (Miklowitz, Goldstein, Falloon, & Doane, 1984).

Further, two independent studies have shown that the subdivision of families in the high EE group into "high EE critical" and "high EE overinvolved" corresponded to differences in affective style. Specifically, high EE critical parents made more critical statements during face-to-face contact with their schizophrenic offspring than did low EE parents or high EE overinvolved parents, while high EE overinvolved parents made more intrusive comments than either of the other two groups (Miklowitz et al., 1984; Strachan et al., 1986). Thus, there is much evidence that the EE ratings of criticism and emotional overinvolvement are significantly associated with their corresponding AS measures of criticism and intrusiveness. This finding raises the issue of whether measures such as EE are, in fact, global labels for complex underlying processes that may have complicated pathways of influence.

Affective Style as a Predictor of Relapse

Studies using the interactional AS measure have provided evidence that this measure is a good predictor of relapse in schizophrenia (Doane, Goldstein, Falloon, & Mintz, 1985) and among bipolar manic patients (Miklowitz, Goldstein, Nuechterlein, Snyder, & Mintz, 1988). This AS measure was also a predictor of long-term psychiatric outcome in a sample of adolescents at risk for developing schizophrenic disorders (Doane, West, Goldstein, Rodnick, & Jones, 1981). One study of recent onset bipolar manic patients found that a combination of the EE measure of parental attitudes toward the patient, plus a measure of AS behavior assessed in family interaction, was a better predictor of relapse than either measure alone (Miklowitz, Goldstein, & Neuchterlein, 1987).

The AS measure can be used as a global, summary count of all the negative verbal comments made during the family discussion task. It can also be used as a categorical variable where families are grouped into one of two discrete categories based on risk for relapse. Benign AS families have a low risk for relapse in the offspring, compared to negative AS families. Interestingly, two studies have found that the categorical designations of benign versus negative AS is statistically independent of the designation of low versus high EE, even though the two measures overlap somewhat (Miklowitz et al., 1987; Valone et al., 1983).

The finding that EE attitudes, as expressed in individual parental interviews, are not necessarily synonymous with AS, as demonstrated in face-to-face family interactions, suggests that some high EE parents may be able to inhibit their behavior when in the presence of the severely disturbed patient, whereas others cannot do so. One report has suggested that patients who return to homes where the parents have both high EE attitudes and negative AS profiles are at particularly high risk for clinical relapse (Miklowitz et al., 1987).

EE and AS as Psychosocial Risk Factors for Severe Psychopathology

Recently, investigators have expanded their study of family emotional climate to a range of other physical and psychological disorders. A large body of carefully controlled studies has implicated family emotional climate in the course and/or treatment of affective disorders (Hooley, Orley, & Teasdale, 1986; Leff & Vaughn, 1981), bipolar disorder (Miklowitz et al., 1988), obesity (Fischmann-Havstad & Marsden, 1984; Leff & Vaughn, 1985), anorexia nervosa (Szmulker, Berkowitz, Eisler, Leff, & Dare, 1987), diabetes (Koenigsberg, Klausner, Pelino, Rosnick, & Campbell, in press), and other medical disorders (Reiss, Gonzalez, & Kramer, 1986).

In addition, EE has been investigated in a number of cross-cultural studies, particularly in developing countries with strong family structures and traditions where a more benign outcome and course for schizophrenia has been observed (Kuipers & Bebbington, 1988; Lefley, 1985). Specifically, an association between relatives' high EE attitudes and subsequent relapse patterns in schizophrenic and chronic psychiatric disorders has been documented in a variety of Western and non-Western cultures, including Chandigarh, India (Leff et al., 1987); a Mexican-American population in Los Angeles (Karno et al., 1987); and an Israeli population (Heresco-Levy, Greenberg, & Dasberg, 1990). Thus, despite the differences in the course of chronic psychiatric disturbance or general cultural attitudes toward it, EE has been found to be a psychosocial risk marker for the exacerbation of severe psychopathology in many cultures.

The Political Side of Family Emotional Climate

Critics have argued that EE and AS as concepts are merely labels that unfairly blame family members who have been burdened with the frustrations of caring for the severely disturbed relative. Joel Kanter and others (Kanter, Lamb, & Loeper, 1987) have argued that the disturbed family member has behaved in ways that have resulted in the development of high EE attitudes or AS behavior in the parent. The alternative explanation for the predictive validity of family emotional climate to patient relapse is the hypothesis that parental attributes such as EE attitudes or AS behaviors are really trait phenomena; and as such, these negative parental attributes may contribute causally to the patient's symptomatic decompensation and return to the hospital. The first argument suggests that EE and AS are state variables and that they recede in the face of improvements in the patient's clinical state. The second position, which argues for a more fixed and unmodifiable view of these variables, would predict that high EE or negative AS in the parent would not necessarily decrease once the burden of the patient's illness had lifted.

The Significance and Limitations of Intervention Studies

During the past 10 years, as EE and AS have been established as nonspecific risk markers that affect the course of a variety of psychiatric disorders, a number of family-based interventions have been developed to target these aspects of family functioning, which have been associated with recidivism in the identified patient. These family treatment programs, which involve psychoeducational models and symptom management in combination with maintenance dose neuroleptics, have been remarkably successful in reducing relapse rates (defined as symptom exacerbation as well as rehospitalization) with schizophrenic patients (Falloon et al., 1982; Goldstein et al., 1978; Hogarty et al., 1986; Leff, Kuipers, Berkowitz, & Sturgeon, 1985; Tarrier, et al., 1988). Relapse rates in these studies ranged from 0% to 19%. Although the relapse rates were impressively low, researchers' understanding of how this protection against relapse actually developed is limited. A number of treatment studies have suggested that reduced rates of relapse are associated with lowered rates of EE and AS in family members (Doane et al., 1985, 1986; Hogarty et al., 1986; Leff et al., 1985).

However, some researchers have shown that for some families, high EE attitudes and negative AS behaviors persist or reassert themselves even after intensive family treatment. Gerard Hogarty and colleagues (1986), for example, found that although family treatment produced a 19% relapse rate during the first year, 49% of high EE parents continued to be high EE after family treatment had ended. Leff and Vaughn (1981) reported that despite a 2-year relapse rate of 20% for the family treatment group of schizophrenics, 50% of high EE parents converted to low EE. Similarly, Doane and colleagues (1985) reported that 33% of families treated with intensive family management continued to have negative AS profiles after three months of treatment. Nicholas Tarrier and colleagues (1988) also reported that 17% to 29% of high EE parents remained high EE after 9 months of treatment, leading the researchers to conclude that longer-term intensive family treatment, rather than short-term psychoeducational models were necessary to reduce EE levels in relatives.

In interpreting the figures just cited, it is important to keep in mind that relatives of patients who relapsed during the 9-month follow-up period were excluded from these rates. Thus, although these studies present a comparison of treatment effects on EE changes that are free of any reactive effect due to relapse, the figures necessarily underrepresent relatives whose EE stayed high throughout the treatment. The findings suggest, but do not demonstrate, that for the majority of families, there is not a simple correspondence between intrafamilial modes of expressing affect and the patient's clinical state. These studies suggest that there are more complex underlying intrafamilial forces that persist even after the patient has stabilized and recovered.

The Dynamics of Family Emotional Climate

Although the constructs of EE and AS have become increasingly reified into theoretical systems with increasingly refined treatments, there is little indication of what actually fuels high EE or negative AS type behaviors. For clinicians, this issue of the underlying dynamics of EE and AS remains an important one, yet to be addressed in the research literature. For many parents, high EE or negative AS may represent the tip of a complex iceberg upon which treatment may founder. Although the value of the two constructs in predicting relapse in a severely disturbed population in multiple cultures and with varied types of psychopathology remains indisputable, the exact nature of EE and AS remains unclear.

Various questions that have arisen in studies have suggested a relationship between EE and AS, and family attachment patterns. First, a number of researchers have questioned whether the three components of the EE index—criticism, overinvolvement, and hostility—ought to be combined in a single global measure of EE, or whether they are in fact measuring different constructs (Hooley, Rosen, & Richters, in press; Kanter et al., 1987; Miklowitz, Goldstein, & Falloon, 1983). Jill Hooley and John Teasdale (1989) have found that the criticism and hostility scales generated from the Camberwell Family Interview do not correlate with the overinvolvement ratings, and further that criticism/hostility ratings are a more efficient and consistent predictor of relapse than are ratings of overinvolvement. In one study of the impact of high EE attitudes on relapse among depressed psychiatric hospital patients, Hooley and Teasdale found that criticism accounted for the major proportion of the variance. Furthermore, they determined that criticism was associated with the age of onset of depression and the number of years the patient had been ill, but not with current severity or with premorbid adjustment. These and other findings suggest that criticism/hostility and overinvolvement may in fact represent two separate constructs or dimensions of family functioning (Hooley et al., in press).

Other findings suggest that criticism and overinvolvement are associated with different patterns of attachment in the family. David Miklowitz (Miklowitz et al., 1983), for example, found that family members who were rated high EE on the basis of emotionally overinvolved attitudes tended to have relatives with poor premorbid adjustment and residual symptoms. However, family members who were rated high on the basis of criticism tended to have relatives whose premorbid adjustment and symptom patterns were consistent with those patients from low EE families. Thus, the overinvolvement of some high EE relatives may represent a particular attachment strategy designed to accommodate the needs of a severely impaired family member, whereas the evolution of highly critical attitudes may reflect a response by parents to a deterioration in functioning and an exacerbation of symptoms in a family member who had previously functioned adequately (Miklowitz et al., 1983). Additional findings by MacMillan and colleagues (MacMillan, Gold, Crow, Johnson, & Johnstone, 1986) suggest that criticism may in fact become more pernicious as chronicity increases, suggesting that critical attitudes may be in part a response to a patient's worsening illness.

EE and Personality Traits

However, some studies (Hooley, 1985; Hooley et al., in press) suggested that the personality characteristics and individual histories of relatives may contribute to patient relapse, even after other factors such as chronicity and duration of the patient's disorder and the extent to which the parents were critical or overinvolved premorbidly have been considered. These findings led to an investigation both of parental personality traits that might fuel EE attitudes and AS behaviors, and of other aspects of the parent-child bond, such as attachment relationships, that might affect EE and AS.

Mary Dozier and co-workers (Dozier, Stevenson, Lee, & Velligan, 1991), for example, found that severely disturbed adults who were characterized by disturbed patterns of attachment tended to have parents who were rated as overinvolved but not critical on EE measures. More specifically, individuals from overinvolved families were more likely to employ two types of disturbed attachment strategies: the repressing strategies, in which individuals present themselves as invulnerable and show little capacity to recollect experiences of parental rejection and neglect; and preoccupied strategies, in which the individuals present themselves as vulnerable and needy, but remain uncertain about whether their attachment needs will be met. In addition, individuals characterized by preoccupied and repressing patterns of attachment also had lower levels of premorbid functioning and were more likely to rate themselves as highly symptomatic than were individuals who employed secure patterns of attachment. Dozier and colleagues hypothesize that for severely disturbed individuals, both preoccupied and repressing strategies are more likely to elicit family members' overinvolved attitudes. In turn, rigid reliance on maladaptive attachment strategies perpetuates heightened familial involvement.

Studies such as the ones just described have led some researchers to question whether high EE and AS might not represent intense, if maladaptive, modes of attachment and caretaking that might even exert a beneficial effect on offspring (Wynne, 1984). Indeed, some studies have failed to confirm the original linkage between EE and relapse, and have even indicated that high EE attitudes and behaviors—particularly, high overinvolvement—might function as a protective factor in families with a physically ill family member (Invernizzi et al., 1991).

Further, a number of investigators have noticed that high EE attitudes and negative AS behaviors often characterize parents who appear in many respects to be likable individuals who are extremely dedicated to their disturbed offspring, and these researchers have suggested that such involved parents are an important resource for the psychiatrically disabled child (Hooley et al., in press; Kanter, 1987; Mintz, Liberman, Miklowitz, & Mintz, 1987; Terkelsen, 1984). Hooley (1985, 1987; Hooley et al., in press) hypothesized that highly critical relatives are those who endorse the culturally sanctioned notion that patients can exert some control over their own illness and recovery process, and Hooley and colleagues have systematically investigated the relationship between the EE status of relatives and their attributions about the extent to which the patient can control his or her disorder and thus is responsible for the disturbed behavior. Briefly, they have found that high and low parental EE profiles are associated with different attributions on the part of parents about the causality and controllability of psychiatric disorder (Hooley et al., in press). Parents who are rated high on measures of criticism and hostility also tend to endorse internal and personal causal attributions about psychiatric disorders, whereas parents who are rated low on EE measures of overinvolvement tend to endorse external attributions and to rate highly on external locus of control measures. On the basis of these findings Hooley and colleagues (in press) have suggested that high EE individuals may be characterized by an internal locus of control (for instance, the belief that one is the cause of the problem or situation and thus is responsible for controlling it), whereas low EE parents are characterized by external locus of control (exemplified by the sense that one is controlled by factors in the external environment).

Such studies thus provide empirical evidence for the following elaborations of the EE and AS constructs: First, criticism and overinvolvement may be two distinct dimensions of family functioning, which entail different types of parent-child attachment patterns and parental personality characteristics. Second, the nature of the relationship EE and AS bear to enduring personality traits or individual histories of the parents has yet to be explored.

The Importance of the Represented Family for EE and AS

In addition, findings by Hooley and Teasdale (1989) suggest that not only is it fruitful to investigate the relationship between parental personality characteristics that may contribute to the maintenance and persistence of high EE attitudes and negative AS behaviors but also that it is important to take into account the way family members are represented in the internal world of the patient. For example, Hooley and Teasdale (1989) found in a study of EE in the marital dynamics of unipolar depressed patients that the depressed individual's perceptions of the spouse's level of criticism, rather than objective assessments of the degree of criticism made on the basis of direct observation of the spouses' interactions, most significantly predicted relapse nine months after discharge. Further, the depressed individual's ratings of *perceived* criticism on the part of the spouse did not necessarily correlate with the independent ratings of criticism made by the researcher.

Thus, these findings suggest that the internal world of the individual, and particularly the ways in which the attitudes and behaviors of significant attachment objects are represented intrapsychically, may be an extremely powerful predictor of the course of severe psychopathology. Yet despite Hooley's provocative findings, researchers working in the framework of EE and AS have yet to recognize the significance of the representational world to the patient's course of disorder.

The Importance of Attachment Theory for Family Research

Although concepts of attachment and bonding have received some attention from family researchers and theoreticians (Byng-Hall, 1991; Dozier et al., 1991; Heard, 1982; Lidz, Fleck, & Cornelison, 1971; Olsen, Sprenkle, &

Russell, 1979; Reiss, 1989; Reiss, Costell, Jones, & Berkman, 1980; Reiss et al., 1986), thus far the conceptual linkages between attachment and family risk factors such as EE and AS have received scant attention from researchers studying family factors in severe psychopathology. The idea that the nature of attachment bonds might influence the developmental course of severe psychopathology originated in research investigations on the families of schizophrenics conducted at the Yale Psychiatric Institute by Theodore Lidz and Steven Fleck. Lidz, Fleck, and Cornelison (1971) found that overinvolved and symbiotic patterns of parent-child interactions characterized families of schizophrenic adolescents and young adults.

Subsequently, several family researchers attempted to incorporate the dimension of emotional bonding into family typologies. Most notably, David Olsen developed a "circumplex model," based in part on concepts of family cohesion (Olsen et al., 1979); David Reiss and colleagues investigated the impact of patterns of connection and disconnection on families with severely disturbed hospitalized adolescents (Reiss et al., 1980) and chronic physical illness (Reiss et al., 1986). Also, Peter Steinglass and colleagues investigated patterns of enmeshment and disengagement in families with histories of alcoholism (Steinglass, Bennett, Wolin, & Reiss, 1987), and W. Robert Beavers and colleagues studied the implications of patterns of closeness and boundary maintenance for varied aspects of family functioning (Beavers & Voeller, 1983; Lewis, Beavers, Gossett, & Phillips, 1976). However, in these family typologies, the dimensions of closeness and attachment are often confounded.

Reiss (1989) has made a major theoretical contribution to the integration of attachment and family systems theory in his call for a reconciliation in family research and treatment of notions of the represented family (i.e, the mosaic of internalized images that each family member holds of significant others in the family) and the practicing family (i.e., the immediate world of family transactions and observable practices and interchanges). Although Reiss acknowledges that these two perspectives derive from divergent observational routes, involve contrasting research strategies, and are based on different units of analysis (in that the represented family is based on inferences derived from in-depth individual interviews or observations of sequences of behaviors in dyads, whereas the practicing family is identified through observed behaviors of triadic or larger family groups), he believes that the two perspectives are complementary, because "every relationship probably has represented and practicing aspects" (p. 194). However, the reconciliation between these two perspectives has yet to be realized empirically.

One major reason for the lack of intersection between studies involving measures of attachment and family concepts such as EE and AS is the exclusively dyadic focus of attachment research, and the fact that the patterns of attachment were developed through research with a normal population. John Bowlby (1969, 1973, 1980, 1988) defined *attachment* as the propensity to make enduring and irreplaceable bonds to significant others. Bowlby emphasized the survival or ethological functions of such emotionally significant bonds, rather than the complex world of family ties and transactions in which they are embedded. Such attachment bonds were thought to function as a goal-corrected control system or cybernetic system, situated within the central nervous system of each partner, which served to maintain proximity of the infant to the caretaker, thus protecting the infant from potential physical and psychological harm.

A number of empirical researchers have operationalized Bowlby's patterns of attachment in laboratory and naturalistic observations of the dyadic interactions between mothers and infants, which set the template for the emergence and internalization of various patterns of attachment. Based on experimental procedures involving a separation and reunion task between infants and their mothers in the Ainsworth Strange Situation, Mary Ainsworth and followers (Ainsworth, Blehar, Waters, & Wall, 1978; Main & Cassidy, 1988; Main & Hesse, 1990) have identified several primary patterns of attachment: secure; insecure-ambivalent (also referred to as ambivalent-resistant), insecure-avoidant, and insecure-disorganized. These patterns of attachment are distinguished by the behavioral and affective expressions of the infant in relation to the mother after a brief separation. Infants classified as insecure-avoidant (Group A) were observed to ignore or avoid the mother upon reunion, turning away from her physically or averting their gaze if the mother sought their contact or attention. In addition, avoidant infants were observed to minimize their affect, showing virtually no distress, fear, or anger upon reunion. Securely attached (Group B) infants actively sought proximity and contact with the mother upon reunion; and these infants expressed a wide range of positive as well as negative feelings, which the caretaker accepted and responded to appropriately. Infants classified as insecure-ambivalent (Group C) were observed to oscillate between seeking and resisting contact with and proximity to mother upon reunion, and they then showed prolonged regressive and exaggerated displays of anger, fear, and distress. Finally, infants classified as insecure-disorganized (Group D) showed random behaviors and often acted dazed and disoriented, or they oscillated in a disorganized fashion between proximity seeking and avoidance in ways that made them unclassifiable in any other distinct pattern.

Thus, empirical investigations of Bowlby's attachment theory involved a categorization of attachment relationships as they are enacted dyadically between mother and infant. The attachment system was originally described by Bowlby as it is organized within the attached person and as it is enacted in the mother-infant dyad; thus, it is not surprising that attachment research has increasingly concerned itself with how dyadic attachment relationships are represented within the individual through what Bowlby terms "internal working models of attachment." (Bowlby 1969, 1973, 1977, 1980, 1988).

Internal Working Models of Attachment

Bowlby (1977) hypothesized that by the end of the first year, "attachment becomes mediated by increasingly sophisticated behavioral systems organized cybernetically and incorporating representational models of the environment and self" (p. 203). Such internal working models of attachment are thought to constitute a set of increasingly complex mental structures by which attachment-related information and events—past, present, and future—are evaluated and processed or anticipated. As Bretherton (1985), Arietta Slade, and Larry Aber (1992) and others have commented, the term *working model* entails dynamic and developmental implications in that these mental structures are being revised constantly to accommodate new attachment-related experiences; but they become increasingly complex, differentiated, and stable as the individual matures.

Bowlby (1988) states that he formulated the theory of internal working models in part to understand the ways in which attachment patterns become internalized during development so that they come to represent an aspect of the child, as well as a relational propensity. However, the emphasis in attachment theory is on the internalization of the attachment *relationship*, and this emphasis on the salience of parent-child interactions for the internal world makes attachment concepts of potential interest to family researchers.

Indeed, attachment research has provided much evidence that the patterns of mother-child attachment observed in a laboratory situation correspond to mothers' ways of interacting with their children in naturalistic observation (Ainsworth et al., 1978; Bates, Maslin, & Frankel, 1985). The correspondence between actual patterns of interaction based on home observations and laboratory-based assessments of attachment has been particularly robust for the families who show disturbed patterns of attachment. For example, in a series of studies that compare reciprocal mother-infant exchanges with infant attachment classification at 12 months, insecure-ambivalent infants were found to have mothers who showed minimal sensitive responsiveness and capacity for reciprocal mutual exchanges. This held true in multiple cultures, as shown in an American sample (Belsky, Rovine, & Taylor, 1984; Isabella, Belsky, & von Eyre, 1989; Lewis & Feiring, 1989), a north German one (Grossmann, Grossmann, Spangler, Suess, & Unzner, 1985), and a Japanese one (Miyake, Chen, & Campos, 1985), as well as in Israeli samples (Sagi et al., 1990; Sagi et al., 1985).

Other studies have implicated a connection between child abuse and maltreatment, and the emergence of parent-child patterns of insecure attachment (Crittenden, 1985, 1987; Lamb, Thompson, Gardner, Charnow, & Estes, 1985; Lyons-Ruth, Connell, Zoll, & Stahl, 1987). Daniel Stern (1989), Arietta Slade and Larry Aber (1992), and others have commented that insecure internal working models of attachment represent adaptations to reality, rather than distortions of reality, in that they occur when the infant must deviate from the expression of normal attachment behaviors and violate normal attachment transactions in order to guarantee or elicit even minimal needs for comfort and security from a caretaker who may present minimal or inconsistent patterns of nurturing. However, it is important to note that parent-child interactions are internalized along with the welter of affects, drives, wishes, and fantasies that accompany them. Thus, such interactions inevitably bear the imprint of the child's subjective world and developmental level, as well as the objective reality of the significant relationships.

Nevertheless, attachment researchers have empirically demonstrated what family therapists and theorists have long hypothesized based on clinical observation: that the representational world of individuals is constituted in part by the internalization of family-based transactions, and that shifts in such transactions may in turn catalyze a reorganization of the representational world.

Transgenerational Transmission of Attachment Patterns

In addition, the centrality of issues around intergenerational continuity and transgenerational transmission of attachment patterns in attachment research is potentially useful for family theorists and therapists, particularly those who have observed the efficacy of family-of-origin therapies, but who have little empirical research to support their theories (Bowen, 1978; Framo, 1992). A number of attachment studies have indicated that internal working models are stable not only within the individual over time (Main & Cassidy, 1988; Main & Weston, 1981; Sroufe, 1983), but also within families and across generations (Fonagy, Steele, & Steele, 1991; Fonagy, Steele, Moran, Steele, & Higgitt, 1991; George & Solomon, 1991; Grossman, Fremmer-Bombik, Rudolph, & Grossman, 1985; Main & Goldwyn, 1984; Main, Kaplan, & Cassidy, 1985; Ricks, 1985; Zeanah & Zeanah, 1989). This group of studies on the intrafamilial, transgenerational transmission of patterns of attachment provides further evidence that interpersonal patterns are reenacted through the generations, with a primary vehicle for such transmission being the mental representation of the self in relation to attachment figures (Main et al., 1985).

One of the most intriguing findings comes from a report by Mary Main and colleagues (1985), who demonstrated that the most powerful determinate of the type of attachment pattern a mother developed with her infant was not the nature of the actual relationship she had with her parents, but the extent to which her mother's internal working model of attachment was coherent, rather than incoherent; integrated positive and negative qualities, rather than being polarized between idealization or denigration; and was readily and easily reevoked during the Adult Attachment Interview (George, Kaplan, & Main, 1985), rather than being blocked out or denied. The mothers of securely attached infants provided coherent narratives of their attachment histories and were able not only to fluently describe negative as well as positive attachment experiences, but to integrate the two and to contextualize negative experiences by presenting them in the light of their own parents' limitations, dilemmas, and conflicts, about which they showed compassion and understanding. The parents of insecurely attached infants were able to present negative attachment experiences but did so in an unintegrated and incoherent manner, so that their interview transcripts showed marked inconsistencies, contradictions, and discontinuities. In the transcripts of attachment interviews of parents of avoidant infants, who tended to be classified as "dismissing of attachment," the structural incoherence often involved contradictions between semantic or general attachment memories that were often quite positive or even idealized (e.g., the mother described as having been all-giving or supportive) and episodic or specific attachment memories elicited through specific probes (e.g., the mother described as having rejected pleas for attention when the child had a physical injury). Finally, the enmeshed parents of insecure ambivalently attached infants appeared to be flooded and overwhelmed by episodic or specific attachment memories, but these parents were unable to structure the memories coherently or to provide semantic or general attachment memories.

The findings just cited on the intergenerational continuity in attachment relationships suggest that the internal working model of attachment functions as the vehicle for the way in which the mother's own attachment history is translated into her attachment behaviors with her child. More recent research has focused on exploring transgenerational linkages among parents' attachment representations of their own parents, parents' attachment representations of their child, the child's attachment representations of the parents, and the correspondence of all three sets of representations with early parent-child attachment behaviors (George & Solomon, 1989; Slade & Aber, 1986; Zeanah, Benoit, Hirshberg, Barton, & Regan, 1991). For example, Charles Zeanah and colleagues (1991) developed a system for classifying the parents' internal working models of the child that corresponds to Main's system for classifying parents' internal working models of their own parents. Specifically, Zeanah and colleagues found that parents whose attachment representations of their own parents were secure or coherent tended to show balanced representations of their child, parents whose representations of their own parents showed a preoccupation with attachment tended to have enmeshed representations of their child, and parents whose attachment representations were dismissing of the importance of attachment relationships tended to be strained in their manner of representing their child. Further, there was a significant association between the nature of the parental internal working models of the child and the quality of the parent-child attachment as assessed in the Ainsworth Strange Situation.

Similarly, Slade and Aber (1986) found that aspects of parental working models of attachment to their children, including coherence in their descriptions of their children and openness about feelings (especially anger) toward them, as well as a conception of the self as able to cope with anger directly and effectively, were related to toddler security of attachment as assessed in a laboratory separation procedure. Finally, Carol George and Judith Solomon (1991) found that the mother's caregiving representation—which includes her conception of herself as capable of providing a secure base for the child and as fostering the child's competence, industry, and autonomy—was related to an interactive measure of mother-child security of attachment obtained in a laboratory reunion situation when the child was 6 years old. In this study the caregiver's representational model of the child was hypothesized to include interrelated self and other components, as well as individual child and parental components. Thus, the caregiver's representational world was evaluated along three dimensions, including the caregiver's willingness to respond, ability to read and understand the child's signals, and effectiveness in fulfilling the child's needs. The studies reviewed suggest that internal working models not only represent the nature of past attachment experiences and transactions in the family of origin, but also forecast the quality of parent-child transactional experiences in the family of procreation, which in turn form the prototypes for new internalized working models across the generations.

Attachment as a Psychosocial Risk Factor

Although the studies just described were conducted with a normative population, a growing number of studies have linked disturbed patterns of attachment with the development of severe psychopathology (Dozier, 1990), including schizophrenic disorders (Parker, Fairly, Greenwood, & Silove, 1982); depressive disorders (Armsden & Greenberg, 1987; Armsden, McCauley, Greenberg, Burke, & Mitchell, 1990; Blatt, 1991, in press; Blatt & Homann, 1992; Parker, 1979, 1981, 1983); borderline personality disorders (Rosenstein & Horowitz, 1993; Sperling, Sharp, & Fishler, 1991); alcohol abuse (Hughes, Francis, & Power, 1989; Kwakman, Zuiker, Schippers, & deWuffel, 1988); and adolescent conduct disorders (Rosenstein & Horowitz, 1993). There are indications not only that attachment classifications in childhood and adolescence place the individual at risk for the development of subsequent psychopathology (Rosenstein & Horowitz, 1993), but also that intrafamilial attachment patterns and their internal representations may constitute a risk factor for relapse (Parker et al., 1988).

For example, Parker (Parker et al., 1982) developed a measure for bonding and attachment (the Parental Bonding Instrument, or PBI) that has been shown to be predictive of relapse in schizophrenia. The patients score their mothers and fathers separately on a 25-item self-report instrument, which is designed to measure different styles of attachment and bonding and their relationship to different parenting styles. The PBI scores permit comparison of four parenting styles: (1) "affectionless control"—low care, high control; (2) "neglectful"—low care, low control; (3) "affectionate constraint"—high care, high control; and (4) "optimal"—high care, low control. Schizophrenic patients who relapsed were significantly more likely to have one or more parents with a high-risk PBI profile of affectionless control. For patients who stayed in contact with their families after discharge, the readmission rate was 75% for patients with one or more high-risk parents, compared with 25% for those who did not have a parent characterized by affectionless control.

Thus, disturbed internal working models of attachment may be associated with or prefigure a number of forms of psychopathology. Internal working models of attachment represent complex configurations that blend affect and cognition, and serve as prototypes to structure attachment relationships and transactions associated with different forms of psychopathology.

The Affective Core of
Internal Working Models of Attachment

The question, of course, remains: What is the derivation of this link between affect and attachment? Recent neuropsychological and infant research studies suggest that affect, cognition, communicative behavior, and object relations develop in tandem (Emde, 1987; Emde, Gaensbauer, & Harmon, 1978; Izard, 1978; Plutchik, 1980; Plutchik & Kellerman, 1983; Stein, 1991). Psychoanalytic object relations theorists have long conceptualized affective exchanges as the fundamental matrix for the development and internalization of object relationships (Behrends & Blatt, 1985; Jacobson, 1964; Kernberg, 1976, 1980, 1990; Sandler & Sandler, 1978). The majority of object relations theorists, regardless of the extent to which they adhere to drive theory, give centrality to libidinal and aggressive strivings as universal and asocial mechanisms that fuel both the search for pleasure and the search for objects (Kernberg, in press). Furthermore, these theorists hypothesize that such libidinal and aggressive strivings are inextricably interconnected with the development of both affects and object relations (Kernberg, 1990; Slade & Aber, 1982). Recent empirical research in infant development and mother-infant interaction patterns has confirmed the centrality of affect for the development of the attachment relationship (Emde et al., 1983; Izard, 1978; Plutchik & Kellerman, 1983; Stern, 1985); but until recently, attachment researchers have failed to develop the subtleties of different forms of affective interchanges for variations in attachment bonds or internal working models of attachment.

We now briefly review the understanding of affect's role in the structuring of self and object representations in psychoanalytic object relations theory. The conceptualization of the relationship between affects and objects in psychoanalytic object relations theory forms the foundation for an understanding of the importance of the affective dimension for the development of internal working models of attachment, since attachment theory, and particularly the concept of internal working models, developed as a "variant" of object relations theory (Bowlby, 1988). Both internal working models of attachment and of self and object representations are considered mental schemata with cognitive, affective, and experiential components that are gradually built up in the course of development as early affect-laden interactions with others are transformed into intrapsychic structures. A comprehensive comparison and critique of ways of conceptualizing the representational world in attachment and psychoanalytic theory are offered elsewhere (Diamond & Blatt, 1994).

Affects and Object Relations

The majority of object relations theorists conceptualize affects as inborn dispositions to subjective experience along the dimensions of pleasure and unpleasure, which are activated simultaneously with inborn or innate behavioral patterns that elicit caretaking by and attachment to significant others. Such experiences of pleasure and nonpleasure involve states of general arousal, which enhance external and internal perceptions of dyadic interactions. A number of object relations theorists (Behrends & Blatt, 1985; Jacobson, 1964; Kernberg, 1980, 1990, in press; Mahler, Pine, & Bergman, 1975) have hypothesized that intense affective experiences form the catalyst for the internalization of primitive object relations, which are initially organized along a positive, pleasurable, all-good dimension and a negative, frustrating, painful, all-bad dimension. In other words, early mother-infant transactions, which form the rudimentary experience of self and other, are imbued with an affective intensity that facilitates the laying down of affective memory traces, and these memory traces include self components, object components, and the affect itself (Kernberg, 1976, 1980, 1990). Indeed, Joseph Sandler and Marie Sandler (1978) have hypothesized that these initial polarized affective responses constitute the two primary objects of the child. "Thus, the first division of the child's world can be regarded as being the division into pleasure and unpleasure per se as objects" (p. 292).

These original and polarized all-good and all-bad experiences occur in the context of undifferentiated self and object representations. However, cognitive and affective development from the fourth or fifth month of life on contribute to the gradual amelioration of such extreme pleasurable and painful states, to the gradual differentiation of perceptions and experiences of the self from those of the object, and to the gradual integration of good and bad self representations into a global concept of self and of good and bad object representations into an integrated concept of the object through the process of separation-individuation (Kernberg, 1975, 1976; Mahler et al., 1975). Thus, affects are thought to have a fundamental and formative relationship to objects and their representations from the outset

(Kernberg, 1976, 1990; Sandler & Sandler, 1978). According to Otto Kernberg (1976, 1980, 1990) and others, every affect state encompasses an internalized object relation, which is comprised of a representation of self in interaction with an object under the impact of a particular affect. Bretherton (1990) refers to such self-object-affect units as "positively or negatively toned interaction schemas that become the basis of self and object representations" (p. 239) and that correspond to working models of attachment.

The Importance of Negative Affect in Attachment Relationships

In developing our conceptualization of attachment and our coding system for assessing attachment (presented in detail in chapter 3), we have tried to consider positive and negative, libidinal and aggressive aspects of attachment relationships. Our attempts to integrate these two aspects of attachment bonds has led us to a return to the object relations root of attachment theory. In repudiating the traditional psychoanalytic dual drive theory in favor of proximity seeking as the primary motivational system (Bowlby, 1969, 1988), attachment theorists have emphasized the libidinal aspects of attachment bonds and perhaps neglected the negative, aggressive aspect of those bonds. The increasing focus on the maladaptive, insecure behavior patterns—particularly the disorganized patterns of attachment that often involve punitive, frightening, chaotic parent-child interchanges (Main & Hesse, 1990) and that have been linked to intergenerational cycles of abuse and maltreatment (Main & Goldwyn, 1984; Zeanah & Zeanah, 1989)—perhaps necessitates a further examination of the origins, impact, and behavioral manifestations of the infant's subjectively experienced painful, frightening, and/or enraged states within attachment relationships. In Kernberg's (1990) terminology, researchers need to explore the aggressively invested line of internalized object relations (whether conceptualized as drive driven or not) that may be "more unrealistic. . . traumatic and more difficult to tolerate in consciousness. . . and to elaborate in the realm of the ego" (p. 128).

Although psychoanalytic theorists have long recognized the importance of the mother's capacity to accept and tolerate the child's rage and aggression for the integration of the representational world, and particularly the resolution of splitting (Kernberg, 1976, 1980, 1990; Mahler et al., 1975), attachment theorists have only recently begun to examine the implications for the mother's capacity to accept and modulate the expression of negative emotions, such as rage, anger, and anxiety, for the way that such emotions contribute to the formulation of different internal working models of attachment. For example, recent studies have indicated that a crucial component of internal working models of attachment is the parents' response to the child's affect (Ainsworth et al., 1978; Kropp & Haynes, 1987). For example, abusive mothers were significantly less likely to identify correctly their own infant's emotional signals as assessed by their tendency to confound negative and positive emotional signals (Kropp & Haynes, 1987), but these mothers were more likely to attribute more malevolent motives to their children (Bauer & Twentyman, 1985). Securely attached mothers, on the other hand, were observed to be attuned to their own infant's negative and positive emotional signals (Haft & Slade, 1989).

The Contributions of Infant Research to Understanding Affect and Attachment

Daniel Stern (1985, 1989, 1990) is one of the infant researchers who has written the grammar for internal working models of attachment in a way that highlights the importance of affective experience. Stern (1985) hypothesizes, first, that the moment of lived interactive experience is encoded in a series of episodic memories, which are then abstracted into a prototypic memory or representation. Second, Stern contends that the salience of such early experiences depends on the degree of affect attunement between the infant and his or her primary caretakers.

Affect attunement can evoke feelings in the members of a dyad that contribute to the affective vitality of the self and how individuals feel about themselves in general. As Stern (1990) points out in his description of a mother and baby engaged in mutual smiling:

> But as Joey and his mother trade smiles, he will probably feel that the gestures are jointly initiated. His mother has willed and executed her own smiles, but he has called them forth. Similarly, he has willed and executed his own smiles, but she has evoked them.
>
> There are many such moments of mutual creation. They are the stuff of being with another person, and they constitute the ties of attachment. So much of attachment consists of the memories and mental models of what happens between you and that other person: How you feel with them. What they can make you experience that others cannot. What you can permit yourself to do or feel or think or wish or dare—but only in their presence. What you can accomplish with their support. What parts, or view, of yourself need their eyes and ears as nourishment (pp. 66–67).

Viewing affect as a central organizing force in the formulation of internal working models of attachment is consistent both with Bowlby's original theoretical formulation on attachment and with the trend in recent attachment research to investigate affect's role in forming and perpetuating patterns of attachment. Indeed, Bowlby (1979) originally conceptualized affects as crucial to the formation, perpetuation, disruption, and renewal of attachment bonds:

> The formation of a bond is described as falling in love, maintaining a bond as loving someone and losing a partner as grieving over someone. Similarly, the threat of loss arouses anxiety and actual loss gives rise to sorrow; whilst each of these situations is likely to arouse anger. The unchallenged maintenance of a bond is experienced as a source of security, and the renewal of a bond as a source of joy. Because such emotions are usually a reflection of the state of a person's affectional bonds, the psychology and psychopathology of emotion is found to be in large part the psychology and psychopathology of affectional bonds. (p. 130)

In his theoretical investigations, Bowlby (1969, 1973, 1980) focused primarily on the functional significance of emotions, that is, their role in appraising, activating, regulating, and terminating attachment behaviors (e.g., fear was likely to activate the attachment system, whereas anger during separation served to bring back the attachment figure).

More recently, attachment researchers have investigated the function of affect within different attachment relationships. A number of research studies have indicated that different patterns of attachment in children and adolescents are associated with different patterns of affect regulation in social relationships (Kobak & Sceery, 1988; Sroufe, 1983; Sroufe, Schork, Frosso, Lawroski, & La Freniere, 1984; Waters, Wippman, & Sroufe, 1979). For example, children classified as securely attached, who had mothers who responded promptly and sensitively to their children's signals for comfort and contact, were able to express a range of both positive and negative affects freely with their mothers in the Ainsworth Strange Situation, and they were observed to modulate negative affects in constructive ways and to generally show less negative affect in interactions with peers (Cassidy, in press; Sroufe, 1983). On the other hand, children classified as insecure-avoidant, whose mothers were consistently rejecting, were generally observed to minimize emotional expression, particularly the expression of negative affects (such as anger or fear) with their mothers in the Strange situation (Cassidy, in press; Main & Solomon, 1986) and in face-to-face interactions with their mothers (Maletesta, Culver, Tesman, & Shepared, 1989), but they expressed hostile emotions inappropriately in other social relationships (Main & Stadtman, 1981; Sroufe, 1983). Finally, children who were classified as insecure-ambivalent, whose mothers tended to respond unpredictably to their attachment signals, demonstrated persistent and exaggerated distress, fear, and anger in the Strange situation (Cassidy &

Berlin, in press) and helplessness and impulsiveness in the school situation (Sroufe, 1983).

The foregoing findings suggest that different working models of attachment involve different organization of affect, which in turn permit different forms of affective expression and regulation. Securely attached children, for example, hold a working model of their parents as capable of tolerating and responding to a range of affects, which in turn allows them to express negative affects and expect an ameliorative parental response. Avoidant infants, by contrast, are thought to hold a representation of their parents as so rejecting and unavailable that they must defensively mute their negative affects such as anger in order to both preserve and minimize contact with the attachment figure in the interests of avoiding further rebuffs. Finally, insecure-ambivalent infants are thought to hold a representation of their parents as so unreliably and inconsistently available that these infants must persist in their negative affective displays in order to gain attention (Cassidy, in press; Cassidy & Berlin, in press).

Further evidence of the centrality of affective organization to working models of attachment is provided by the different affective organizations shown by parents on the Adult Attachment Interview (Main et al., 1985). The parents of most securely attached infants expressed a range of positive and negative feelings in an open, integrated, modulated way on the Adult Attachment Interview. The parents of most avoidant infants, however, showed a restricted range of affective expression. They either denied any negative feelings toward their parents, whom they tended to idealize rigidly, or they minimized their own negative responses to their stories of parental abuse and neglect. Finally, the persistent and exaggerated displays of ambivalently attached infants corresponded to their parents' chaotic presentation on the Adult Attachment Interview as overwhelmed with anger and conflicts about their own parents, which they were unable to resolve or even analyze (Cassidy & Berlin, in press).

The convergence of different working models of attachment with different styles of affect regulation and the relationship of both to the quality of representations of self and others were found in another study of adolescents' attachment representations (Kobak & Sceery, 1988). Rogers Kobak and Amy Sceery (1988) gave the Adult Attachment Interview to a sample of 53 college students, collected self-report measures of perceptions of self and others at two points, and obtained peer ratings of each individual's affect regulation and social adjustment over a year. Adolescents who were rated as "securely attached" on the Adult Attachment Interview also reported higher social competence and higher levels of support from their family, and they were assessed as lower on anxiety in comparison with both "insecure" groups, and on hostility in comparison with the "dismissing of attachment" group. In contrast, adolescents who were rated as dismissing of attachment on the Adult Attachment Interview were rated as higher on hostility by peers and, overall, tended to view relationships as distant and unsupportive. The dismissing of attachment group, however, did not differ from the secure group in self-reported measures of social competence, which was interpreted as consistent with the pattern of denial and compulsive self-reliance evident among those dismissing of attachment. Finally, the adolescents who were categorized as "preoccupied with attachment" were rated as higher in anxiety than either of the other two groups by their peers, and those preoccupied with attachment depicted themselves as lower in social competence on self-report measures. Kobak and Sceery (1988) hypothesized that working models of attachment are closely linked with representations of self and others, and with affective regulation in actual interpersonal transactions, and these researchers called for further research on how working models of attachment affect the quality of affective communication in current attachment relationships.

Intergenerational Transmission of Attachment Patterns

In research with a clinical population, Diana Diamond and Jeri Doane (in press) investigated the relationship between parents' working models of attachment (as assessed on the Five Minute Speech Sample and Parental Bonding Instrument) and the expression of negative affect among a group of severely disturbed adolescents and young adults and their families during long-term treatment. The researchers found that parents who had disturbed (negative or ambivalent) attachment representations of their own same-sex parent were significantly more likely to exhibit negative affect in the form of critical, guilt-inducing, or intrusive comments in face-to-face interactions with their disturbed children than are parents who are securely attached to their own parents. Further, Doane and Diamond found that many parents with disturbed attachment histories persisted in expressing negative affect over the course of treatment regardless of patient improvement, which led the researchers to stipulate that negative affect is not only embedded in the parents' own disturbed attachment histories and representations, but also functions as the vehicle through which disturbed patterns of attachment may be transmitted across the generations (in press). In addition, there was evidence that such negative affective patterns and their linkage to the disturbed internal working models of attachment functioned outside of the participants' conscious awareness, in that the parents' verbal attachment representations of their children (as assessed through a Five Minute Speech Sample) did not necessarily correspond with the degree of negative affect that they displayed in actual interactions with them.

In sum, previous research on attachment suggests that encoded in internal working models of attachment are affects that are generated through attachment experiences, which may linger and become the driving force for the transgenerational transmission of such experiences. In the YPIFS, we explored whether disturbances in attachment between parent and patient or between parents and their own parents are associated with the persistence of negative styles of relating as measured in face-to-face interaction with adolescent or adult offspring.

We have maintained that neither the EE coding system nor the AS interactional measure of family emotional climate actually measures attachment. Despite some points of overlap between attachment and EE-related constructs such as overinvolvement and negative affect, it is important to remember that both of these coding systems involve unidirectional assessment of parental criticism and rejection of the patient, whereas attachment involves a bidirectional process in which both parties are drawn into reciprocal bonding and interaction (Doane, Hill, & Diamond, 1991). In general, family researchers have neglected the bidirectional nature of affectional bonds that may exist or have failed to develop between the patient and his or her family of origin. Empirically, we have found that attachment ratings between parent and child and measures of family AS are not always overlapping, and that these two aspects of family functioning reflect distinct domains of family emotional climate that can make valuable contributions to understanding the emotional atmosphere of families with psychiatric disorder in one of the members. Our research investigations have been guided by the idea that affective exchanges within families function as the vehicles through which attachment patterns are conveyed through the generations.

An Epigenetic Model of Relational Systems

As the preceding research review indicates, both a negative emotional environment and a disturbed attachment between parents and their child may contribute to the development and maintenance of severe psychopathology and to recurrent relapse. Thus, it is important to understand how these two sets of family attributes might combine to result in different familial constellations of protective and risk factors. In the clinical arena, our experience has been that issues concerning disturbances in attachment between one of the primary parents and the patient take priority over other problems such as verbal criticism, hostility, communication difficulties, or deficits in problem-solving skills.

This formulation is consistent with Lyman Wynne's (1984) notion that there is an epigenetic model for understanding the development of enduring family relational systems. In this model, four major processes are outlined: attachment and caregiving, communicating, joint problem solving, and mutuality. The initial epigenetic layer, attachment and caregiving, is primary; and when attachment has not taken place, a shared cognitive and affective perspective necessary for more advanced and complex relational modes of relating, such as joint problem-solving, cannot be established. With a nonexistent or negative attachment, the family may be arrested at the first stage of the epigenetic journey. The patient and parents have no shared base of positive affective history that each can take for granted when attempting to send and comprehend complex verbal and nonverbal communications. When secure attachment bonds characterize the family, communication styles become prominent in the family's day-to-day concerns. As Wynne points out, however, family members must first be sufficiently emotionally attached to one another before they are willing to come together to learn communication skills or anything else. Joint problem solving, an even more complex form of relating, presupposes not only an attachment but also the acquisition of relatively successful communication skills among family members. Joint goal setting and problem solving are key components of many forms of family-based treatments for severely disturbed individuals (e.g., Falloon, Boyd, McGill et al., 1984; Goldstein, Rodnick, Evans et al., 1978).

Wynne (1984) has suggested that the two major components of EE, emotional overinvolvement and criticism, can be understood as "special forms of attachment/caregiving that are likely to lead to dysfunctional communicating, problem-solving, and intimacy" (p. 304). The clinical implications of this theoretical linkage, which combines attachment and EE constructs, has not been fully developed by Wynne. Our research findings, which are presented in significant detail in chapter 3, suggest that EE and AS are better understood as vehicles of family communication through which intrafamilial attachment problems are perpetuated. Therefore, our model of treatment necessitates that we first evaluate whether disturbed intrafamilial attachment patterns are present. The extent to which problems around attachment bonds have been positively resolved in the initial epigenetic layer of family relationships provides the context for understanding and treating the family's problems in the realm of expressed emotion or affective style. In our studies of intergenerational family attachment patterns, we have used the AS ratings because the family transmission processes occur primarily through family interactions, and thus necessitate measures that go beyond the attitudinal level into the realm of family transactions.

In our empirically derived family typology and the method of treatment on which it is based, we thus stress the importance of assessing the nature of family attachments and caregiving across generations. Also, we contend that therapists need to assess the representations, or internal working models, that individuals hold of such attachment experiences before attempting to understand and treat the dysfunctional high EE or negative AS patterns of family communication.

CHAPTER 3

The Yale Psychiatric Institute Family Study: Research Design and Methods

I
N THIS CHAPTER we outline the design of the Yale Psychiatric Institute Family Study and provide a comprehensive overview of the clinical assessment instruments and procedures used to address our central research questions. The more clinically oriented reader may wish to move directly to chapter 5, which introduces the family typology derived from the research methods and findings presented in chapters 4 and 5.

In designing the Yale Psychiatric Institute Family Study (YPIFS), we intended to explore in depth the process of change in families of patients undergoing treatment for major psychiatric illness. We wanted to focus on some of the unanswered questions about the sequence and patterns of individual and family changes, and about linkages between family risk and patient characteristics. Previous research, as discussed in chapter 2, had clearly established a statistical link between certain dysfunctional patterns of relating in families and psychiatric outcome in patients diagnosed with disorders such as schizophrenia, bipolar disorder, and depression. Prediction studies pointed to the family emotional climate as a potential pathogenic factor in the patient's recovery efforts. Certain assumptions followed from the family research, particularly from research on expressed emotion (EE) done in Great Britain, where patients were assumed to be the victims of an overly critical, overinvolved, and hostile family environment. Many of these original investigators believed that EE (overly critical or overinvolved attitudes) was primarily a unilateral force, stemming from within the parent, that directly exerted a negative influence on the recovering patients as they were struggling to recover from a florid episode of the disorder. The alternative explanation—that patients, due to the burden of their psychiatric disorder, caused the relatives to become excessively critical or involved toward them—had been voiced primarily by self-help support groups such as the National Alliance for the Mentally Ill (NAMI).

This issue of reactivity versus causality had become further complicated by numerous treatment studies that combined maintenance dose neuroleptics and family therapy interventions aimed at providing parents with skills for managing the illness in the sick family member. Although these studies had successfully demonstrated that family intervention had dramatically reduced the relapse probability for the patient, they had not addressed the basic question about what exactly had changed in the patient or in the family.

In virtually all of these treatment studies, the relapse rate for the group of patients receiving family treatment was significantly low. Yet a significant number of the patients remained high EE despite several months of family treatment (Doane et al., 1986, in press; Hogarty et al., 1986) This suggests that for some parents, high EE attitudes, as well as behaviors, may reflect relatively enduring qualities in many families.

Why are some parents persistently critical of a severely disturbed or psychotic child? Are they overwhelmed and overburdened with the strains and stresses of caring for someone so impaired? Were these family members highly critical and overinvolved before they had a severely disturbed child to contend with? Or were they just average parents, fairly even in their tendency to be critical, who became involved in their child's illness in an emotionally intense way that left them so frustrated and overwhelmed that they became angry, critical, overintense reactors to their own situations? If the patient were to make a recovery and act in a more socially appropriate and nonsymptomatic way, would the high EE attitudes of the parents then abate?

And what about the relationship between parental attitudes and actual parental behaviors? Does it matter if parents secretly hold the rejecting attitudes but are able to curb these attitudes in face-to-face interactions with their disturbed offspring? Once parents change their negative attitudes, do those attitudes disappear completely, or do parents revert to negative attitudes again when the patient becomes symptomatic again? The foregoing questions inspired the design of our research study.

The questions' importance lay in their implications for treatment. In today's climate of brief treatment, it is increasingly important to find the optimal way to allocate limited treatment resources. The more we understand how risk factors in the family work, the more effective we can be in designing interventions that lower the patient's risk for relapse.

The YPI study design and conceptualization evolved out of the unanswered research questions that had emerged from studies by Jeri Doane, the principal investigator, regarding the prediction of relapse in chronic psychiatric patients. The primary purpose in carrying out the YPI study was to generate understanding of the phenomenon of change, rather than merely to predict outcome or to increase the precision with which prediction studies could be carried out. Existing instruments for assessing relevant dimensions of family functioning such as EE and AS had proven to be limited because they had not provided data about the underlying processes involved in the family, or because they had focused more on performance of certain skills or behaviors and less on the specific problems unique to each person's situation. Therefore, some new measures were formulated for the YPI study, many of which were designed to be carried out at a reasonable cost by ordinary clinicians in typical treatment settings.

In this chapter the focus is on the design and the empirical methods used. In chapter 4 we present some of the core research findings, with a focus on critical research questions about as the validity of the instruments and the predictive utility of the measures in identifying cases that may be more vulnerable to clinical relapse. While the empirical approach to studying these phenomena is a necessary component for identifying cases at risk, it is important to remember that these ways of synthesizing and organizing information are not necessarily the most useful ways of organizing data for the development of treatment models. Another way of using these research data is to draw conclusions from the pool of empirical results that have implications for clinical practice. In the clinical chapters that follow this one, we present a family typology based on the empirical findings and measures reported in the following sections.

Overview of Study Design

A total of 53 patients consecutively admitted to the Yale Psychiatric Institute participated in a prospective, longitudinal study of change occurring during a relatively lengthy inpatient treatment (average length of 1 year). None of the patients had evidence of parental retardation (IQ below 70), organic brain syndrome, or substance abuse that appeared to be implicated etiologically in the patient's primary psychiatric diagnosis. Patients met criteria for one of three diagnostic groups.

Schizophrenia Spectrum

All but two of the 22 patients in this group met the criteria for schizophrenia specified in the *Diagnostic and statistical manual of mental disorders* (3rd edition, revised), or *DSM-III-R* (American Psychiatric Association, 1987). The remaining two patients had diagnoses of schizoptypal disorder and schizophreniform disorder, and both had clear features of schizophrenia but had not yet developed a definite syndrome. The patients were between 17 and 29 years of age. Schizotypal disorder was included in the schizophrenia-spectrum groups (one case), based on the findings from Scandinavian data in which evidence of genetic links between schizophrenia and schizotypal disorder was found (Kender, Gruenberg, & Strauss, 1981).

Young Adult Affective Disorder and/or Borderline Personality (ADBL)

This group of 18 patients included individuals whose primary diagnosis was affective disorder (9 patients), borderline personality disorder (5), or substance abuse (4). Half of the patients in the affective disorder group (and all of the substance abusers) also had a borderline or mixed personality disorder. The patients were between 17 and 29 years of age. Eighty percent of all the patients in this group also had diagnoses of substance abuse.

Adolescent

This group of 13 patients ranged in age from 14 to 16. The primary diagnosis for patients in this group was borderline personality disorder. Many of the adolescents had transient psychotic features, but none were chronically psychotic.

Diagnostic Assessment

Patients 18 years and older were administered the Structured Clinical Interview for DSM-III-R (SCID), developed by Robert Spitzer and Janet Williams (1985) for generating DSM-III-R Axis I diagnoses. Younger patients were administered the Schedule for Affective Disorders and Schizophrenia for School-Age Children, Epidemiologic version (K-SADS-E) (Orvaschel & Puig-Antich, 1987). One of the parents was also interviewed with the K-SADS-E in order to obtain a full diagnostic picture. A system for making DSM-III-R diagnoses from the K-SADS-E interview, which Karen John developed for epidemiologic studies of high-risk children (Weissman, Gammon, MeriKangas et al., 1987), was used. This procedure involves algorithms for assignment of probability levels of DSM-III-R diagnoses on the basis of the number of criterion symptoms met, and the duration of these symptoms. Trained interviewers included a psychologist and a psychiatrist who were experienced in diagnostic interviewing. Interrater agreement on diagnosis was high (90%), with few differences between major diagnostic categories. Diagnoses were made from the SCID and K-SADS-E, and supplemental information was also reviewed for corroborating evidence of the accuracy of the diagnosis (information from previous hospital records and consultation with the patient's treatment team). In situations where disagreements arose, they were resolved by a third experienced clinician.

All patients were administered the Personality Development Examination (PDE), which had been developed for deriving Axis II diagnoses (Loranger, Oldham, Russakoff, & Susman, 1987). This instrument is a structured interview that allows the investigator to check systematically for the presence or absence of the various criteria used to make the diagnosis of the individual personality disorders in the DSM-III-R. The instrument systematically surveys the phenomenology and life experiences that are required to make these diagnoses in the subject. The format, which resembles a clinical interview more than a questionnaire, is designed to maintain rapport and encourage valid replies from the subject. We piloted this instrument during the first year of the study, and analyses showed excellent reliability with Axis II diagnoses assigned by the treating clinicians. Interrater reliability was excellent (intraclass $r = .89, n = 11$).

Patient Characteristics

Patients in the adult subgroups ranged in age from 17 to 29 years of age, and they had a mean of 3.6 (schizophrenics) and 1.1 (adult affective disorder/borderline) previous psychiatric hospitalizations. Thus, this was a fairly young, seriously disturbed group of patients. The adolescents had a mean of one previous admission; thus, this group was severely disturbed for their age cohort as well. Socioeconomic status ranged from lower-middle to upper-middle class.

Like most other patients treated at the YPI, these patients had third-party insurance carrier coverage of their hospital care. Sixty percent of the families were dual-parent; 40% were single-parent families. The sample was predominantly Caucasian; 6% were black, and 2% were Hispanic. Further details on demographics are provided in Table 3.1.

Before the specific measures and modes of assessment used in the study

TABLE 3.1

Sample Characteristics

	Schizophrenia Spectrum (*n=22*)	Adult Borderline/ Affective Disorder (*n=18*)	Adolescents (*n=13*)
n	22	18	13
Primary Diagnosis Affective Disorder	—	9	—
Primary Diagnosis Borderline PD	—	5	13
Primary Diagnosis	—	4	—
Mean Age	20.4	19.7	14.9
Sex M/F (%)	8/14 (36/64)	14/4 (78/22)	7/6 (54/46)
Ethnicity (%)			
White	21 (95)	18 (100)	10 (77)
African American	0	0	3 (23)
Hispanic	1 (5)	0	0
Family Composition (%)			
Single-parent	9 (41)	6 (33)	7 (54)
Dual-parent	13 (59)	12 (67)	6 (46)
Age at Onset of Illness (Mean + SD)	17.6 + 3.2	18.8 + 2.7	13.5 + 1.6
No. Prior Hospitalizations (Mean + SD)	3.6 + 3.6	1.1 + 1.5	1.0 + 1.2
Length of Stay Index Admission (Mean + SD)	13.8 + 8.1	11.5 + 5.8	12.2 + 6.3

are described, a brief description is needed of the setting in which the patients were treated, including the approach to inpatient hospital treatment at the YPI at the time the study was carried out.

The YPI

The YPI provides intensive, long-term psychodynamically oriented treatment for severely ill young adults and adolescents. At the time of this study the average length of stay at the YPI was 12 to 18 months.

The YPI treatment philosophy emphasized helping patients build interpersonal skills and develop realistic ways of managing the problems and limitations imposed by their illness. On the long-term treatment units of the hospital, successful amelioration or elimination of overt symptoms (e.g., depression, anxiety, hallucinations, delusions—ones that might entail a psychiatric diagnosis on Axis I) was only an initial treatment goal. The overarching aim for all patients was to help them develop the requisite skills and strengths necessary for extended non-hospital-level residence. The YPI was one of a very small number of psychiatric institutions that offered treatment that focused on this particular outcome goal.

Such a treatment goal involved targeting not only the major psychiatric symptoms exhibited by the patients, but also their longstanding interpersonal difficulties, usually resulting from severe character pathology in conjunction with Axis I disorders, which made it difficult for them to sustain their functioning as outpatients or to use the mental health system effectively. The convergence of severe psychiatric symptoms with intractable character pathology was thus a hallmark of YPI patients, and this necessitated multimodal treatment involving individual and family therapy, as well as educational and vocational counseling.

Description of the Family Treatment

All patients and their families participated in weekly family therapy, in addition to other treatment modalities, including thrice weekly individual psychotherapy, group therapy, and occupational and recreational therapies. The psychotherapeutic approach was psychodynamic and rested heavily on developmental object relations theory; that is, the patient's pathology was conceptualized as resulting from the confluence of developmental failures and psychiatric disorder. Patients with clearcut chronic psychotic disorders were educated about their disorder and were helped to understand how their characteristic patterns of managing their symptoms necessitated repeated hospitalizations. Most patients also received pharmacologic treatment.

An initial goal of family treatment was to provide the family with information about the nature and course of the patient's disorder so that all family members could better accept the realities of the disorder. In addition, the family therapist assessed structural aspects of the family system such as generational boundaries, strength of the parenting coalition, strength of the marital coalition, and presence of triangulation. The family therapist also assessed the family's characteristic coping style (e.g., the ability to communicate clearly, to express a range of affects, and to cope with the periodic crises of the patient's disorder).

Family therapists drew on a broad range of treatment techniques, and they did not adhere to a specific intervention strategy for every case.

Rather, family therapists were encouraged to tailor their interventions to fit a specific family's style, with the particular treatment goals and their timing growing out of the therapist's assessment of the family. For example, a therapist might begin a family treatment by exploring the family's communication style; shift to assigning tasks to facilitate an improved parental coalition; and, later in the treatment, move to exploring the marital relationship. The modification of behaviors such as those assessed by affective style (AS) or expressed emotion (EE) methods was not a specific focus of the family intervention.

The general theoretical orientation of family treatment tended to be a blend of family systems and object relations approaches that emphasized verbal communication, expression and subsequent clarification of feelings, strengthening of appropriate boundaries in the family, and improvement of the family's reality testing and resistance to stress. Although behavioral techniques were sometimes used, the approach was not traditionally behavioral. All of the family therapists had undergone training in both psychodynamic principles and system-based family assessment and therapy.

A psychodynamically oriented emphasis on the exploration and sharing of feelings and conflicts, along with the historical roots of these in individual and family history, was common; but the family therapy tended to be eclectic. None of the therapists focused on a strictly psychoeducational model of treatment, although the parents were informed about the nature of the patient's problems and symptoms. Staff social workers, advanced psychiatry residents, and postdoctoral fellows in psychology served as therapists. These individuals varied in their level of experience and training in family therapy. All therapists were supervised by an experienced family therapist in weekly supervision.

Repeated Measures Design

Aspects of the patient's functioning and course of illness and aspects of the family's functioning and interaction patterns were studied independently in a quasi-naturalistic, multiple repeated measures design. This particular design incorporated features of rigorous laboratory measurement and measures derived from the "natural environment." With the latter measures, nurses, family therapists, and case coordinators who had regular, ongoing contact with the patient on the hospital ward where he or she was living with others and dealing with the social world reported these measures.

Our team made family laboratory assessments at the time of the patient's admission into the hospital, three months later, nine months after admission, and at the time of the patient's discharge into the community. From observers who could provide us with a window into how the patient was doing and how the family reacted, we obtained monthly or bimonthly measures of patient and family factors, similar conceptually to those being studied in the lab setting, from the patient's admission to his or her discharge. The patient's primary nurse on the ward and the family therapist who saw the family and the patient for weekly family therapy sessions acted as our informants.

This tracking aspect of the design permitted us to look at how patients and families change in a point-counterpoint fashion. For example, we could ask whether families tended to become less hostile and critical once the patient began to show some solid clinical gains, or whether the family's rejecting attitudes or behavior persisted in the face of obvious clinical improvement. Patient symptoms and social functioning deficits were independently assessed each month, which allowed us to study how these two lines of change covaried over time. Studies were carried out to establish the reliability and validity of these measures.

We were interested in exploring the nature of family risk factors across generations. Each parent in our study participated in a 1.5-hour to 2-hour semistructured interview designed to elicit systematic information about how affective styles varied in the family of origin, as experienced and reported by the parent, and about the quality of the attachment bonds between the parent and his or her own mother and father. We included in this intergenerational assessment two instruments used to collect data on the patient's attitudes toward and perception of the parent—the Five Minute Speech Sample (FMSS), from which attachment was measured, and the Parental Bonding Instrument (PBI), which provided an additional measure of perceived nurturance and protection. These intergenerational measures provided us with parallel data collected in identical ways across three generations. In examining these data, our goal was to begin to explore intergenerational transmission of risk factors in families. As with the measures on family emotional climate, these attachment measures were also subjected to reliability and validity studies.

We also had parents complete genetic pedigree interviews. A systematic family history of mental illness interview (Thompson, Kidd & Weissman, 1980; Thompson, Orvaschel, Prusoff, & Kidd, 1982) was used to collect information about psychiatric illness in the parent's first- and second-degree relatives. Gathering these data allowed us to compare the degree of overlap between biological risk or stress in the parent's family and the type of psychosocial risk factors present (negative ways of relating emotionally and disturbed patterns of attachment).

Assessment as a Therapeutic Experience

Each family participated in a 2-hour intensive initial family assessment carried out in a laboratory setting at the hospital. This assessment provided data about how the family functioned with regard to a number of dimensions. First, we wanted to know how parents in the family handled a situation when they were emotionally stressed and talking face-to-face with the patient about some aspect of his or her behavior or attitude that they did not agree with. In particular, we were interested in the expression of feelings—especially, critical ones, including guilt-inducing or intrusive remarks, as well as positive emotions, as reflected in empathic statements, praise of the patient, and the expression of warmth. The AS system of coding direct interaction was used to measure this aspect of parental behavior toward the patient.

However, we were also interested in attitudes, not just the behavior. The Kreisman scale of rejecting attitudes was used to assess parental negative attitudes, because it could be administered fairly quickly and because several of the scale items had obvious construct validity with the AS coding system. Having measures of both attitudes and behaviors allowed us to address questions such as "If therapy alters only the AS behavior and not the attitudes, will the negative AS behavior be more likely to return?" Or, "Do parents of borderline adolescents have equally negative attitudes toward the patient as do parents of chronic schizophrenic patients?"

Family Interaction Task

The family interaction task used is a modification of Fred Strodtbeck's (1954) revealed differences technique, which elicits samples of clinically meaningful family affective behavior during an emotionally charged discussion about a current problem or unresolved issue in the family. The task involves first separating family members into different rooms, where each family member is interviewed individually to generate problem issues that focus on family conflicts idiosyncratically relevant to that particular family. After an issue is identified, the interviewer asks the family member to pretend that the person involved in the problem is sitting in the room with him or her and to verbalize the issue while the tape recorder is running. This audiotaped recording of the family member's issue is then taken to the respective family member to whom it was directed, and he or she listens to the statement and is asked to respond to it. This response is recorded immediately after the initial statement. Two issue-and-response sequences are generated for each family member.

The family members are subsequently brought together into a lab, where they listen to one of these audiotaped sequences of statements. The family is then directed to discuss this problem for 10 minutes, to express their thoughts and feelings about it, and to try to solve the problem while the experimenter is out of the room. After 10 minutes the family is asked to discuss the second problem. One of the issues is generated by the patient, and the other is generated by one of the parents. The order of presentation is counterbalanced across families. This procedure generates a family discussion that is emotionally meaningful for the entire family. Approximately 45 minutes of assessment time is invested in generating a family discussion that is relevant for that particular family. We have found this investment of time to be essential to generating a meaningful sample of family interaction.

The majority of our families spontaneously remarked to us that the family interaction task was helpful to them and that they experienced it as therapeutic. Many of them said that it was more helpful than a regular family therapy session. The interactions differed from family therapy in that the family was focused on a fairly narrow issue, but then they were left alone to try to work on the problem. Many parents reported a sense of accomplishment at having been able to engage their son or daughter and discuss a meaningful issue without having to have a therapist's help. These family interactions were audio and video recorded. The entire family assessment package took about 2 hours to complete.

AS Risk Profile

Verbatim, typed transcripts were made from audiotapes of these interactions and are coded for AS (Doane et al., 1985). As noted in chapter 2, Affective Style (AS) is a coding system that was designed to capture clinically meaningful affective attitudes and behaviors that were verbally expressed toward a patient during a face-to-face family interaction task, and some of the system's codes overlap with the EE dimensions of criticism and emotional overinvolvement. Measures of different forms of parental support for the patient are also coded. For purposes of illustration, examples from three categories of the AS coding system are presented: criticism, guilt induction, and intrusiveness.

Personal Criticism

The criticism has one or more of the following qualities: unnecessary or overly harsh modifiers; reference to broad classes or behaviors; or reference to the child's character or nature.

Examples: "You have an ugly, arrogant attitude." "We're just saying that the way you act is bad." "Usually your answers have been right off the cuff—quick and phony." "It's just slovenliness on your part, right?"

Guilt Induction

Statements with a guilt-inducing impact have two components: They convey that the child is to blame or is at fault for some negative event and that the parent has been distressed or upset by the event.

Examples: "You cause our family an awful lot of trouble." "And now you've got me feeling bad, because here I thought you were doing so well." "You're being unfair to your mother." "Most of our fights are because of you."

Intrusiveness

Intrusive statements imply knowledge of the child's thoughts, feeling states, or motives when, in fact, there is no apparent basis for such knowledge.

Examples: "You're not mad; you're just depressed." "I know that you are feeling upset about what happened last night and trying to hide it, but don't let it ruin your day." "Every time I walk away I cringe inside and I know that you feel it too." "You won't take your medication because you're afraid it isn't helping, right?"

There are two different kinds of criticism codes: Personal Criticism (as just illustrated) and Benign Criticism, which involves lower-key critical remarks. In addition, a measure of intrusion is obtained that, like guilt induction, has no direct parallel in the EE system of coding. Many guilt-inducing remarks in the AS coding system are considered critical remarks in the EE coding scheme. The interpersonal analogue of emotional overinvolvement may be reflected, at least in part, by the parent's excessive intrusiveness. With intrusion, one person speaks as the supreme expert concerning the listener's thoughts, feelings, and motives, with little regard for the autonomy of the inner world of the other.

The AS data can be reduced in two ways. First, a categorical designation for each parent can be assigned, based on whether or not the parent uses one of the negative marker codes of AS previously shown to be associated with increased risk for a poor course of illness (i.e., personal criticism, guilt induction, or excessive intrusiveness). Parental AS profiles are either *benign* (no negative marker codes used in either interaction) or *negative* (at least one negative marker code is used). These parental classifications can then be used alone to group individual parents as low-risk or high-risk for AS, or the classifications can be combined with the spouse's AS profile to generate a family AS pattern categorization. Patients from negative AS pattern families (where at least one parent has a negative profile) have been found in several studies to be at risk for poor course of illness (Albers et al., 1986; Doane et al., 1981, 1985; Doane & Becker, in press; Miklowitz et al., 1988). Benign AS families are not necessarily adaptive or particularly healthy; rather, the benign designation indicates merely the absence of negative AS marker codes.

Total AS Score

Change in the way that family members express criticism and other negative feelings may occur subtly. This change might be clinically meaningful, yet not so obvious as the overtly hostile criticism reflected in the relatively low frequency marker codes. The AS profiles rely exclusively on the presence or absence of certain low-frequency marker codes. The total AS score is a more broadly defined measure of affective communication that may be more sensitive in picking up subtle, yet perhaps meaningful, changes occurring in the quality of affective verbal exchange in families as they progress through treatment. The total AS score is a summary measure of all of the negatively toned affective remarks occurring during the interaction, irrespective of whether they were the low-frequency harsh codes or relatively benign ones (e.g., benign criticism, occasional neutral intrusiveness). Using AS this way, one can think of a total of all of the four negative AS codes (personal criticism, benign criticism, guilt induction, and intrusion) as a combined score, reflecting the general family emotional atmosphere or climate.

Positive AS

The positive AS codes have not been particularly useful as predictors of course of illness in any study thus far. We had expected the positive AS measures to be more fruitful in this particular study, because we were obtaining assessments of AS at intervals spanning several months of family treatment. We thought that because families were receiving relatively lengthy treatment, the positive AS codes might emerge as significant family variables after extensive family work had occurred and presumably the family relationships had improved to the point that support would play a significant role in the family discussion. As discussed later, this did not turn out to be the case. In fact, family support and positive remarks often remained remarkably low throughout extensive periods of treatment. In cases where clear changes for the better were observed in the family's style of interaction, however, positive AS did emerge, but typically this was not until after 9 or 10 months of family therapy.

A total AS score was calculated for the positive AS codes by summing all of the positive codes for each parent across both interactions. This measure reflects the number of times a parent is able to stand back from the conflictual discussion to say something supportive or positive to the patient. This category of AS includes codes such as statements of unqualified support, compliments, acknowledgements of improvement on the patient's part, praise, references to the idea that other people have the same kinds of problems, empathic statements, and statements of love for the patient. Interestingly, in our study the typical parent made very few positive remarks to the patient, even months after treatment had begun. Although the experimental procedure "pulls" for conflict and negative affect, it seemed surprising that a parent often made 8 to 12 negative remarks, but only 1 or 2 positive statements, if any. Similarly, we were surprised to see that even when the number of critical statements was reduced after three months of family treatment, the number of positive remarks did not increase—it remained low.

Repeated Measures of Family Interaction

As noted in chapter 2, the family interaction task was repeated 3 months after treatment had begun, again 6 months later, and again when the patient was discharged from the hospital. This repeated measures aspect of the design allowed us, first, to explore several questions: Did an AS profile of the family predict relapse, as it had in previous studies? If so, did the initial assessment, the 3-month assessment, or the final discharge assessment have the best predictive utility?

Second, this design aspect allowed us to look at how AS and other variables such as rejecting attitudes and attachment to the patient changed during a lengthy treatment period. We could look at issues such as differential patterns of change based on diagnosis, a patient's ability to progress in treatment, and a patient's compliance with the type of medication prescribed. We were also able to investigate whether parental AS shifts to a more benign pattern once the patient has sustained significant improvement in his or her clinical state and social functioning.

Attitudinal Measures of Affective Style

We also tried to assess parental attitudes related to AS by obtaining parental responses to the Kreisman Scale of Rejecting Attitudes (Kreisman, Simmons, & Joy, 1979), a questionnaire designed to assess parents' negative attitudes toward their children. This 24-item questionnaire was originally designed to assess family emotional attitudes similar to expressed emotion (EE), as measured by Vaughn and Leff (1976a). Each item is a statement read to the parent expressing commonly held attitudes family members have about a mentally ill relative. A prototypical example would be, "I'm tired of having to organize my life around him." The items are accompanied by a 7-point scale, which is used to score how frequently the parent reports that he or she feels the same way about his or her own son or daughter.

In the YPIFS we were interested in identifying parental attitudes that might be considered consistently negative or particularly strong. Therefore we adapted the scoring procedures for the Kreisman instrument as follows: Parents who agreed with the negative attitude "never" (score of 1); "almost never" (score of 2); or "occasionally" (score of 3) were given a weighted score for that item of 0, because it was felt that most parents would theoretically have occasional negative attitudes about their children. Thus, if parents replied "occasionally" to an item such as "I am increasingly more irritated with [him]," they received a weighted score of 0 for negative AS on that item.

If, on the other hand, the parents replied "sometimes" (score of 4), this was felt to reflect some minimal degree of consistency in negative attitudes, so a weighted score of 1 was assigned. Increasing agreement was assigned a weighted score as follows: "a lot of the time" (score of 5) was assigned a weighted score of 2; "almost always" (score of 6) was assigned a weighted score of 3; and "always" (score of 7) was assigned a weighted score of 4.

Ten items from the original 24 were selected in a pilot study to use as an index of negative AS attitudes. These 10 items are statements that would be scored within the AS coding system as critical remarks if they were spoken directly to the patient during a face-to-face discussion. The sum of the weighted scores for the 10 items was calculated to reveal a summary score called the 10K score, which ranged from 0 to 40 theoretically, but from 0 to 29 in this sample. A natural break in the distribution of scores suggested a cutoff to divide parents into low and high 10K scores—parents whose scores were 8 or above were said to have definite negative AS attitudes about the patient. This method of grouping parents is fairly conservative; only one third of the parents were classified as high 10K. Having measures of both behavior and attitudes permitted us to examine how much overlap between the two existed and whether any lack of overlap was clinically meaningful.

For example, we wondered whether parents with highly rejecting attitudes were slower to change their AS behavior toward the child as treatment progressed. Similarly, would parents whose Kreisman attitudes were relatively benign respond to family therapy more rapidly than parents with entrenched negative attitudes? Because the Kreisman scale takes only 10 minutes to administer, it was incorporated into the repeated measures assessment package, which was administered each time the family interaction task was administered.

Attachment Measures

As part of the initial family assessment, each parent was also administered an FMSS task in which he or she is asked to speak spontaneously and without interruption for 5 minutes about the patient, what kind of person the patient is, and how they get along together. During the intergenerational interviews, each parent was also asked to give an FMSS about each on of his or her own parents, in which the parent described how he or she and the parent got along together during childhood, adolescence, and adulthood.

Such spontaneous descriptions frequently elicit themes related to attachment, bonding, and closeness or distance. This approach is consistent with previous research by John Bowlby (1982), Mary Ainsworth and colleagues (1978), and others who posit attachment as a central dynamic in human relatedness. Diana Diamond (1986) developed a coding system for measuring attachment, which is designed to make a distinction between parents who show a positive, secure attachment—as assessed through the expression of loving, caring feelings toward their child—and those who demonstrate ambivalent, indifferent, or overinvolved feelings and attitudes. This coding system, along with reliability and validity studies, has been presented elsewhere (Diamond & Doane, in press), but is summarized here as well.

As is the case with much recent research on attachment (Main, Kaplan, & Cassidy, 1985), the FMSS attachment coding system is designed to assess the individual's representations of attachment relationships based on verbal descriptions, rather than laboratory- based experimental procedures (e.g., mother-infant nonverbal reunion behaviors, as observed in the Ainsworth Strange Situation [Ainsworth, Blehar, Waters, & Wall, 1978], that elicited the original mother-infant attachment patterns). Previous researchers (Main, Kaplan, & Cassidy, 1985) have suggested that such verbal representations of attachment experiences provide a window into what Bowlby (1982, 1988) terms "internal working models of attachment," as described in chapter 2.

FMSS Attachment Coding System

The FMSS attachment coding system bears some similarities to the prevailing paradigms that have emerged in attachment theory and research (Ainsworth, 1978; Bowlby, 1980; Main et al., 1985). The coding system includes the following six categories:

Positive Secure Attachment

Statements are coded for positive attachment if they contain evidence of an enduring emotional bond, the expression of loving and caring feelings, and a sense of the individual's unique significance and/or irreplaceability. Positive, secure attachment can also be expressed through statements that emphasize that the parent (or parent figure) can be relied on to be available, responsive, and helpful in adverse or difficult circumstances, or that the individual can evoke the emotional bond to the parent in such circumstances. Positive attachment is also sometimes indicated through empathy, or the capacity to intuit, understand, and identify with the other person's feelings, thoughts, or motives.

Example: "My mother is a warm, caring, loving person. There were hugs and kisses when I was a kid. She always made me feel secure. . . when she was around I always felt secure."

Example: "I think he's a very nice guy and I really love him. His life is really hard and he's sacrificed a lot to make me and my brother happy. . . . . He's had a rough life himself, and when he's had problems helping me, it's because he's had difficulties in his past life and problems with his own family."

Negative Attachment

Statements are coded for negative attachment when they convey a negative affectional bond based on rejection, hatred, or dislike, or a nonexistent bond based on indifference to the other. Negative attachment is also coded when the individual expresses an expectation of being rebuffed when he or she seeks care.

Example: "Well, I've come to realize... how much of an influence my mother played by her just not being there for me."

Example: "I just wanted love like a father and son would have, and that never happened."

Example: "She just wasn't there for me. She's never been there for me. . . . If she were to die today, I don't know what I'd feel."

Example: "He told all of us that we weren't worth much. . . . He is an uncaring person. . . . He didn't want children; my mother did. He always says he should have never had any kids. . . ."

Ambivalent Attachment

Statements are coded for ambivalent attachment when they involve unintegrated oscillation between positive and negative, secure and insecure attachment, without either predominating. Ambivalent attachment can also be expressed through uncertainty about whether the parent will be responsive or rejecting when the patient seeks care or faces aversive, difficult situations.

Example: "I'd love her and I'd hate her. It was like a see-saw."

Example: "I developed and still have to this day I think what one would call um, a love-hate relationship for him."

Example: "I have no strong emotional attachments to her, but I feel that she really was warm and affectionate and loving to us, but she also sometimes pushed us away."

The first three categories—positive, negative, and ambivalent attachment roughly correspond to Ainsworth's (Ainsworth et al., 1978) attachment categories of secure, insecure-ambivalent, and insecure-avoidant attachment patterns, and to their adult counterparts identified through the Adult Attachment Interview (Main et al., 1985). Some conceptual overlap between our attachment codes and patterns of attachment observed in infancy and childhood by Bowlby, Ainsworth, and others was expected, because the ethological underpinnings of Bowlby's theory suggest that there are a finite number of attachment patterns that result when the child exercises his or her environmentally stable propensity to seek and maintain proximity to a caretaker. When a child's biologically based attachment-seeking behaviors are accepted and responded to and reciprocated, a secure mother-infant attachment pattern results; when they are rebuffed or avoided, an insecure-avoidant pattern emerges, and when they are alternately rebuffed and reciprocated, an insecure-ambivalent attachment pattern ensues (Ainsworth et al., 1978).

We have expanded the avoidant attachment category to include negative bonds based on rejection or dislike, as well as bonds characterized by the maintenance of distance or separateness. Previous theoretical work (Kernberg, 1975, 1990) and research (Sperling, Sharpe, & Fishler, 1991) have suggested that negative hostile attachment bonds, as well as avoidant or resistant/ambivalent attachment patterns, are prevalent with severely disturbed (borderline) patients.

In addition, disturbances in attachment are captured through codes on overinvolvement, parentification, and triangulation, which is consistent with Bowlby's (1977, 1980) aforementioned theories of the triadic variations, which disturbed patterns of dyadic attachment may take in later childhood and adolescence.

Overinvolvement

Statements are coded for overinvolvement when they reveal the parents' excessive preoccupation with or overinvestment in their child, such that the individual's emotional life is almost entirely oriented around the patient to the exclusion of other interests and involvements; or when the parent is excessively overprotective and/or overcontrolling toward the child, as in the following:

Example: "I tend to, or I guess I do, overprotect her and overcoddle and maybe overbaby her, and she's always pushing me away."

Parentification

Statements are coded for parentification when there is evidence of a role reversal in which the parent has abdicated parental functions and cast the child in the role of caretaker, surrogate spouse, or friend, in ways that clearly inhibit the child's development.

Example: "I think that when my father divorced her, she needed me, and she didn't let me develop. . . and she let my problems get worse. I think she was afraid to be alone and I had to take care of her and stay with her."

Triangulation

Statements are coded for triangulation when the child clearly is in the middle of parental conflict such that he or she inevitably betrays one parent if he or she affirms or sustains an attachment to the other.

Example: "If I loved my mother, I had to hate my father. If I hated my father, I had to love my mother, because they always took up battle with me in the middle."

Example: "It was only after my mother died that my father became more interested in me. When she was alive, he was afraid to because my mother would get angry. I was always pulled in between them and asked to take sides in their arguments. Neither parent believed that I could have any loving feelings toward the other."

The FMSS attachment codes are designed to make a distinction between parents who show positive secure attachment to their own child or parents, and those who demonstrate a rupture or disturbance of attachment (e.g., negative, overinvolved, weak, or ambivalent attachment assessed through the expression of contradictory, conflictual, rejecting, and indifferent feelings toward the child or parent). The coding system involves a critical incident model of coding, whereby only those statements thought to be reflective of the affectional bond or relationship between parent and child are coded.

A study establishing the interrater reliability and validity of the FMSS attachment coding system has been carried out and is described elsewhere (Diamond & Doane, in press).

Patient Perceptions of Family Relationships—The PBI

Attachment was also assessed through the PBI, a 25-item self-report measure that reflects the subject's perceptions of his or her mother or father along two dimensions relevant to attachment: care (perceived nurturance) and protection (perceived control) (Parker, Tupling, & Brown, 1979). The two scales may be intersected to yield four possible patterns of parenting: neglectful (low care, low protection), affectionless control (low care, high protection), affectionate constraint (high care, high protection), and optimal parenting (high care, low protection). The PBI has been shown to have good reliability and validity both as a measure of perceived parental characteristics (Parker et al., 1979) and actual parental characteristics (Parker, 1981). The affectionless control pattern has the most overlap with the concept of EE, and recent studies have associated this pattern of parenting with depression (Parker, 1983), early onset schizophrenia (Parker et al., 1979), and schizophrenic relapse (Parker, Fairley, Greenwood, Jurd, & Silove, 1982). Parents fill out the PBI on each of their parents at the time of the parental family-of-origin interview, and patients complete the instrument on their parents at admission, and at the 1-year follow-up.

The PBI and FMSS attachment codes are conceptually overlapping, but distinct. As a self-report questionnaire, the PBI is tapping into the individual's conscious assessment of how well his or her parent mastered basic caretaking and nurturance tasks. The FMSS, on the other hand, is designed to elicit more extensive spontaneous verbalizations about the patient's parent and that person's relationship with his or her own parent, and thus may reflect more primitive underlying emotional reactions.

Patient Symptom Severity and Social Functioning Deficits

The dimensions of patient symptom severity and social functioning deficits are both important when assessing change in individuals with major psychiatric impairment. Contemporary treatment philosophy emphasizes pharmacologic intervention, often to the exclusion of psychosocial interventions. The basic assumption is that when one pharmacologically treats the core symptoms of the illness, the individual ought to be able to survive outside of the hospital setting—that is, that improved social functioning follows decreased symptom severity. We wanted to explore the validity of this assumption in our sample. The YPIFS treatment philosophy at the time of this study was that pharmacologic treatments, while often necessary components of treatment, often do not produce sufficient change in patients to permit them to function in the social world outside of the hospital.

Symptom severity measures were obtained monthly from ratings made by the patient's treatment coordinator, who had no information about any research data collected on the patient. Key symptoms for each patient were identified, and the average of these ratings was used to track change in the patient's symptomatic status as treatment progressed.

Two measures of social functioning were obtained at monthly (for the first 3 months of inpatient treatment) and bimonthly (thereafter) intervals throughout the duration of the inpatient phase of the study. The first measure was the Social Behavior Adjustment Schedule (SBAS), developed by Stephan Platt (1980) in London for use with patients who had chronic psychiatric impairment. Doane adapted this interview for use in the present study by adding some additional items to capture more fully the range of social skills assessed in these patients. The items on this instrument have 3-point scales that rate the severity of impairment from 0 (not a problem at all) to 2 (definite impairment). In the YPIFS, this scale provided data about how well the patients could perform basic social skills, but it did not provide an indication of whether the patient was improving in those areas in which he or she was most deficient.

To assess relevant changes in each patient, the Target Social Deficit measure (TSD) was developed that allowed us to identify the patient's three most severe social deficits that prevented him or her from getting along in the social world. In general, we did not use symptoms to define each problem, but social deficits such as "social withdrawal," "is argumentative with peers," "behaves impulsively," "is rude and obnoxious in conversation," "denies he has any problems whatsoever." Each of these targeted social deficits was rated each month by the patient's primary nurse on a 13-point scale ranging from 13 (this was constantly a problem) to 1 (this was almost never a problem). The average of these three scores was calculated each month or each 2 months throughout treatment to track the patient's progress in becoming more socially appropriate. If the patient sustained a gain of 2 or more points on the scale for at least 2 months, a period of improvement was said to have occurred. The interval of 2 points was chosen because it was felt that this constituted a very obvious, easily noticeable change in the patient's functioning—one that would probably be noticed by anyone having contact with him or her, including his or her family.

Although the nature of the TSD method complicates the exact comparison of numerical scores from patient to patient, it is possible, with this measure, to capture a clinically meaningful measure of each patient's progress in learning how to get along with and be accepted by others in the social world. More direct testing of differences in actual levels of performance on discrete social behaviors can be obtained from the SBAS data.

Medication Issues

Roughly 80% of the patients in the study received some kind of psychotropic medication during the hospitalization. Detailed records of these medications were kept, and profiles of responses to somatic interventions were constructed for each subject. These data allowed us to look at how medication effects interacted with the other psychosocial measures in the study.

Tracking Changes in the Family's Affective Style

Direct observation or recording of family therapy sessions was not feasible in this setting. Therefore, a set of scales for assessing aspects of family functioning related to EE and AS was developed for use by the family therapists who were treating patients in our study. A 20-minute interview was carried out monthly (for the initial 3 months) and bimonthly (thereafter) with each patient's family therapist, during which the therapist described the central themes or focus of the work during the previous interval. The therapist also participated in researcher-guided ratings on three scales that assessed the degree of parental criticism expressed directly to the child in the sessions, the degree of emotional overinvolvement or disengagement displayed toward the child during the sessions, and the extent to which the parent reacted in an emotionally labile or constricted (or flat) way during the sessions. These scales allowed us to look at how the parents changed during the treatment. Further details of these scales, the Family System Functioning scales (FSF), can be found elsewhere (Doane, Hill, Kaslow, & Quinlan, 1988).

A study of interrater reliability and validity was carried out on these scales, and the scales were shown to have good construct validity and concurrent validity with the affective style measures obtained earlier in a laboratory setting. Just as we compiled longitudinal profiles of patient social functioning and symptomatic functioning, so we constructed longitudinal family profiles of FSF scores on criticism and emotional involvement for the duration of inpatient treatment for each family. This allowed us to study change in the family and change in the patient, in a counterpoint fashion, and to address issues such as the sequential linkages between patient improvement and improvement in familial attitudes and behavior.

One-Year Follow-Up Interview

After the patients were discharged from YPI, they entered the 1-year follow-up period. At the end of this year, each patient was interviewed for 2 hours about his or her symptoms, social functioning, intimate relationships, family relationships, treatment history, work functioning, and perceptions of their own coping skills. Patients were also asked to reflect on any changes they had made and to comment extensively on their perceptions about how their inpatient treatment had affected their lives.

During the first 12 months, and prior to the follow-up interview, the patient and his or her family were contacted by phone at 3-month intervals to track progress prospectively, assess family relationships, and monitor medication compliance, including precipitants to periods of medication noncompliance. Patients were also asked about their treatment and their general functioning.

After the follow-up interview, each patient provided two FMSSs, on his or her mother and father; in addition, each patient filled out the PBI about each parent. These data allowed us to examine the nature and quality of the parent-child attachment, and to assess how these patients had consolidated an internal working model of their parents, and their relationships with these parents, after extensive psychotherapy and hospitalization. Many of these patients were remarkably articulate and sophisticated in their ability to portray very rich pictures of their parents. These measures enabled us to explore the relationship between patients' internal working models of their patients and the parents' internal working models of their own parents.

After the follow-up data on relapse were collected, laboratory-based family measures such as AS were used to predict clinical outcome to determine whether previous predictive relationships between family AS and relapse could be replicated in this sample of individuals treated with long-term inpatient treatment. Readmission to the hospital was the basic outcome variable used to get a sense of general ability to survive outside of the hospital. We were also interested in other aspects of outcome, however; and in order to measure these, a set of scales were developed to measure outcome (Doane, Johnston, & Becker, 1989). Included in these scales were aspects of patient functioning such as resiliency (a general ability to bounce back after crises or setbacks in recovery), unfulfilled yearnings and longings, attitudes toward medication, and likability, as well as scales typically used in outcome studies, such as work adjustment and quality of peer relationships.

The interviews were videotaped, and an experienced clinician later rated the interviews independently on these scales.

CHAPTER 4

The Yale Psychiatric Institute Family Study: Research Findings

B ECAUSE NO MAJOR differences between the sexes were found in any of the Yale Psychiatric Institute Family Study analyses, the results are presented for both males and females combined. We also did not find major differences between the borderline adolescent group and the young adult borderline personality and/or affective disorder adult (BLAD) group; therefore, these two groups were combined for data analysis. There were no significant differences found on any of the key demographic or patient illness variables for affective style (AS) family groupings.

Diagnosis and One-Year Outcome

The first question concerned the relapse rates of the three diagnostic groups. Table 4.1 contains the outcome data for the first year following discharge from the study. As seen in Table 4.1, 64% of the schizophrenics relapsed during the first year, 28% of the Affective Disorder/Borderline (ADBL) group, and 38% of the adolescents. These figures suggest that long-term inpatient treatment was relatively effective for patients with ADBL, whether they were adults or adolescents. Long-term treatment was less successful in preventing rehospitalization for patients with schizophrenia.

No differences were found between survivors and relapsers on patient illness variables such as severity of symptoms, or number of previous

TABLE 4.1

First-Year Rehospitalization (n=53)

	No. Survived	No. (%) Rehospitalized
Schizophrenia Spectrum (n=22)	8	14 (64)
Young Adult Affective/ Borderline Disorder (n=18)	13	5 (28)
Adolescents (n=13)	8	5 (38)

hospitalizations. A 64% relapse rate for the schizophrenic group compares unfavorably with results from recent studies that employed management-oriented, behavioral, and educational models of intervention for schizophrenics and their families (e.g., Falloon et al., 1985; Hogarty et al., 1986; Leff et al., 1985). However, an important distinction between the foregoing studies and the YPIFS research is that the studies that employed psychoeducational measures also provided prolonged family treatment during the aftercare period while the patients were out of the hospital.

The YPI results would support the position that although extensive *inpatient* family treatment for schizophrenia might have benefit, it does not dramatically reduce relapse in the absence of solid family intervention during the aftercare phase of the disorder. Most of the YPI schizophrenic patients did not receive regular or sustained aftercare family therapy. Many contemporary inpatient settings employ a model of treatment for schizophrenia that focuses on brief inpatient treatment, followed by the patient returning to outpatient treatment in his or her community. The YPI data suggest that this strategy may not be very effective, as most of the YPI patients did not follow through with aftercare plans or were not able to connect with and attach to community-based clinicians. A treatment program that provides continuity of both individual and family therapists may be a more effective way to treat this population.

For the nonschizophrenic group, however, the benefits of long-term inpatient treatment may be more lasting. The relapse rates for this group were dramatically low (28% of the ADBL group and 38% of the adolescents), compared to the hospitalization rate for these groups in the year prior to their entering YPI. During the year prior to entering the study, 100% of the young adult nonschizophrenic patients had been hospitalized, as had 85% of the adolescents and 100% of the schizophrenics. These results are consistent with results from Tom McGlashan's (1986) study of the long-term inpatient treatment of patients hospitalized at Chestnut Lodge, because McGlashan also found evidence that borderline patients, but not schizophrenics, benefited from such treatment.

AS Profile as a Predictor of Relapse

AS was significantly related to rehospitalization for patients in the YPI study, but only when AS was measured at each patient's time of discharge from the hospital. The relapse rate for negative AS patients (61%) was twice the rate for patients from benign AS families (32%) (see Table 4.2). When the data were analyzed separately by diagnostic group, the relationship between AS and relapse for schizophrenics was significant at the .05 level. Eighty-three percent of schizophrenia patients from families characterized as hostile, guilt-inducing, or intrusive (negative AS) at the time of discharge were rehospitalized within 1 year of discharge, compared with only 40% of those returning to families that were nonhostile, more low-key, and nonintrusive (benign AS).

The analysis for patients with nonschizophrenic diagnoses did not reach statistical significance. However, the negative AS relapse rate was higher (44%) than the benign AS rate (27%). The difference between diagnostic groups and the way the cases are distributed across the 2 x 2 cells is interesting. In the schizophrenia group, the negative AS profile carries the predictive value (83% relapse), whereas in the nonschizophrenic group, the benign AS profile has more discriminative power—73% of the cases do *not* relapse. Thus, for the nonschizophrenic patients a benign family atmosphere seems to have some protective effect; but this was not true for those who had a schizophrenic disorder. The findings on AS and schizophrenia replicate previous reports (Doane et al., 1981; Doane et al., 1985) of a significant predictive effect of AS on outcome in schizophrenic patients. The relapse rate for patients from negative AS families was double (83%) that of the rate for patients from benign AS families (40%) (see Table 4.3).

TABLE 4.2

Discharge Family Affective Style (AS) as a Predictor of Rehospitalization:
Total Sample (n=53)

	No. Survived	No. (%) Rehospitalized
Benign AS	17	8 (32%)
Negative AS	11	17 (61%)

p < .03, Fisher's Exact Test

TABLE 4.3

Discharge Family Affective Style (AS) as a Predictor of Rehospitalization

	No. Survived	No. (%) Rehospitalized
Schizophrenics (n=22)		
Benign AS	6	4 (40%)
Negative AS	2	10 (83%)

p < .05, Fisher's Exact Test

	No. Survived	No. (%) Rehospitalized
Nonschizophrenics (n=31)		
Benign AS	11	4 (27%)
Negative AS	9	7 (44%)

p = ns, Fisher's Exact Test

The fact that it was the final assessment of AS that had the predictive validity, and not the initial or the 3-month assessment point, suggests that the closer in time to the outcome criterion point the data are obtained, the more valid the prediction of outcome will be. These statistics imply that for schizophrenic patients, the high-risk families are the ones with unrelenting negative affect who have not shifted to a benign style of affective expression even after a lengthy period of hospitalization for the patient and weekly family therapy for themselves.

For the patients with borderline disorder or affective disorders, however, the persistence of negative affective style at the end of treatment is not a good predictor of relapse. Instead, families with a benign affective climate have particularly low relapse rates (27%) (see Table 4.3). Thus, patients returning to families where change in family AS has been achieved after lengthy treatment may indeed benefit from the shift from a more hostile to a more amiable family environment. Perhaps, for patients with schizophrenia, the biological components driving the illness are so powerful that they override any potential benefit of a benign family environment. The data would support this interpretation, because the relapse rate for the schizophrenic patients returning to benign AS families was 40%, not an impressively low figure.

If we hypothesize that the borderline or affective disorder patient has more ego strength and perhaps a more coherent (if not necessarily benign) internal working model of attachment, then these trends in the data might suggest that the ADBL patient is able to benefit actively from the benign

AS parent in a way that the patient with schizophrenia cannot. Similarly, relapse in the ADBL patients may have more to do with other factors such as life events, stress, and so on than with the negative effects of an excessively critical or intrusive mother or father. The schizophrenic, on the other hand, may be unable to use the benign parents as a buffer against relapse because the biological press of the illness may be sufficiently intense to override the salutary impact of a benign or supportive family affective climate; at the same time, the presence of a hostile, intrusive parent may interact with biological induced stress from the schizophrenic disorder itself, in ways that escalate the patient's anxiety or reduce his or her capacity to cope with psychotic symptoms.

Parental Rejecting Attitudes as a Predictor of Relapse

The next YPIFS area examined was the predictive utility of the attitudinal measure of AS as derived from the Kreisman Scale of Rejecting Attitudes data. Families were grouped on the basis of whether one or more parents had a hostile, rejecting attitude toward the patient or the patient's illness. A cutting score of 8 and above on the weighted sum of the 10 key items was used to group parents, as this score was the cut-score for the upper third of the distribution.

When families were grouped in this way, the relapse rates for the two groups did not differ. Thus, this briefer, quick assessment of attitudes was not useful in predicting relapse. Employing a less conservative cutting score did not improve the predictive validity of the Kreisman scores. Although the Kreisman scale items share some conceptual overlap with the EE and AS measures, the instrument cannot be assumed to capture the same quality of attitudinal expression as that reflected in the Camberwell Family Interview (CFI), which was used to elicit EE attitudes (see chapter 2). Perhaps this more intense, personalized interview context produces emotional attitude measures that have more predictive validity.

Medication Compliance and Outcome

Analyses of medication compliance and its relationship with relapse were carried out next. A total of 42 patients were discharged on a psychotropic medication that was to be taken on an outpatient basis (20 of the 31 ADBL group and all 22 of the schizophrenic patients). Medication compliance was tracked prospectively in telephone calls by the project principal investigator, Jeri Doane, every 3 months. Patients were designated as either

TABLE 4.4

AS Profile and Medication Compliance as Combined Predictors of
One-Year Rehospitalization: Schizophrenic Patients (n=22)

	Rehospitalized	
Risk Group:	No	Yes
Benign AS/Compliant	5	1 (17%)
Benign AS/Noncompliant	1	3 (75%)
Negative AS/Compliant	2	1 (33%)
Negative AS/Noncompliant	0	9 (100%)

compliant or noncompliant (i.e., stopped medication for more than 3 days and did not resume taking it) based on data obtained during these phone calls. Of those schizophrenic patients who remained compliant, 22% (2 of 9) relapsed, compared to 92% (12 of 13) who stopped medication. Compliance status and discharge family AS profile were combined to yield the four groups shown in Table 4.4. For schizophrenic patients, 100% of those who had negative AS families and who stopped their primary medication were rehospitalized during the first year after discharge from the hospital. Three of four noncompliant patients from benign AS families also relapsed, despite the low-risk family environment. Thus, for patients with a schizophrenic illness the effects of stopping medication are obvious. Patients who took their medication and who had low-risk families (the benign AS/compliant group) had the lowest risk of relapse (17%). No clear overlap was observed between AS profile and compliance.

In Table 4.5 similar trends are observed for patients with ADBL. Noncompliance with medication was once again obviously associated with relapse (36% of compliant patients relapsed, compared with 78% of those who stopped). Eighty percent of the benign AS/noncompliant group and 75% of the negative AS/noncompliant group relapsed. Again, the best outcome was in the group with compliant patients in a benign family environment.

TABLE 4.5

AS Profile and Medication Compliance as Combined Predictors of
One-Year Rehospitalization: Nonschizophrenic Patients (n=20)

	Rehospitalized	
	No	Yes
Benign AS/Compliant	4	0 (0%)
Benign AS/Noncompliant	1	4 (80%)
Negative AS/Compliant	3	4 (57%)
Negative AS/Noncompliant	1	3 (75%)

We examined these findings for the prevalence of bipolar disorder compared to borderline disorder and could not find any differences that would explain the trends in the data. Thus, we might conclude from these data that, at least for this study, medication compliance is just as important for patients with borderline or bipolar disorder in preventing relapse as it is for schizophrenics. Further, although family AS was also a powerful predictor of outcome in our sample, it was not a superior predictor to medication compliance.

An important implication of this finding is that even long-term hospitalization and extensive, prolonged family therapy are not enough to prevent relapse in patients who remain unconvinced about the necessity of taking regular medication. These patients and their families received care that is considered high quality by most standards. The treatment was conducted in a university setting, where therapists were either experienced or were receiving supervision by highly trained clinicians, who were often foremost authorities in their field. Although the families did not receive a lot of formal psychoeducation, they did receive extensive support and education from a family therapist, on a weekly basis. The family therapist also spent a great deal of time helping the family cope with crises, work on communication problems with the patient, and prepare the patient and the family for discharge. The YPI data suggest that for many families, family risk factors persisted, despite treatment. This speaks to the need for continuation of family-based care during the aftercare period.

The YPI data also suggest that adding a component of treatment specifically focused on relapse prevention might help prevent noncompliance. A series of workshops or sessions could be offered to prepare the patient and his or her parents for the inevitable moment when the patient wants to reduce or stop his or her medication. Walking the family through the likely course of events once this happens might exert a preventive effect by helping them to anticipate crises around medication, and teaching them ways of dealing quickly with those.

Our finding that medication compliance played an important role in outcome, and that it was as good a predictor as AS, differs somewhat from the findings usually reported in the EE literature. Several features of the YPI study may account for this discrepancy. First, we did not control medication in our study, but we did carefully track both the way it was prescribed and the patient's compliance with the regimen. In contrast to many other studies, we collected this compliance data prospectively, which may have resulted in detecting more noncompliance situations. We found that our prospectively collected and verified (through parental report) data about noncompliance often differed from what the patient reported to us during his or her 1-year follow-up interview. It was not unusual for our schizophrenic patients to have forgotten entire episodes of illness, and to have reversed the sequence of stopping medication and beginning to become symptomatic. Also, schizophrenic patients often could not accurately recall the events leading up to their readmission to a psychiatric hospital. Second, our sample was a fairly disturbed one, and thus these extremely disturbed and symptomatic patients may have been even more susceptible to relapse without the protection of neuroleptics than the average schizophrenic.

It is not possible from this study to understand why negative AS and noncompliance resulted in a 100% relapse rate. One hypothesis, however, might be that the patients who are toying with stopping their medication might not want to discuss that with negative AS parents, and when the patients began having difficulty with a return of symptoms, they might not feel especially comfortable seeking assistance from parents who might be critical, guilt-inducing, or intrusive. Thus, the negative AS parent might be part of a stress "equation" that includes a negative representation or internal working model of that parent in the patient's internal world, as well as an actual absence of emotional resources. This hypothesis cannot be tested here, but it deserves further study.

These findings should be tempered by the fact that the YPI approach to the prescribing of medication during long-term hospitalization may differ from the usual practice in a short-term psychiatric unit. It is possible that a number of YPI patients who were discharged without medication would have received prescriptions if they had left after three weeks. A total of 11 patients, most of whom received medication while in the hospital, were not prescribed medication for the aftercare period. Three of the 11 patients refused medication at discharge, although they had taken it during the inpatient phase. In the other cases, it was judged that medication would not be necessary. None of these 11 cases relapsed, and none were bipolar. All had diagnoses of either borderline personality and/or major depression.

Those who did receive aftercare medication, therefore, may have been patients with disorders that clearly necessitated medication for control of the disorder. The strong association between compliance and relapse found in the YPI study would be consistent with this. Another possibility is that because the patients were treated with medication during a lengthy inpatient stay, they became dependent on it as part of their ability to resist relapse, and that once they stopped it, they were primed for relapse.

Despite these qualifications, the data support the role of both family AS and medication compliance in predicting relapse. Although this finding departs somewhat from the existing research literature on EE types of studies, it fits with the experience of many clinicians who work with severely disturbed patients such as those in this study.

Change in Family Risk Factors over Time

AS tends to decrease over time, for both mothers and fathers, beyond the initial three months of treatment (see Figure 4.1). For fathers of ADBL patients, a slightly different pattern was observed.

As indicated in Figure 4.2, these men tended to get worse before they got better—that is, they became more verbally critical with their children at the 3-month point, after which their level of criticism declined. It is important to note that for both groups, parents seemed to continue to benefit from family therapy past the 3-month reassessment point. This would suggest that treatment benefits continue to accrue beyond what is usually provided in short-term treatment programs.

Previous studies have suggested that positive AS was not changed in the first 3 months of treatment. Figures 4.3 and 4.4 show the same repeated measures analyses, except that positive AS was used as the dependent variable. Positive AS consisted of the raw sum of all of the supportive or positive verbal remarks the parent made to the patient during the family lab assessment. The very low incidence of supportive verbal remarks—which was true for both mothers and fathers, regardless of diagnosis, and regardless of how much family treatment had taken place—was striking. The low incidence in spite of family treatment was somewhat surprising, given the amount of treatment the families received. We might have expected that parents would become more warm and supportive once the acute stresses of the patient's decompensation and symptom exacerbation had resolved.

Affective Style and Patient Illness Characteristics

The next task involved assessment of the relationship of the AS measure to other patient measures that might help explain the predictive validity of the AS measure. Specifically, we asked whether patients from families where parents were critical or intrusive were more disturbed to begin with than patients from benign families. We looked at both the degree of social functioning deficit and the severity of symptoms, as measured at the time of entry into the study. The severity of symptoms at baseline was not correlated with the degree of social functioning deficit as measured by the

FIGURE 4.1

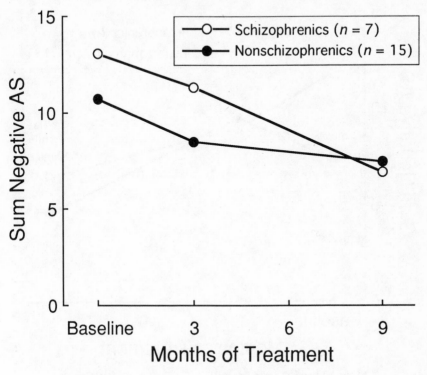

Mothers' Negative Affective Style

Main Effect, Time, $p < .09$, $F\,(2, 40) = 2.56$

Target Social Deficit (TSD) index. This finding applied equally to schizophrenics and nonschizophrenics. Further, neither the severity of social functioning deficits nor the severity of symptoms was related to AS at the time of entry into the study. No differences were found for AS and the number of previous hospitalizations, the age at onset of illness, the specific type of symptoms, or social deficit.

The Relationship between Affective Style and Course of Illness

In the last set of analyses, we wanted to explore the hypothesis that negative AS in the parents is primarily something that occurs *in response to* the stress and burden of having to deal with a severely ill or disturbing individual. If AS were more a reflection of the parent's character or nature,

FIGURE 4.2

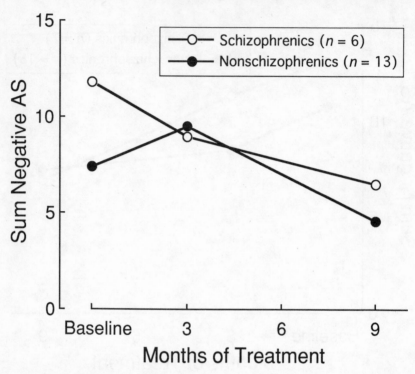

Fathers' Negative Affective Style

Main Effect, Time, $p < .07$, $F(2, 34) = 2.86$

then we would expect that AS would not improve in the face of major improvement in the patient's symptomatic status or the extent to which he or she has major social deficits. Conversely, if AS is more of a state variable that reflects the acute stress of attempting to cope with the ill patient, then we would expect AS to subside as the patient's florid symptoms remit and as his or her social functioning improves.

To explore this issue, a 2 x 2 plot was constructed for each patient and his or her family that spanned the entire period of hospitalization. Assessments of family scores of criticism and involvement, as measured by the monthly and bimonthly Family System Functioning (FSF) scales, were plotted against the average TSD score, as rated by the patient's primary nurse, at the same points in time. Similar analyses were done using the average symptom severity score, as rated by the patient's primary clinician (a psychiatrist or clinical psychologist). These grids allowed us to

FIGURE 4.3

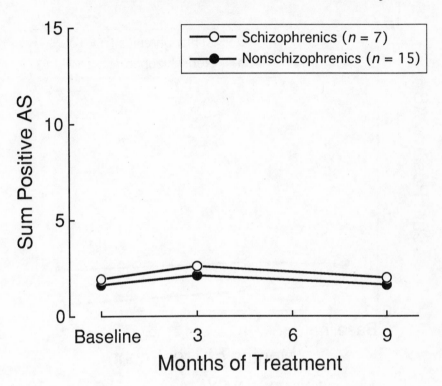

Mothers' Positive Affective Style

examine, on a case-by-case basis, whether changes in the family variables preceded, accompanied, or followed changes in the patient's symptomatic status and social functioning level.

Our interest was to look at the directional shifts in the two sets of variables (patient measures and parent measures) relative to each other, since the data in the grids did not lend themselves to parametric statistical techniques. Sequential analysis, for example, would have required pooling the subject's data, since there were not enough data points collected on a single case to permit a sequential analysis. This strategy would mask any patterns having to do with the direction of change during sequential shifts in the two lines of data. We categorically grouped cases based on the patterns observed regarding change in the two sets of measures. Improvement for the patient was reflected in scores on the TSD measure and on the mean symptom score. Improvement on the parental dimension was defined as a reduction in observed criticism, a lessening of emotional over-

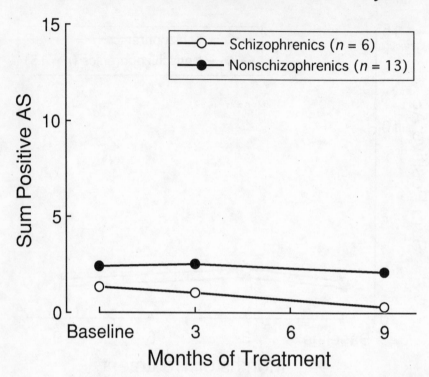

FIGURE 4.4

Fathers' Positive Affective Style

Repeated Measures ANOVA, $p < .06$, $F(1, 17) = 4.10$;
9-Months, $p < .05$, Duncan's post-hoc test

involvement, or emotional connecting in disengaged parents, as measured by the therapist-rated FSF scales.

When the 53 cases were examined for change, seven distinct patterns were observed that best reflected the different patterns seen in the entire sample. Table 4.6 contains a list of these patterns, with the rehospitalization rate for cases in each group. It is often argued that variables such as AS or EE are best understood as the family's reactions to the stresses and strains of caring for a disturbed or severely ill relative. The group that reflects this position is the affect falling (AF) group, in which parental criticism and emotional overinvolvement were observed to drop as the patient's symptoms and level of functioning improved. The AF group had a dramatically low relapse rate (11%). In the AF group, one might say that the family AS was more a state phenomenon, something that emerged when the patient was floridly symptomatic. Of particular interest is the

TABLE 4.6

Patterns of Change in Parental FSF in Relation to Patient Improvement (n=53)

Pattern	n	% of Total Sample	Rehospitalization Rate
Affect Falling (AF)	9	17%	11%
Affect Rising (AR)	11	20%	45%
Low Key (LK)	7	13%	71%
Continuously Disengaged (CD)	6	12%	67%
Continuous Criticism (CC)	7	13%	57%
Under-Over (UO)	7	13%	57%
Unstable Chaotic (UC)	6	12%	50%
	53	100%	

fact that only 9 (17%) of the total sample of 53 families displayed this pattern. In contrast, the affect rising (AR) group displayed the reverse pattern. In these families, parental criticism and emotional overinvolvement increased as the patient improved. We found this pattern somewhat surprising, particularly since it occurred among 20% of the families.

Low-key (LK) families (13% of the sample) were ones in which parental criticism and emotional overinvolvement were short-lived and declined quickly in the first month of treatment. Also included in this group were families where the parents never exhibited excessive criticism, emotional overinvolvement, or excessive disengagement during the patient's hospitalization. Despite this, the relapse rate for this group was 71%.

In the remaining four groups, the parents displayed continuous negative affect throughout the hospitalization and did not alter their behavior as the patient's clinical state changed (49% of the sample). The continuously disengaged (CD) group had a fairly high relapse rate (67%). Parents in this group were not overly critical of the patient at any time during the study, but they remained emotionally disengaged or distant from the patient, no matter how the patient's state changed.

Patients from families with parents who were continuously highly critical (CC) of the patient regardless of improvement, had a fairly high relapse rate (57%) also. A similar rate was observed in the unstable chaotic (UC) group, in which the parents were alternating between low levels of criticism or emotional overinvolvement and high levels. These fluctuations were not related to patient variables, or to any particular external stress or life events.

The last pattern characterized fairly rigid, polarized families in which one parent remained very emotionally overinvolved with the patient while the spouse remained disengaged (under-over). No shifts in parental scores in response to changes in the patient could be detected. Families of this type had a relapse rate of 57%.

The overall relapse rate for the 53 families was 47%. One can look at deviation from this rate to estimate the relative risk of each of these patterns. The LK, CC, CD, and under over (UO) groups all had relapse rates at least 10 percentage points above the 45% rate for the sample as a whole. The AF group was the only one for which the relapse rate was meaningfully lower than the overall rate. Patients in this group of families were as disturbed as patients in the other groups; they did not differ on length of stay, nor on any of the other demographic or previous history variables.

Thus, it could be hypothesized that the parents in this group were different, that they responded to treatment differently, or that they received therapy that differed from what those in the other groups received. We examined the latter possibility by examining the results of monthly and bimonthly interviews with the family therapists about the nature of the work being done in family treatment. No unique or unusual treatment factors could be identified. Extensive review of these cases, and of the parents' characteristics, did not reveal anything unique about them, as compared with parents in the other groups.

Our results do not support the position that parental AS is a reaction to the stresses of dealing with a severely ill relative. Our data suggest that this is true for a minority of the families in the YPI study. Only 17% of our families fell into this category (see Table 4.6). Another 13% were fairly low-key families in that their initially negative AS behavior responded rapidly to treatment, and they continued to relate to the patient in modulated, benign ways, throughout. Together, these two relatively benign groups comprised only 30% our families. The other 70% continued to exhibit excessive criticism, emotional overinvolvement, or emotional disengagement throughout treatment, regardless of the patient's clinical state. In 20% of the cases, the parents actually became more critical when the patient made improvements. Although we expected to find some portion of the sample with relatively unremitting negative interaction patterns, we did not expect this to be true for 70% of the cases.

These results have important treatment implications. They suggest that for the majority of families, variables such as AS reflect relatively enduring, treatment resistant aspects of the family environment that are not closely linked to how well the patient recovers, or how well his or her medication controls the symptoms. Nor does it AS seem linked to how much improvement the patient makes in social skills. Notably, some YPI parents seemed not to perceive very obvious improvements that the patient had made. In other cases, parents clearly did comprehend gains the patient had made, but the negative affect tended to persist anyway. These data suggest that AS may be linked to fairly entrenched, underlying patterns of experiencing affect and coping with affect. The patterns, in turn, may have less to do with the specifics of the psychiatric illness itself than with some emotional "drama" of sorts that becomes unleashed when the patient and parent confront each other. This hypothesis would suggest that variables such as AS may be linked to internal dynamics and ways of experiencing affect in the parent. Thus, reducing AS in the family may involve, first, understanding what is generating the intense affect in the parent, rather than making assumptions (because of preconceived beliefs or theories) about the cause.

Because the behaviors reflected in the AS variable clearly increase the risk of relapse, because they are not easily eradicated, and because they do not appear to be linked to the patient's clinical state, a reasonable hypothesis is that they reflect an aspect of the parent's internal world. This hypothesis and the research findings based on it are presented in the following section on AS and attachment.

We did not see an increase in positive AS in the families in this study. In fact, the very low rates of positive remarks observed in family interactions are quite striking when one compares those with the high rates of negative AS. What accounts for this discrepancy between rates of positive and negative AS? A partial explanation may be that the nature of the family interaction task, which is structured around discussion of unresolved family issues or problems, pulls for negative affect. Yet, our research findings show that even with the resolution of some family issues and with the decrease in the most acute aspects of the patient's symptomatology, many parents continue to display a great deal of negative affect and fail to increase their supportive remarks to patients in family interactions. Also, positive affect and warmth may not be as easily measured through verbal channels. These attitudes may reflect aspects of the attachment bond, and therefore may be captured more readily through nonverbal measures. Because nonverbal measures were not included in the YPI study, we cannot answer this question. Nevertheless, the question of the role of warmth remains an intriguing one. We know very little about the role of warmth in preventing relapse in psychiatric illness, yet clinical intuition tells us that it is vital.

In summary, our results suggest that variables such as EE or AS are more reflective of enduring qualities in the parents than they are of transient emotional states that devolve from the frustrations of having to deal with a severely disturbed relative. The enduring nature of the AS in some parents may be the result of cumulative frustrations, however. We cannot address this question in our study, but it deserves further attention. We would propose an alternative hypothesis—namely, that a persistent tendency to use negative AS with the patient may reflect the result of cumulative frustration, but a frustration that has as one of its major components the internal world of the parent himself or herself, complete with unresolved frustrations from his or her own family experience. These may then interact with a disturbed and disturbing patient-child relationship to generate new frustrations and disappointment in the parent. The parent's internal world acts as a screen that blocks positive changes in the patient from view, and thus an excessively critical response ensues. In the next section, empirical findings from intergenerational measures of attachment and bonding are presented that support this hypothesis.

It is perhaps ironic and untimely that a research report should advocate long-term family treatment when the economic realities of clinical practice dictate the opposite. In this regard, we should emphasize that our data do not support the value of lengthy inpatient treatment for people with disorders such as schizophrenia, at least when using rehospitalization as a criterion of outcome. Longer-term outpatient family treatment is a possibility for many families, however. Our data suggest that for some it may be a necessity. Finding ways to deliver effective, low-cost forms of treatment continues to challenge our field.

Disturbed Attachment and Negative Affective Style—Intergenerational Findings

The relationship between the quality of the parents' attachment to their own parents and the quality of AS they exhibited in interaction with their severely disturbed son or daughter was examined in a sample of 49 families from the core sample. Detailed findings from this study, including reliability and validity of the measures, appear elsewhere (Diamond & Doane, in press). The most important results are replicated here.

Attachment and AS

In order to investigate the extent to which AS and attachment are overlapping measures, we assessed whether parents who have disturbed attachment on the FMSS toward their children were more likely to exhibit negative AS in face-to- face interactions with their disturbed offspring.

In these analyses a critical incident model was used to group parents as low and high risk for disturbed attachment, depending on whether their Five Minute Speech Samples (FMSSs) on their children at 3 months had one or more indicators of disturbed attachment codes (i.e., negative attachment, ambivalent attachment, overinvolvement, triangulation, or parentification).

Our hypothesis was that parents who have disturbed attachments to their own parents (high risk) are more likely to exhibit negative AS in face-to-face interactions with their disturbed young adult and adolescent offspring than are parents without evidence of disturbed attachments to their own parents (low risk). Examination of the intergenerational attachment data reveals significant differences between the amount of negative AS demonstrated by the high- and low-risk attachment groups at 3 months after admission. As indicated in Figure 4.5, mothers who have disturbed attachments to their own mothers (high risk), as assessed through the FMSS attachment codes, are significantly more likely to direct negative affectively toned remarks to their disturbed offspring than are mothers with less disturbed attachment histories. These analyses again use the presence or absence of the disturbed attachment codes as a grouping variable, with parents designated as low or high risk for disturbed attachment, depending on whether their FMSSs on their own parents had one or more indicators of disturbed attachment codes.

For mothers, there is a dramatic difference in mean negative AS remarks between high- and low-risk attachment groups (a mean of 10.1 for high-risk attachment groups, versus a mean of 4.2 for low-risk ones on negative AS). For fathers, the difference between the means of negative AS for low and high risk for disturbed attachment groups did not reach statistical significance; nonetheless, there is a notable trend for fathers at risk for disturbed attachment to their own fathers (but not to their mothers) to show almost twice the amount of negative affect in interactions with their own child, as shown in Figure 4.5.

Negative Affect as a Vehicle for Transmitting Risk

These results suggest that disturbed intergenerational parent-child attachment may constitute a psychosocial risk factor that affects the course of illness and treatment for severely disturbed young adults and adolescents. The linkages between disturbances in the parents' attachments to their own parents and the degree of negative affect that they display toward their disturbed offspring suggest a conceptual model for the transgenerational transmission of psychosocial risk factors related to attachment.

FIGURE 4.5

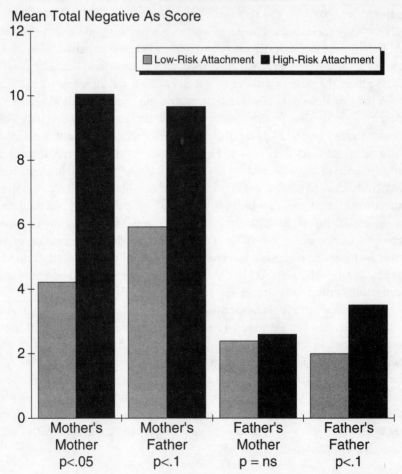

Disturbed (High Risk) Intergenerational Attachment as a
Predictor of Parental Negative Affective Style After
Three Months of Treatment

This model is more fully developed in another publication (Diamond &
Doane, in press), but in brief it stipulates that the expression of affect, particularly negative affect, may be the vehicle through which patterns of
attachment are transmitted across the generations. Disturbed patterns of
attachment may not be immediately discernible in the conscious attitudes
that parents hold toward their children. Rather, parents may inadvertently

reenact and recreate with their own children their own disturbed attachments to the parents of origin. We have found that when the parents' own internal burdens and unresolved negative attachments to their own parents are evoked in stressful family interactions with their disturbed offspring, the parents inadvertently direct negative affect toward their children, about whom the parents may actually hold relatively benign attitudes. Research findings presented in this chapter suggest that such negative affective reactions are not linked to the vicissitudes of the patient's course of illness, but rather appear to be linked to the parents' own disturbed attachment histories.

The research findings also suggest a model of treatment that takes into account parent-child relationships in both the family of origin and the family of procreation. The linkages between intergenerational attachment measures and AS behaviors imply that a treatment model that attempts to focus only on communication skills and the expression of criticism may be inadequate for some families. In the following chapters, we present a family typology that evolved out of blending the empirical research findings presented thus far with our YPI clinical work with patients and families.

CHAPTER 5

Family Typology

W E HAVE USED the empirical research data and the assessment methods described in chapter 4 to identify three distinct family types that have different characteristics in terms of two key dimensions: (1) the quality of parent-child attachment and (2) the way that affect is expressed among family members.

By combining these two dimensions of family environment, we have been able to deepen our understanding of the relational patterns in the families of patients with major psychiatric disturbance. These three family types have distinctly different treatment needs.

The first group, which we called the *high-intensity* family, is characterized by attachments that are strong and positive, if intense, and by interactions among family members that are overinvolved and sometimes highly critical, or intrusive. A second group of families, called *low-intensity*, is characterized by parents who are positively attached to the patient but who are also fairly low-key in terms of family affective climate—that is, they show little evidence of the entrenched criticism or intrusiveness toward the patient, expressed either in terms of attitude or behavior.

The third group of families, called *disconnected*, is characterized by family interactions in which one or both parents are noticeably disengaged from the patient or his problems. This fundamental emotional disconnection manifests itself through a wide range of family interactions. Some parents appear to be highly critical or overinvolved with the patient, whereas others appear to be totally uninvolved or mildly detached. Research measures, however, suggest that regardless of the surface presentation, the parental bond with the patient is often disrupted or disturbed. At first glance the family interaction patterns in disconnected families may look identical to families in the high-intensity group, but the underlying nature of the familial relationship is quite different. In disconnected families, the intensely negative affective climate masquerades as overinvolvement; in fact, affectional bonds are usually impaired or nonexistent.

The methodological pathways by which these groups were empirically derived involved a discrete blend of conceptual thinking and empirical sorting of research data. In this chapter we describe in detail these three family types and illustrate their characteristics with actual examples from our research data. In our experience it is sometimes difficult to decide whether a sample of family interaction or parental interview data fits one family type rather than another. We have included extensive quotes from families in our study in order to give the reader an intuitive grasp of the kinds of clinical material one encounters when working with each family type.

Families in each of these three groups show different and distinct patterns of intergenerational relationships. Therefore, in the descriptions that follow, we provide clinical material from data obtained through various levels of assessment, including data from the family of origin as well as the family of procreation. We include data from directly observed family interaction between the patient and his or her parents, parental interview data when each parent spoke about the patient in a Five Minute Speech Sample (FMSS), and data from parental interviews in which each parent was interviewed about personal experiences with his or her own mother and father.

Before we elaborate further on these three family types, we need to review the criteria that clinicians may use in their clinical work to assign patients and their families to one of the three groups.

Criteria for Family Assessment

In the previous chapter we described a variety of measures used to assess aspects of the family emotional environment and focused on research findings related to the prediction of relapse and assessment of change. In this chapter we shift the focus to a description of key family attributes that the clinician can use to group families according to the dimensions of attachment and emotional style of relating. Because we wanted to use easily administered instruments, we chose not to use the affective style (AS) measure of family emotional climate, which requires an elaborate, time-consuming procedure involving video-taped live family interaction, tasks best carried out in a family research laboratory rather than in clinical practice. Instead, we chose four measures that, when combined, yield data about the family's style of expressing affect and the family's emotional attitudes toward the patient, the nature of their attachment bonds, and the level of emotional overinvolvement or disengagement in the family system. These measures provide information about primary attachments between each parent and the patient, and also between each parent and his or her own parents. We review the four measures, even though they were presented in detail in previous chapters.

Kriesman Scale of Rejecting Attitudes

We were interested in identifying the negative or rejecting attitudes that parents hold toward the patient that might be considered consistently negative or particularly intense. As noted in chapter 4, the sum of the weighted scores for the 10 Kriesman items that were particularly useful in identifying negative AS attitudes was calculated to reveal a summary score called the 10K score, which ranged from 0 to 40 (theoretically), but from 0 to 29 in this sample. A natural break in the distribution of scores suggested a cut-off to divide parents into low and high 10K scores; parents whose scores were 8 or above were said to have negative AS critical attitudes about the patient. This method of grouping parents is fairly conservative in that only one third of the parents were classified as high 10K with this method. For clinical purposes here a parent was said to have critical, rejecting attitudes toward the patient when he or she made enough critical comments on the Kriesman scale to achieve a score of 8 or higher. This allowed us to identify parents who openly acknowledged a number of critical attitudes toward the patient in a number of statements on the Kriesman scale. Parents who made one to two critical remarks were thus excluded from the grouping. In our sample, only 8% of high-intensity patients had a high-risk parent on the Kriesman.

By contrast, in low-intensity families, 20% had a high-risk parent, and in the disconnected family, 63% had a high-risk parent.

Attachment Measures in the Five-Minute Speech Samples

As part of the initial family assessment, attachment was assessed through an FMSS task in which the parent was asked to speak spontaneously and without interruption for 5 minutes about the patient, what kind of person the patient is, and how they get along together. Examples of the attachment codes include (1) positive attachment, coded for statements that include loving, caring feelings toward the child; (2) negative attachment, coded for statements that express negative, rejecting, or indifferent feelings and attitudes; (3) ambivalent attachment, coded for statements that express contradictory, conflictual attitudes toward the child; and (4) overinvolvement, coded for statements that express an excessive preoccupation with, overprotectiveness toward, or overinvestment in the child; (5) triangulation, coded for statements that convey the sense that the child is caught in the middle of parental conflict such that he or she inevitably betrays one parent if he or she affirms or sustains an attachment to the other; and (6) parentification, coded for statements that indicate a role reversal in which the parent has abdicated parental functions and has cast the child in the role of the caretaker, surrogate spouse, or friend in ways that clearly inhibit the child's development.

In the high-intensity family, the parent-child attachment tended to be characterized by positive attachment, often in the context of overinvolvement and idealization. Negative attachment, parentification, and triangulation were usually absent in these parents' descriptions of their child. Overall, low-intensity families had fewer negative attachment codes than families in the other two groups, particularly in parent-child attachment ratings, which were predominantly positive. In the intergenerational parental attachments, no particular pattern of attachment predominated. In the disconnected family, negative attachment, parentification, and triangulation were prevalent, but disconnected parents tended not to have overinvolved, idealizing, or positive attachment codes.

Intergenerational Assessment of Attachment

Extensive historical data were obtained for families in the study, and part of this procedure involved obtaining two FMSS for each parent—one in which the parent spoke about his or her relationship with his or her mother, and the second, about his or her father. These protocols were then scored using the Diamond (Diamond & Doane, in press) coding system just described. These data, in conjunction with the parental FMSS data on the child, permit us to examine some elements of the intergenerational nature of intrafamilial attachment and bonding patterns.

Emotional Involvement and Disengagement in the Family Therapy Setting

Ratings of parental emotional involvement with the patient were made using the Family System Functioning (FSF) scales, developed by Doane and colleagues (Doane, Hill, Kaslow et al., 1988) and described in chapter 4. The family therapist based these researcher-guided ratings on the weekly family therapy sessions through the first month. The rating on the involvement scale permitted us to divide families into two groups: (1) families in which both parents (or the single parent) were emotionally involved to some extent, ranging from an appropriate level to an extremely overinvolved level; and (2) families in which at least one parent was rated as disengaged from the patient, ranging from a tendency to be underinvolved to a pervasive lack of involvement. Further details of the FSF scale can be found elsewhere (Doane et al., 1988).

Among the high-intensity families, 100% had a parent who was rated as overinvolved on the FSF. In the low-intensity families, most of the FSF ratings were either neutral or mildly involved. Two patterns appeared among the disconnected families: (1) a disengaged rating on the FSF or (2) an overinvolved rating. Most of the families who had an overinvolved rating also had negative attitudes toward the child, as expressed on the Kriesman.

Family Types

Data from the four domains of assessment just described were pooled to determine which family type each family most closely approximated. The family grouping criteria outlined in Table 5.1 are derived from a combination of conceptual thinking and empirical data. Further elucidation of the criteria for these groups are presented later. Briefly, however, a key feature of this three-way grouping is that the disconnected group of families differs from the other two groups in that a disturbed attachment, as measured by the FMSS, exists between at least one parent and the patient. As shown in Table 5.1, the family types differ with regard to the family emotional climate. The way that these two dimensions overlap or diverge has implications for treatment. Although disturbed attachments in the family of origin are sometimes accompanied by disturbed attachments in the family of procreation, as well as by a negative emotional style of relating, this is not always the case, as indicated in Table 5.1.

Diamond and Doane (in press) have reported group analyses showing that disturbed attachment in the family of origin is often associated with negative affective style in the family of procreation. Attachment between the patient and the parent is a starting point for generating a family profile and typology. We assume that disturbed parent-child attachment has a different quality or meaning when the parent has unresolved or disturbed

TABLE 5.1

Family Types: Attachment and Family Emotional Climate

Type	Attachment to Patient	Family Emotional Climate	Attachment in Family of Origin
LOW-INTENSITY	Positive	Low-Key	Usually Positive
HIGH-INTENSITY	Positive	Highly critical or Emotionally overinvolved	Positive or Negative
DISCONNECTED (Low-key)	Negative	Low-key	Positive or Negative
DISCONNECTED (High Criticism)	Negative	Highly critical	Positive or Negative

attachment with his or her own parents, as opposed to when the parent has a disturbed attachment to the patient but has successfully resolved intergenerational attachment issues. Differential treatment plans that take such differences into account permit the therapist to address these issues in an intergenerational context.

In Table 5.1, areas of intervention focus are enclosed in boxes. Following an epigenetic approach to treatment, one would address the attachment disturbances first during family therapy (the second and fourth columns in Table 5.1). The intergenerational attachment problems indicated for some parents in the high-intensity group are not enclosed in boxes because with high-intensity parents, when intergenerational disturbances in attachments are present, they are not accompanied by similar disturbances in attachments to the patient. Instead, the attachment to the patient is positive, perhaps overinvolved, but not negative or ambivalent. In the further discussion of the typology that follows, both disconnected types of families (low-key and highly critical) are combined for purposes of discussion, since, although they differ in family emotional climate, they share in common the attribute of a primary disturbance in attachment between one of the parents and the patient.

We have assigned a developmental priority to attachment, in part because our empirical analyses indicate that attachment constitutes a psychosocial risk factor that affects the course of pathology, and may, with borderline patients at least, exert a protective influence (in the case of families that have positive attachments) against relapse. It is also clear from our empirical findings and clinical experience that attempts to treat high EE or negative AS families who also have attachment problems are not very successful when the attachment difficulties are not addressed in the treatment.

In sum, in assigning a family to a given group, we used the attachment coding system to determine the quality of the parent-child attachment. A similar intergenerational assessment of attachment was also made based on FMSS interviews with each of the parents. The FSF scale of family inter-action on criticism and emotional overinvolvement then provided data about how the parents related to the child. The adapted Kriesman scale of rejecting attitudes provided data about whether the parents held exces-sively negative attitudes toward the patient. Data from these measures were examined case by case to determine the most appropriate designa-tion for the each family.

Empirical Findings

To test more rigorously the validity of our grouping assignments, we com-pleted a series of one-way ANOVAs on the raw FSF scores for each parent on the degree of criticism in the family and the degree of emotional involvement, as rated by the family therapist. We also had available inde-pendently measured AS scores for each family. This laboratory based mea-sure of family interaction provided summary scores on the total number of negative verbal remarks (e.g., criticism, hostility, guilt induction) made by the parent to the patient during 20 minutes of intense family discussion. A summary score of all supportive remarks (e.g., praise, warmth, empathy) was also calculated for each parent. Details of the AS coding system can be found elsewhere (Doane et al., 1985).

No significant differences were observed between the groups on the summary negative AS score (AS based on family interactions) for either mothers or fathers. Although negative AS was lowest in the low-intensity group, this difference was not statistically significant. Positive remarks to the patient were twice as likely in families of low-intensity and high-inten-sity mothers, as compared with mothers from the disconnected group. The difference was not statistically significant, however. A similar pattern was observed for fathers; those from disconnected families had the lowest mean number of positive remarks made to the patient.

Regarding negative AS attitudes (as measured by the Kreisman scale, a structural self-report measure of rejecting attitudes), however, the dif-ferences between the groups are sharper; mothers of disconnected fami-lies had significantly more rejecting scores (mean = 9.5) than mothers of high-intensity (mean = 2.9) or low intensity (mean = 7.5) families. A simi-lar pattern was observed for fathers, but the results were not statistically significant.

These patients' family therapists rated the high-intensity mothers as significantly more emotionally overinvolved ($p<.01$, $F[2, 38] = 5.67$) than were mothers in the other two groups of the FSF involvement scale. Paralleling the findings on negative AS, no differences between groups were found for the FSF criticism scale.

The lack of clear overlap between AS and our grouping was expected, because our grouping criteria involve multiple levels of data and include measures such as attachment and attitudes toward the patient. In addition, our grouping of families is based on the entire family's data, not just the mother's or the father's data, as reported here. Thus, to find any validity for the AS measure and the clinical groupings for mothers alone or fathers alone is impressive. The section that follows contains a more comprehensive discussion of the three types of families, which therapists can use to generate clinical portraits of the kinds of issues that each family type probably will raise.

The High-Intensity Family

High-intensity families are characterized by highly or overly intense modes of feeling and relating. The emotional intensity in these families is usually generated by a network of strong, positive attachments and represents an expression of such secure affectional bonds. The parents seem deeply involved and interested in the patient and what he or she is saying or doing. In such families, emotional expression appears to be open and free-flowing, and family members are verbally and expressive, if not always verbally fluent. Members are emotionally attuned and highly reactive to one another's words, affects, and expressions.

TABLE 5.2

High-Intensity Families

Toward Patient:
  Positively Attached
  Emotionally Overinvolved Attitudes
  Infantilizing Attitudes
  Behavior: High Criticism, High Emotional Overinvolvement;
    No Disengagement

Family of Origin:
  Positively Attached
  Emotionally Overinvolved Attitudes
  Idealization of Parents

One of the most salient problems for members of high-intensity families is that the family members are quick to *react* emotionally. When tension builds in such families, the interest and concern seem to get buried in floods of affect, particularly when the parents feel overwhelmed by the patient's illness or disturbance. In conflictual family discussions, family members may criticize the patient, sometimes both extensively and harshly. Similarly, guilt-inducing and intrusive remarks are made fairly often. In the family treatment setting the clinician often observes that this emotional overinvolvement is treatment resistant—it persists throughout fairly lengthy periods of family therapy and frequently appears to be relatively intractable.

Clinicians, understandably, often misinterpret the negative affect in these families as springing from resentment of the patient, or of the patient's illness or disturbed behavior. In fact, the consistently high degree of emotional overinvolvement in such high-intensity families appears to be rooted in a network of positive and sometimes idealized attachments through the generations. The confrontation with reality that occurs during family interaction often breaks the fantasy of the patients' perfection or the parents' idealization of the parent-child bond and results in bursts of criticism or intrusiveness. Typically, members of high-intensity families express strong, positive attachments to the patient and to each other, as assessed by the sometimes effusive statements they make, expressing loving feelings, empathy, and caring. When parents in high-intensity families speak about their child in the context of a brief interview with an examiner (in the FMSS), they spontaneously verbalize this sense of an intense, positive, gratifying attachment, as the following statement from the FMSS of Ms. Russell, the mother of a schizophrenic adolescent, Gina, illustrates.

> Well to start out at first—as an infant, I think we got along very well. We hit it off right away. Through her younger years of childhood, we got along excellent—we've always had fun together. She always loved me and enjoyed being with me, we always did a lot of things together, and we did things as a family. . . . She was always a lovable thing and I think I was always lovable for her. She was always a good kid until her problems started. We always had fun together. We were always very close to each other. I tried to help her with everything I could. . . socially and emotionally.

Statements such as these indicate that a largely positive internal working model of attachment exists. In other words, in high-intensity families the parent carries an internalized image of the patient that emphasizes primarily his or her good qualities, despite evidence of the parent's sense of being overwhelmed by the patient's illness or disturbed behavior. In fact, parents often idealize the patient and ignore the problematic or troubled aspects of his or her behavior.

For some parents this tendency to idealize the patient might sustain or reinforce a sense of total commitment to the patient, regardless of the vicissitudes of the disturbance. However, for most parents a major component of this idealization of the patient is their lack of integration of the patient's psychiatric illness or disturbed behavior into their view of the patient. Their understanding and acceptance of the patient's illness is often a veneer that conceals a fixed belief that the patient will someday revert to his or her former self. Ms. DeLeo, the mother of a schizophrenic young woman, whom we will call Rebecca, expresses such nostalgia and longing for a restoration of the past self of the patient in the following excerpt from the FMSS:

> She is a good person. She was a good girl when she was little. And now she's able to talk to me better. I think she feels better and I feel better too. And I just hope that she can help me with the cooking again. When she was 10 years old, before we found out that she has this problem, she liked to cook and I was happy. . . .

Just as the parents tend to describe the patient (their son or daughter) in such idealized terms, which often deny the current reality of the patient and the illness, so also do they tend to present an idealized, one-dimensional view of their own parents. The parents' descriptions of their own parents reflect not so much a blatant denial of difficulties but an inability to integrate experiences of conflict, distress, or hardship into their version of family-of-origin relationships. There is a notable absence of complexity and/or differentiation in the parents' descriptions of their own parents, whose good and bad qualities are not acknowledged and reflected upon. Instead, there is often a rigid adherence to a view of the parents' goodness, righteousness, or perfection, despite considerable evidence of conflict, deprivation, parental loss, and/or abandonment.

Such an idealized view is often mixed with the parents' depiction of their own parents' overinvolved attitudes and behaviors, which often may be the only area of difficulty, conflict, or imperfection that the parent will acknowledge and explore. For example, the following statement of Ms. McLellan, the mother of a borderline daughter, Eva, illustrates the confluence of positive attachment, intrusiveness, and guilt-induction in the relationship with her own mother:

> My mother, she loves her family. She liked to take me everywhere. Basically, she liked to control everything about me, including my friends. She very often would pick me up after school when I wanted to go out with friends and she wanted me to come home. We had a big television set, and to her this was an exciting afternoon. I think, actually, she would be jealous if I did things with my friends. She always told me I was her best friend. . . . I hid things from her though because she wanted everything to be perfect. . . . She

overreacts, you know, if I was upset about something she would overreact. If I ever got angry with her, she would sulk and withdraw, so it wasn't worth it. . . . She made me feel that everything was for me. Basically, I grew up in a very close kind of existence, protected, but protected too much.

Often such overinvolved behaviors and attitudes on the part of the parents, the only dark cloud over an otherwise idealized childhood, extend to the relationship with grandchildren or the patients in our study. Sometimes a grandmother is so involved and emotionally reactive to the state of the patient, her grandchild, that this affects how the mother feels, often exacerbating the mother's emotional reactions to the disturbed child. Such emotional overinvolvement may ricochet through the generations. The following statement from one research participant, Ms. Stern, describing her own mother's extreme emotional involvement with the vicissitudes of the patient, Melanie's, psychiatric disorder and symptoms, illustrates how such overinvolvement can be intimately intertwined with attachments through the generations:

> My mother, I love her, and she was helpful to me all the time. She was caring and always there if I had a problem, like when I was cold or scared of dogs; she brought me everywhere so I wouldn't have to confront one. And she loves to be involved with Melanie. When Melanie starts to hallucinate or get paranoid, Mom would get more unglued than I was. She would call me or Melanie's doctors constantly, and would bombard me with articles and books about Melanie's condition. I was constantly trying to reassure her that Melanie would recover, even when I wasn't so sure myself, and was feeling pretty hopeless. But I just hated to see my mother so upset. When things would be going a little better with Melanie, her mood would bounce right back.

Thus, such overinvolved attitudes in the context of positive attachments are transgenerationally transmitted relational patterns in high-intensity families. However, whereas the parents tend to highlight the positive attachment and downplay or minimize the overinvolved attitudes in their families of origin, the patients in our study tended to focus more on the overinvolved attitudes in their descriptions of their own parents. Indeed, while the patients generally express positive attachment with their parents, they sometimes show an inordinate involvement with and concern for their parents' feelings. This concern and worry about their parents is often indicative of overinvolved attitudes, as the following excerpt from an FMSS of a borderline adolescent, Dana, describing her mother, Ms. Jordan, shows:

> I think she's a very nice woman. Her life is really hard. And she sacrifices a lot to make me and my sisters happy. She's always there if I need help. I'd like to make her proud of me, but it's hard because I keep blowing it. I'd like

her to be proud of me before she dies, you know. I feel bad that I'm making her feel so upset.

Many times the patients find the overinvolvement component of their strong affectional bond to their parents uncomfortable, as shown in the following quote from the FMSS of a borderline adolescent, George:

> My mother's always watching what I do. She won't let me have any privacy on the phone. She's constantly cleaning my room, arranging things. She treats me like a pampered guest—asking me whether I want this or that. Ever since Dad left, she's always spoiling me. She doesn't know how to show her love to me, but she loves me.

In high-intensity families, these measures of family relationships converge to define a familial presentation in which strong and positive affectional ties among family members are pervaded with overinvolved attitudes. This combination of positive attachment and overinvolvement is represented differently through the generations. In the parents' descriptions of their own parents, positive attachment often eclipses overinvolvement. In the patients' descriptions of their own parents, however, the overinvolved attitudes are often emphasized, although the attachment component is almost always a strong, if secondary, theme.

Regardless of the balance between strong affectional bonds and overinvolved attitudes in the representations that members of the family hold of each other, in the directly observed family interactions, the overinvolved attitudes break through directly. Whereas the emotional overinvolvement may be curtailed or denied when family members are describing each other in the individual interviews, in the family interactions, the physical presence of family members appears to incite almost immediate overreactivity. The following excerpt from the family interaction of the Blakes, the family of Tom, an angry borderline young man, illustrates this point:

TOM: What else did she [the therapist] talk to you about me? Did she say anything?

MR. BLAKE: She said you were doing very well.

MS. BLAKE: Very well, I felt very bad when I left last week and you went to the TV room. I was so upset. I had a hard time driving home, it was dark, I was so upset.

TOM: Yeah. Oh.

MS. BLAKE: I don't want you to walk away depressed from me. I think about you all week like that. I want to think of you as happy, you know, that you're glad to see us, that we had a nice day.

In the family interaction situation, these families typically generate a lively, if not chaotic or overstimulating, discussion that may appear confusing or stressful to the observer. And although family members may express disappointment or sadness, these affects are not the predominant emotional overtones present in the family. Instead, the interactions often seem too close or too intense.

Family interactions in high-intensity families often evince overinvolvement in the form of parental preoccupation with the patient's ideas, thoughts, or feelings. Sometimes the parent speaks in ways that imply a "privileged knowledge" of the patient's internal states or motives, as with Annette, a schizophrenic woman in her 20s, and Mr. and Mrs. Kane, her parents.

ANNETTE: I don't want to be away from home. I haven't been home you know for a long time.

Ms. KANE:You want to be home, but when you get there you can't seem to take the stress there that's bothering you. It's you that puts this stress on yourself from what I can gather.

ANNETTE: Yeah, it's my fault, I admit it.

MR. KANE: You seem like you get so many things in your mind. . . 'Well, what do I do now, I'm home, I have to go to the gym, I have to do this, I don't want to stay home.' All these things start getting on your mind and it seems like it sets you back.

Ms. KANE: You just have to work on yourself. . . So you're sitting there right now thinking about it and it's causing you stress, right now. . .

MR. KANE: I can see it in your face.

ANNETTE: I know, it's getting down to my neck, too.

The foregoing examples from the FMSSs and the family interactions illustrate that in high-intensity families, positive attachment converges with and is often expressed through overinvolved attitudes. In our sample research families, there was a prevalence of schizophrenic patients whose families were categorized in the high-intensity group. These families often present a picture of the "enmeshed family" written about by early observers of families of schizophrenics (see, for example, Singer & Wynne, 1963; Wynne, Singer, Bartko, & Toohey, 1977). In high-intensity families, the positive attachments are often characterized by an element of fusion or extreme closeness that comes through in the intrusion, mind reading, and emotional overreactivity observed in the family interactions. In this study, the majority of parents in the high-intensity group had a child with schizophrenia. Nevertheless, only half of the schizophrenic cases in our sample were in the high-intensity group.

In our analysis of the high-intensity family, we have attempted to illustrate the complexities of such overinvolved attachments—for example, the ways that they are represented internally and enacted behaviorally. Although most of the high-intensity families had a schizophrenic member, this blend of strong positive attachment in the face of overinvolved attitudes and behaviors was also found, although to a lesser extent, in the parents of borderline individuals and patients with affective illness, as well as those with schizophrenia.

Regardless of the patient's diagnosis, it is clear from our data that both the patients and their parents contribute reciprocally to the maintenance of overinvolved patterns. In most high-intensity families, the patient exhibited a superficial or pseudo acceptance, or at least tolerance, of parental overinvolvement. Perhaps the child senses the intermingling of positive attachment with the overinvolvement and fears that if the child confronts the latter too strongly, he or she will lose the former. If this were the case, it might help explain why these families are particularly slow to change. Therapists who quickly move in and challenge the parental overinvolvement may receive an icy or hostile reception from the family, which may coalesce further and even close ranks against the therapist. These kinds of families often evoke intense feelings of frustration in a therapist who harbors ambitious fantasies of change for the family.

The foremost therapeutic task with high-intensity families is to make the family aware that their mode of expressing intense attachment bonds is maladaptive and needs to be ameliorated.

In the high-intensity family, one wants to gently loosen attachments and transform emotionally overinvolved ways of relating that are less helpful into ones that facilitate the patient's recovery. Attachment issues and intergenerational issues, while they may be of interest to the clinician, are not necessarily the primary target for intervention.

The Low-Intensity Family

Low-intensity families are characterized by positive, differentiated attachments to both the family of origin and the family of procreation without the excessive emotional overinvolvement and reactivity that characterize the high-intensity group. In the family interactions, emotional overinvolvement tends to be minimal or short-lived, and criticism of the patient, low or moderate.

Low-intensity parents appear to have a genuine capacity to modulate their affect in their interactions with the patient, regardless of the vicissitudes of his or her illness or disturbance. Further, the steadfast insistence on seeing the patient in an extremely positive and often idealized fashion is not evident in low-intensity families. Rather, there is a more balanced view of the patient that emerges in the individual interviews—a view that

TABLE 5.3

Low-Intensity Families

Toward Patient:
   Positively Attached
   Behavior: Low/Moderate Criticism, Moderate Emotional Overinvolvement;
      No Disengagements

Family of Origin:
   Positively Attached
   May be Emotionally Overinvolved
   Mastery Experience as Parentified Child
   Differentiated View of Parents

integrates both positive and negative qualities, and strengths as well as weaknesses, and that encompasses the patient's areas of disturbance as well as areas of competence and intact functioning.

Similarly, the tendency to minimize conflicts, hardships, and deprivations in the family of origin is not present. Low-intensity parents appear to have derived a sense of mastery out of coping with difficulties in their early lives and relationships, and hence do not back off from or avoid acknowledging such difficulties in their own parental descriptions. Occasionally, the parents may express anger or negative feelings about their own parents, or overinvolved or infantilizing attitudes toward the patient; but overall, the tendency for negative attributions of any kind is diminished in this group. It should be noted that this type of family was the least common in our study.

The following examples from the FMSSs of low-intensity parents illustrates the capacity of families in this group to present a balanced, integrated view of the patient.

Mr. Pine speaks about his young adult schizophrenic son, Roger, as follows:

> He makes every situation a happy one. He's had this for four years—it's been very hard for me to realize that he is sick, because when he's not going through an episode, I feel I'm talking just the way I would to a normal friend. He's just been a joy in our lives since the day he was born. Until this happened, which is when he finished his first year of art school, he was absolutely all you could ask for in a person. I admire him, and we've always gotten along. There's been no friction between us. He doesn't always talk much, but there's no reason he should. So that perhaps I don't know him as well as I think I do. He can still function in many ways, in his painting and all the surface things. When he is ill, he is away from reality and it's very difficult to talk with him at all. He will just go up to his room and paint.

Such a balanced, integrated view of the patient is also evident in the statement of Ms. Davis, the mother of a borderline young adult, Jana:

> After sharing 15 years of life with her, I would say that she is fun, entertaining. She has a lot of enthusiasm and she's a fabulous dancer. On the negative side is that she is very sad, and this is hard for her to deal with. She has a hard time deciding how much of her real self to let people see.

As these examples indicate, parents in the low-intensity group show an acceptance of the vicissitudes of the patient's illness or difficulties. This greater tolerance does not devolve from any characteristics of the patients in the low-intensity group. Patients in these families do not differ from those in the other groups on any of the patient variables such as severity of illness, diagnosis, length of preexisting illness, number of previous hospitalizations, or on demographic variables. However, the intergenerational patterns of relationships in these families do appear to be distinct.

The parents' relationships with their own parents are often characterized by positive attachments and occasionally some overinvolvement with one of the parents. In this sense they are similar to the parents in the high-intensity group. Interestingly, however, they differ from the high-intensity families in that the parents' view of their own parents is much less idealized and one-sided than was the case with parents in the other group. Low-intensity parents can acknowledge some of the negative or problematic aspects of their relationship with an overinvolved parent.

Low-intensity parents also have the capacity to see and understand that intrafamilial patterns of overinvolvement are rooted in their parents' weaknesses and impairments. In fact, in a surprising number of parents in this group, there has been some major illness or impairment in another member of their family of origin. Typically, these parents talk freely and without bitterness about the impact of such parental impairment on their own childhood and earlier familial experience. This, is turn, might suggest that these parents are somewhat more differentiated with regard to the overinvolved family patterns and problematic family characteristics that they grew up with, and that the overinvolvement in the family of origin was not necessarily egosyntonic (comfortable or consistent with their view of themselves, or with their typical defensive structure). They are able to tolerate negative or ambivalent reactions to at least some aspects of their parents, and thus perhaps do not have to resort to covering attitudes of idealization either toward their own parents or toward their children. In many cases the parent was parentified as a child, but he or she seems to have undergone some kind of mastery experience in the process.

In the following excerpts from parental speech samples, one can detect a certain maturity in the speaker's attitude that suggests that the parent has somehow been able to integrate both the negative and the positive aspects of their own experience as children in their families.

This integrative capacity is evident in the following maternal description of Ms. Reich, the mother of a young adult schizophrenic son:

> My mother was a wonderful companion, a lot of fun. But it was hard for me because it seemed her whole interest was on me. When I was small, she was very nurturing. We went through very hard times together monetarily, financially, and every other way. When I was very young, she was nervous because she was having money troubles. . . . I always felt close to mother. I liked to talk things over with her very much. She was brave and she had a wonderful sense of humor. . . . I admired her very much, and she was a wonderful woman.

Mr. Rotter, the low-intensity father of a schizophrenic son, describes his mother in similar terms:

> I've already mentioned that mother had a bad temper, and when she got into her downers or bad temper periods, they didn't upset me for some reason. Early on, I took the role of supporting mother and trying to get her through her depressed periods. I tried to stick close to her and tried not to get angry myself or get upset. And of course, that made us very close because she appreciated that. She was a wonderful cook, and I used to help her cook dinner every night. We used to do a lot of things together, and I always felt a sense of harmony with her, even when she had her difficult periods.

Similarly, Mr. Kaplan, the father of a schizophrenic adolescent, Joseph, shows an understanding and acceptance of his own father's limitations, in the context of a representation of a secure, gratifying attachment.

> My father was 50 years old when I was born. . . . And he was always very gentle and kind, he never spanked me, although he didn't have to spank me because all he had to do was. . . just the tone of his voice was enough to straighten me out. I loved him very dearly and he loved me very dearly. But as I grew a little older, into my teens, his health began to worsen. He also had troubles with my older sister, who was somewhat of a wild one, and I knew all those things and realized that he simply didn't have the time or the strength to devote too much close attention to me. And he often told me that he had great confidence and faith in my ability to take care of myself, and he seemed to think that I had a certain amount of personal strength that would enable me to make my own decisions. . . . He was a very comforting man because he was so steady and so gentle.

Just as the parents in the low-intensity families were often accepting of their parents' problems, so the patients describe their parents in positive, appreciative tones. The patients often express deep gratitude toward one or both parents for being able to accept their illness or disturbance. For example, Tom, a schizophrenic young adult speaks about his mother, Ms. Eigen, as follows:

> My mother's always been a very good mother to me. She's affectionate, warm, nurturing, a good listener. She often speaks her piece. She doesn't intrude on my business. She gives me a feeling that she's there when I need her and she's not overpowering. I care for her very much. And I enjoy her company.

The same appreciation and gratitude are evident in the maternal description by Keith, a borderline adolescent who speaks about his mother, Ms. Phillips, as follows:

> My mom's cool. That's the only word for it. She taught me how to roller-skate, swim, and horseback ride. She likes the music I like. I could talk to her about anything. She lets me live my own life, and that's cool, but she was always there for me.

In general, the low-intensity parents often seem able to differentiate between the child when well and the child when ill. The parents keep the relationship on an even keel—that is, they maintain a steady level of relatedness that does not falter; the illness does not rupture the parent-child bond. Perhaps these parents have somehow worked through or risen above their anger at and disappointment in their own parents, and in their children. This is no easy task, of course, which may help to explain why this category of family is relatively infrequent, compared to the other two.

In the family interaction setting one observes a tone of moderation—the parents may be critical of the patient, but they are not excessively hostile. They are connected with the patient in a positive way and may be slightly overinvolved, but those attitudes do not persist. A countering move by a therapist or even by the patient to confront parental overinvolvement usually brings on a change in the parent's behavior. One also observes that the parent usually does not emotionally overreact to the patient's provocation, whether intentional or inadvertent.

In the following excerpt from a family interaction task, Ms. Smith, the mother of Jason, a schizophrenic young man, is able to identify and differentiate the components of a given problem and engage the patient in seeing how a step-by-step approach to working on the problem might bring better results. Despite the fact that her son is severely disturbed, there is little evidence of emotional overreaction to him or his psychiatric disorder. Although the mother is herself stressed, she does not appear to be overwhelmed:

JASON: And, you know, if I had a car and my license and stuff like that, I'd be able to go to go to town and I could've found some more jobs.

Ms. SMITH: Yeah, I think you said something there. I know you won't get up for the bus. You have a hard time getting up in the morning.

JASON: That's 'cause I go out and party all night like a fool.

Ms. SMITH: Yeah, but Jason, there were times you didn't go out and party all night, but I always felt that if I didn't get you up and get you out of the house that you'd lose the job. So that's where my anxiety was coming in.

Another feature of the low-intensity family is that the parents seem able to step back from the conflict at hand and reflect on their own contribution to it. In the following example, the father, Mr. Paglia, accepts responsibility for his role in the current difficulties of his borderline son, Jim, but he does so in a way that does not make the patient feel guilty or bad.

MR. PAGLIA: There are times when we argue that you have very strong, definite ideas; I have very strong, definite ideas; and we don't know how to take these ideas and be able to listen to the other person. I sometimes. . . I get impatient listening to you because I've heard it all before, and that's not fair to you. I sometimes don't give you the opportunity to talk to me because I've already heard it. There's always a crisis it seems—it's either Grandma, or it's my sister. My energies are a lot of times spent dealing with all these other crises going on, and I feel that I've kinda short-changed you because I don't have any more energy by the time it gets to be your turn.

JIM: Yes.

MR. PAGLIA: Plus I also think that maybe sometimes we don't have a lot to talk about because I don't know whether you're really interested in what I do.

JIM: You know, I wish there were some school that I could go to like teach me to talk to people—because I don't talk to people.

MR. PAGLIA: There've been occasions that you've had a job that you felt decent about, could talk about it. Maybe you just don't have enough subject matter to talk about.

In sum, in the low-intensity families, the family members' positive differentiated attachments are translated into an interactional style characterized by a low level of emotional reactivity and a capacity to regulate emotional involvement in ways that enhance, rather than disrupt, the affectional bonds. Guilt inducement and hostility are absent from family discussions. Further, there appears to be a crucial intergenerational substrate to this interactional style that involves the parents' capacity to tolerate their own parents' sometimes quite substantial impairments without a major disruption of affectional ties.

Although there were few low-intensity families in our study, there were a number of individual parents married to disconnected spouses who were not included in this group of low-intensity families because the presence of only one disconnected parent automatically classified the family in the disconnected group, which is described in the next section.

Treating low-intensity families is usually easier than treating families in which the parents are disconnected or high-intensity. Clinicians working in contemporary settings where the biological aspects of psychiatric illness are emphasized sometimes develop a tendency to overgeneralize about the families of people they treat. Often clinicians assume that *all* families of patients with schizophrenia, for example, are dysfunctional only to the extent that family members are uninformed about the nature of the illness and how to manage it. Parents are seen as victims of previous mental health professionals who neglected to educate them about the burdens of the illness. Sometimes blatant problems in relating or attitudes are minimized or completely discounted. When this happens, the therapist risks relating to the family's problems superficially, so that meaningful change in the quality of the family environment will not occur once the assistance and protection of the hospital or clinic ends. The converse is also common: the clinician—often trained in the nuances of family systems theory, psychodynamic object relations family theory and therapy, or behavioral techniques—might automatically focus on the negative aspects of family interactions. In so doing, the therapist may not look carefully at the relational context of or substrate to the behavior, which might in fact be relatively benign and functional, as is the case with the low-intensity family.

The secure, positive attachment bond and consistent, low-key style of affective expression enables many low-intensity family members to grasp psychoeducation principles quickly. Treatment may well be brief, because there generally is less work to do regarding attachment disturbance and styles of conveying criticism to the patient about himself or herself, or the illness. Many low-intensity families were able to make solid gains in the therapy hour that generalized and persisted after only one or two sessions. In our experience of working with families of severely disturbed patients, the low-key, mature, modulated low-intensity family does exist, but it is not as common as the other two family types. The point here is that when these families do appear, a briefer course of treatment can be planned. Interventions based on education and instruction in management skills are ideally suited for these families.

With the low-intensity family the therapist is fortunate to have, from

TABLE 5.4

Disconnected Families

Toward Patient:
  Negative/Weak/Non-attachment
  Triangulated
  Infantilized
  Behavior: Continuous or Unpredictable Criticism or Low Criticism; At Least
    One Parent is Emotionally Disengaged

Family of Origin:
  Tend to have Negative/Weak/Non-attachments
  Triangulated

the outset, family members who are potential treatment collaborators. When the clinician is able to capitalize on the family members' strengths, optimal results can be achieved with less elaborate types of family intervention.

The Disconnected Family

In contrast to the high-intensity family, in which emotional intensity appears to be generated by positive, if overinvolved, attachments, the disconnected family is characterized by affect that seems linked to disturbances or ruptures in the attachment bonds between family members. What distinguishes disconnected families from those in the other two groups is that one or both of the parents are emotionally disengaged from the patient—that is, a certain degree of distance, aloofness, or disconnection between one or both of the parents and the patient exists. The degree or intensity of the disengagement varies, ranging from overt rejection to mild estrangement.

Because these families have disturbance at the level of attachment between family members, we view them as facing a developmentally earlier task than families in the high-intensity group. The disturbance or developmental arrest in the disconnected family exists at a more basic level of relational disturbance. In these families there is a lack of bonding or positive attachment between parent and child that colors the emotional atmosphere of the family environment. It is against this relational backdrop that other attributes of the family, such as negative affective expression, should be viewed.

In the current study, two thirds of the families in the sample fell into the disconnected group, which includes patients from all three diagnostic groups: the schizophrenic group, the adult borderline and/or affective disorder (ADBL) group, as well as the adolescent borderline group. Regardless of diagnosis, at least one of the parents in these families appeared to have a disturbed attachment to the patient. When the parents were asked at admission to complete the FMSS, they often spontaneously focused on a negative aspect of their relationship with the child.

When parents did not provide spontaneous verbal descriptions of the disturbed parent-child relationship, their negative attitudes about the patient were revealed in high scores on the Kreisman scale. Thus, for parents in this group of families, there appears to be a negative, disturbed, or weak attachment to the patient, not only in terms of observable behavior but also at the level of conscious attitudes. The predominant internalized image of the patient has a negative valence; the attachment may be strong but intertwined with rejecting attitudes toward the patient. In these families, the parent's disturbed, damaged, or undeveloped connection with the patient on the attitudinal level is visibly enacted in the family interaction. During the parent-child interaction, the family therapist may be aware of an almost palpable relational distance, often accompanied by themes of disappointment and resentment, or overt criticism.

Sometimes these disturbances of attachment are readily obvious, as in the following paternal description offered by James, a young adult suffering from major depression.

> I don't really remember him being involved with me as a child. I keep seeing him in my head as being angry and screaming. As I got older, he told me that I was dumb, stupid, couldn't do anything right; he was always just knocking me down. I was good at sports though when I got older, and he liked that. He never criticized me for that. But I always respected him. I mean, I still do. I respect him very much. He's a writer, very intelligent man, but he's got a hell of a lot of hang-ups.

Similarly, in the following example, Ms. Lang's description of her 28-year-old bipolar son conveys a relatively fixed negative view of him and of their relationship:

> My son has an incredible sense of humor, and its always been a way to get attention. When he was little, it was always very amusing; now it's not at all. We have a very orderly home, and I think that he has a great deal of difficulty dealing with authority figures. He's always got to battle with me about almost everything. He has a great deal of difficulty with my husband and I being together and our way of raising him. He's been angry and stubborn and very difficult to deal with. He's been a source of great pain, I think, for the whole family, and for me in particular.

In many cases, the disruption in attachment is more subtle, as evidenced in this FMSS of a father, Mr. Oates, speaking about his borderline adolescent daughter:

I would say our relationship at times is distant, simply because she is looking for approval that she thinks that she doesn't get. She says I'm overly critical and demanding. If she's got a personal problem, she doesn't come to me. She doesn't feel comfortable talking to me for some reason.

In some disconnected families one of the parents may appear to be extremely overinvolved with the patient, but the overinvolvement is accompanied by criticism or guilt-inducing remarks to the patient. The clinician often mistakenly assumes that the intense involvement reflects the parent's deep, emotionally overinvolved stance, similar to that observed among the high-intensity parents. When the therapist makes this assumption, a tactical error in treatment can occur—that is, the therapist may embark on the task of helping the patient separate and individuate from the presumably overattached parent.

Our research data suggest a different interpretation of the intense affect and involvement seen in the disconnected families, however. We view this overinvested kind of behavior not so much as intense emotional overinvolvement with the patient but as intense *preoccupation* with the patient—particularly with his negative attributes or behavior. This focus on the aspects of the child that are unacceptable or irksome to the parent may stem in part from the fact that many of these parents continue to grapple with some residual negative feelings derived from problematic interactions with their own parents, as expressed in the following excerpt from a FMSS from Mr. Weisburg, the father of Theresa, a young borderline woman:

My father was an impossible man. He wasn't interested in me. He seemed to keep to himself much of the time, except for holidays, when he was around more. But even then he would shout at one of us and tell us how that everything we were doing was wrong, and that we would never amount to anything. I wanted him to be a father to me, but it didn't happen. I once told him that I really wanted him to spend more time with me and asked him to do some things with me—like play sports or even just go for hikes together—you know father-daughter things, but he just continued to ignore me most of the time, when he wasn't criticizing me or yelling at me.

This is an example of the blatant negative images that some of the parents in this group have about their own parents. When the parents react with frustration or rejection to their disturbed children, we can hypothesize that this reaction may be fueled, at least in part, by the painful residue these parents carried with them from interactions with their own parents.

Another mother of a schizophrenic young man, Ms. Thompson, describes the negative attachment she had with her mother and also alludes to the merging or blending of issues of control, blame, and overinvolvement that is often found in the histories of parents in this group:

> When I was small, my mother seemed to be a major controlling figure in my life. She was the one that was always blaming me for everything that went wrong. When my mother didn't get what she wanted, she would have a tantrum. Sometimes she might throw dishes or slap me or one of my sisters. My sister talked back to her a lot, but that just seemed to make her more angry, and so I was afraid to.

When intense anger at the patient is expressed spontaneously during the FMSS, it is important to explore the roots of such intense negative feelings in prior suppressed or repressed family-of-origin relationships. We have found threads of remarkable continuity in the parent-child relationships of the previous generation. In the preceding excerpt, for example, Ms. Thompson's own mother was depicted as being an emotional and neglectful, yet very controlling, woman who was not able to put her own needs aside to take care of her daughter. In the following FMSS in which Ms. Thompson describes her schizophrenic son, Michael, it is clear that she finds especially frustrating these aspects of her son that are reminiscent of her mother.

> He would always do the opposite of what I wanted; he did it just to make me lose my temper. We have always had conflicts. I don't know why. We never were able to see things the same way. And I have never forgiven him for making me lose control of my temper, and scream at him. It's never been a nice relationship. Everything revolves around him. He's a very self-centered child. Everything has to revolve around him, and if it doesn't, he throws tantrums. My husband always gave in to him, but I didn't, even though at times I've been afraid of him. And so I was the one he always fought with. I just found it frustrating.

In this FMSS one can also see that Ms. Thompson seems unaware of the link between her own past experience with a difficult and tyrannical mother, and her current frustrations with her son. These issues were addressed in the treatment by having mother-son family sessions early in the treatment. During these sessions the focus was on Ms. Thompson's frustrations and disappointments with her own mother and how these got translated into her relationship with her son, particularly in her tendency to blame him for her temper and in her reactions to him that mirrored her own mother's responses.

Parents with these kinds of attachment problems may have difficulty relating in a caring, sensitive way to their child unless they explore the intergenerational sources of their own attitudes and behaviors. Psychoeducation or skills-training approaches probably will not have an enduring or meaningful impact on such entrenched attitudes. Our approach would dictate an intergenerational strategy in working with this woman's buried and archaic hostility and resentment. The therapeutic task would be to explore the mother's experiences with her own mother and the legacy of disappointments in the family-of-origin relationships that have influenced her extreme distress and disappointment in her son, as well as her tendency to hold him responsible for her behavior.

An Intergenerational Spiral

Our observations of the similarity across generations regarding disturbed, damaged, or negative attachments led us to speculate that perhaps the stresses involved in dealing with the psychiatrically impaired child activate preexisting internal problems of the parent that involve disappointments and burdens experienced with his or her own parents. The ill child then may serve as a catalyst for reactivating old "unfinished business" for the parent. This theme of intergenerational transmission of risk factors through processes of projection and expression of negative affect is central within disconnected families.

In the following example one can see the intergenerational process commonly observed in disconnected families in which painful or negative aspects of the parent's own history are intertwined with negative affect and reenacted in the context of the parent's current relationship with the patient-child. The mother, Ms. McGregor, describes her own mother as follows:

> My earliest memories of her are when I was about 3 years old. I was all dressed up and waiting for her to take me to a birthday party. I was sitting in the swing with my kitty, and I wanted her to come and see us together in the swing, but I didn't because I was afraid she would get mad at me. And I can remember her later yelling into the window at me, telling me to put the cat down and not to get my dress dirty. I was always trying to be very good, but no matter how hard I tried, my interactions with her were very unpleasant. She had been training as a concert pianist, and she had given up her career when she got married. And she was very bitter about this, which resulted in her always wanting me to be perfect, and always finding fault with everything I did. Sometimes she would say things like, 'I wish I'd never had children.' She was an unhappy person who was impossible to satisfy. As I got older, I avoided her and rarely told her anything about myself because I knew that she would inevitably say or do something to make me feel rejected.

Jessica, Ms. McGregor's daughter, similarly describes her own mother as a woman who was rejecting, intrusive, impatient, and unavailable.

My mother and I look alike and we have other things in common too, which is why we don't get along. We're both rigid and don't like being pushed around. She was always calling me on the carpet for being inappropriate. I always did or said the wrong thing. She was always giving me lectures about the things that I did and said that embarrassed her. We fought a lot, especially about my friends. She always compared me to her friends' daughters and tried to get me to be like them and to be friends with them, but I wouldn't do it. My mother doesn't know how to deal with me. She doesn't talk about her mother, and I think that she is bitter about her own mother. I don't know why. She didn't turn out so badly. She's smart, she's a doctor, she's sensitive to all of that, I guess, but she doesn't know how to deal with me.

The comments from this mother-daughter pair highlight the unwitting recreation of negative relational patterns and rejecting attitudes.

These disconnected families also show us how powerful negative introjects can be in shaping current interactions in the family of procreation. The introjection of objects refers to the process through which the subject transposes experiences and images of others and their intrinsic qualities so that they come to constitute an aspect of the self. In the following excerpt from the FMSS of Stan, a borderline adolescent boy, one is struck by how fresh and painfully alive early childhood images can be, and how they can persist even in the absence of current interactions, which is often the case in families where divorce or desertion has occurred:

Okay, well, Dad was cool for a while. He was there and he was okay, but I didn't see him that much. He was always working; he was never really home a lot. I didn't really spend any time with him at all until they got divorced. Then he came every Friday night. He picked us up. Then he dropped us off at two o'clock on Saturday. Now he only comes once a month, and I never see him at all. He was never a big family person. Once I hit 15 there was a complete change—he no longer came up to see me regularly. He disowned me. And that took a while to accept because he was always like 'daddy' and I always put him up on this big pedestal. It was like it hurt really bad. And it was like I couldn't accept that he didn't love me anymore, that I was just a financial responsibility more than anything else. He didn't like hugging. He put one arm around my shoulder, he'd give a quick squeeze, and then he'd let go. He never said, 'I love you.' I was never close to him.

In disconnected families the negative aspects of the internalized image or representation of the parent-child relationship get enacted in different ways during face-to-face discussions in the family. Sometimes the family interaction is almost isomorphic with the representational world, as can be seen in the following excerpt from family interactions in the Thompson family, which was quoted extensively earlier in this chapter:

Ms. THOMPSON: But I think that you don't have a lot of respect for yourself.

MICHAEL: Respect is something that you earn.

Ms. THOMPSON: Respect is something you have when you respect yourself, and you ask other people to respect you. You ask a lot of people but you don't care. You ask a lot of your brothers, but you never do anything for them.

MICHAEL: Not true. I do a lot of things .

Ms. THOMPSON: I'm not talking about material things. I'm talking about giving. You don't give. You don't seem to care about anybody but yourself. Everything revolves around you. You do it with me, you do it with your brothers.

MICHAEL: I've had problems.

MR. THOMPSON: I think it's really more important that you should move ahead; you have to forget the past. Look at Derek and Tom [brothers]— you've gotten on with them.

Ms. THOMPSON: I can't forget the past.

MR. THOMPSON: Well, yes, you have to.

Ms. THOMPSON: I can't.

MR. THOMPSON: What do you mean you can't?

Ms. THOMPSON: I just can't.

In this excerpt, Ms. Thompson is overly angry about her son's inability to meet parental expectations, but her attributions about his selfishness and his failure to take the other's needs into account are reminiscent of unresolved, painful issues in this mother's history with her own mother (see earlier quote). The projection of these attributes onto her son Michael, followed by the mother's angry attack, provides an arena for the mother's own unresolved issues with her own mother to be reenacted. The intense drama in the mother-son dyad is so powerful that it quickly overshadows the father's futile efforts to intervene more constructively.

Not all family interactions are openly hostile, however. In some cases parents seem to feel overwhelmed by their burden, and a guilt-inducing message is conveyed to the child, as in the following interaction between Ms. Lesser and her severely depressed 25-year-old daughter, Joanne.

Ms. LESSER: We can't even get out one night a week. You get scared that I'm going to leave you, and then you start whining and complaining. And you won't eat right. You're so skinny.

JOANNE: Can't help it.

Ms. LESSER: Remember I was at work and you called me and begged me to come home? I hope nobody ever has a kid with all your problems. It's really not easy. Your brothers are a problem, too, but this is much worse.

JOANNE: How do you think I feel? I'm doing the best I can.

Here Ms. Lesser's intense affect masquerades as emotional overinvolvement. The real issue, however, is the extent to which Ms. Lesser experiences her daughter as burdensome. Ms. Lesser is annoyed and angry because she perceives the patient as causing the curtailment of her freedom. In fact, Joanne's helplessness and dependency may be seen as desperate attempts to engage a mother who really was not that involved. In fact, Joanne did not need her mother there each night; Joanne had spent a year attending community college night classes prior to her most recent hospitalization.

The preceding excerpt from a family interaction task is marked by a relatively calm tone to the interaction, but a sense of distance between the parents and the patient is evident. In the excerpt from the family interaction that follows, the mother, Ms. Wolf, is able to acknowledge openly her tendency to withdraw from her son, Ken:

MS. WOLF: I feel like I'm kind of cut out from your life. And I know a part of that is because I withdraw. Because we don't talk, I have insecurities 'cause I don't really know what's happening in your life. Not only do I feel left out, I feel anxious. I feel like a failure, which then causes me to withdraw.

KEN: Why does that cause you to withdraw, then?

MS. WOLF: Well I'm not saying that this is a good reaction on my part. Obviously, this is something I have to work on. But this is what happens, you know.

After reviewing this mother's FMSS, the therapist hypothesized that Ken, a borderline adolescent, felt a lack of attachment to his mother, and this relational lacuna shortcircuited any real contact between them from occurring during family therapy. In some disconnected families, the parents are encouraging, yet they continually allude to how much of a hardship the patient's illness has been for them. The message is not really a mixed message, but it contains enough criticism or guilt-inducement of the patient that he or she probably would walk away feeling responsible or guilty for causing the parents so much trouble. There is a quid pro quo quality to their interaction, in which it seems that the parent is "keeping score" about suffering, payoff, and the value, if any, of struggles. This type of score keeping in family interactions in disconnected families suggests an atmosphere of unmet needs and unfulfilled longing in the parent's family-of-origin experiences, a common characteristic of disconnected families. Although some of the families have quite negative ways of relating, characterized by harsh or too frequent criticism, or seeming emotional overinvolvement, not all of them are what might be labeled "high expressed emotion families." The quality of the family interaction in these families varies from mild aloofness to overt hostile rejection of the patient.

If one were to intervene with a plan organized around helping the patient in the disconnected family separate from his or her highly critical, overinvolved, or disengaged mother, the ruptured mother-child bond would be further widened, perhaps leaving the patient feeling even more desperate or despondent than he or she did before. Since a secure, positive parent-child attachment was never consolidated in the first place, it would be premature and therapeutically incorrect (according to our model) to intervene in ways that result in a separation or break between parent and child.

In the disconnected family the first task is to mend, develop, or strengthen the patient's relationship with the estranged parent. The next level of intervention will depend on whether or not the family is actively critical or hostile, or more low-key and modulated. When an intergenerational network of disturbed attachments exists, then this aspect of the family's life ought to be incorporated into the treatment strategy. The development of communication skills, including alternatives to high EE styles of relating may also be part of the treatment plan. In any case, with the disconnected family one begins with the task of trying to build or repair a ruptured bond—that is, the therapist wants to create or construct something that is lacking.

In the next three chapters we elaborate on the particular challenges and pitfalls posed by each of these family types in the treatment arena. We also present and further explicate the treatment strategies that we have found most effective with each type, using more extensive case material to illustrate our treatment approaches with these three family types.

CHAPTER 6

Treatment of the Disconnected Family

IN THE PRECEDING chapter, we presented data to illustrate that the disconnected family has many interactional characteristics similar to those of the high-intensity family, but that it differs in important ways along the dimension of attachment and bonding between the patient and the parents, and between the parents and their own parents. In our own clinical work with families of young adults and adolescent patients, we have found that treating patients from disconnected families often poses formidable challenges to the family therapist, regardless of the diagnosis of the patient, or index family member. Patients from these families are at high risk for a poor course of functioning when the attachment-caregiving deficits in the family are not adequately addressed.

For treatment purposes it is useful to distinguish between two sub-groups of families within the disconnected group: (1) the hostile, critical, disconnected family, in which one or both parents are especially hostile or pervasively critical in their remarks during family interaction, and (2) the low-key disconnected family, in which criticism is benign and somewhat understated. Disconnected families can also be further divided into those in which intergenerational attachment problems exist, and those in which the parents' attachments to their own parents are relatively benign. Treatment issues become more complex, and intervention becomes more challenging, when families are pervasively hostile or critical and/or have intergenerational disturbances in attachment. In such cases, the intergenerational difficulties are usually accompanied by similar disturbed attachments toward the patient; in such families the attachment problems are best conceptualized as an intergenerational problem.

Therapists must take into account these two aspects—the degree of emotional intensity in the interactional style and the presence or absence of intergenerational attachment disturbances—when planning what type of treatment strategy to take with the family. Families in which one of the parents is poorly attached to the patient, the interaction is not hostile or critical, and intergenerational problems are not prominent are relatively easier to treat because the therapist does not have to cope with the projection onto the patient of intensely negative feelings, which often devolve from layers of buried resentments.

In brief then, when assessing the family, one initially determines whether an attachment problem between one of the parents and the patient exists. First, when attachment problems exist, an assessment of intergenerational disturbance in attachment bonds with the family of origin is in order—indeed, is especially significant. Second, an estimate of the family style of emotional relating is made to determine whether the family is actively critical or hostile toward the patient, and whether parents are emotionally overinvolved or disengaged from the patient.

In working with families that evince problems with attachment alongside negative ways of expressing affect in face-to-face discussion, the therapist often must make a decision about what to address first in the family. As discussed in chapter 2, Lyman Wynne's (1984) epigenetic model of relational systems provides a useful guide for thinking through how to sequence intervention strategies in these multiproblem families. The four major processes outlined in this model—attachment/caregiving, communicating, joint problem solving, and mutuality—must be addressed sequentially if lasting change is to occur. As noted in chapter 2, the more complex cognitive, communicative, and affective tasks involved in the latter three levels presuppose that attachment issues in the initial epigenetic layer have been resolved. With a nonexistent or negative attachment, the family may be arrested at the first stage of the epigenetic journey. When severe disturbances or disruptions in the attachment bond exist, the patient and parents have no shared base of positive affective history that each can take for granted when attempting to send and comprehend complex verbal and nonverbal communications. Because communication becomes the arena through which attachment problems are played out, they can become rigidly fixed. Conversely, when family relationships are characterized by secure attachments, communication styles become more flexible and more easily and directly addressed. As Wynne points out, however, family members must first be sufficiently emotionally attached to one another before they are willing to come together to learn communication skills or anything else.

Intergenerational Considerations

Nearly 20 years ago, Murray Bowen (1978) wrote about the implications of remaining entangled in one's family-of-origin issues and relationships. Bowen contended that at the heart of many issues that emerge in the family of procreation was an unresolved, often unconscious connection or enmeshment between the parents and certain aspects of their family-of-origin relationships. If one explored carefully and diligently, one could discover and explore buried connections and conflicts, and such efforts would result in the individual's being able to separate and individuate from the undifferentiated family ego mass. Bowen's ideas attracted many followers among the burgeoning ranks of family therapists during the 1970s. However, Bowen was primarily a clinician, and many of his ideas have not been tested empirically, in part because of the methodological complexities of operationalizing and assessing multigenerational family patterns (Reiss, 1989). In this chapter we explore and further develop some of the theoretical aspects of intergenerational transmission processes that are the legacy of Bowen's concepts, particularly those that involve projection across generations.

Projective Process

One of the more clinically fascinating and often challenging aspects of treatment of the disconnected family concerns the role of projective processes in the transmission of disowned aspects of the parents or disowned aspects of the self. Although a complete discussion of projective processes lies beyond the scope of this chapter, most family clinicians will recognize that projective identification is a frequent dynamic among marital couples. One partner projects unacceptable and unacknowledged aspects of the self onto the spouse, who then overtly manifests the behavior, attitudes, or traits disowned by the other. For example, a husband may project his own feelings of neediness and dependency onto his insecure wife, who then begins to interrogate him about his whereabouts, thereby meeting his unacknowledged needs for dependency. In this way the husband's dependency needs are met without his having to deal with them directly.

In disconnected families, a similar process occurs *across* the generations between parent and child. In this situation, the child becomes the repository of some split-off aspect of the parents, who then overtly condemn the child while covertly identifying with the child's expression of their own forbidden impulses or dreaded traits. Reminiscent of Adelaide Johnson and S. A. Szurek's (1952) formulation of the superego lacunae, the interactions we have witnessed in disconnected families go beyond the commissioning of certain behaviors. Projection in disconnected families tends to encompass the whole personality of the child, who becomes a receptacle for the discarded, unwanted, and despised aspects of one or both parents, or of the parents' parents. As in the more classic expressions of projective identification, both parent and child are gratified by the process in that it engages central, though despised, aspects of the self, although it frequently manifests itself as a chronic irreconcilable conflict that binds them. For example, a teenage daughter who flaunts her sexuality may be enacting the covert fantasies of her repressed mother, who simultaneously envies and condemns the daughter for her burgeoning sexuality.

Projective processes in the family are sometimes difficult to observe, especially for the beginning family therapist. When the clinician does recognize these processes, he or she is often deeply impressed with the powerful influence that these maneuvers have on the family. The parent becomes anxious in the face of some stimulus presented by the child because it threatens to stir into awareness the unwanted, discarded aspects of the self that the parent struggles to avoid experiencing. For example, a mother, whose obese, mentally ill daughter reminds her of her own difficult childhood experience of caring for a psychotic mother, may feel anxious when reflecting on her own mother's abandonment of her; and her sadistic, angry feelings toward her severely disturbed mother may become activated. These feelings create intense anxiety for the mother, who cannot tolerate thinking of herself as someone who is not compassionate, forgiving, and understanding. The unconscious subtle message to her daughter is that she should behave in a defiant, disrespectful way. When the daughter begins to show this kind of attitude and behavior, the mother's anxiety is decreased as her own rage is transferred *into* the daughter and can then be managed by less threatening or disorganizing means involving the expression of contempt for the daughter and criticism of her behavior. The mother is left gratified and relieved on two counts—she has rid herself of the intolerable and near-unbearable sense of loss, rage, and deprivation in relation to her own mother, and she can punish her daughter for exhibiting problematic behaviors that resemble aspects of her mother's behavior that she was never able to criticize as a child. The daughter is rewarded because she has warded off her mother's anxiety and has reconnected, albeit negatively, with her emotionally aloof mother.

Case Example of Projective Processes

The only child of socially prominent and well-to-do parents, who owned a chain of department stores, Joanna Jackson was born and raised in a small New England community. Her mother was an aloof, cold, and angry woman who seemed to take little interest in her only daughter, Ms. Jackson. Ms. Jackson's mother developed muscular dystrophy when her daughter was 13, and thereafter became even more emotionally unavailable, except to express anger at her daughter and husband for being part of her disappointing life as a wife and mother, and anger about her deteriorating physical condition. Ms. Jackson experienced her mother as a demanding, infantile woman who always thought of herself and her own needs first, and who used her illness to control and dominate her family.

Ms. Jackson's father, a quiet, conventional man, was preoccupied with managing the family business, and was only intermittently available as a nurturant object for Ms. Jackson, in part because of he traveled frequently, but also because he could not tolerate his wife's increasing invalidism and chronic physical complaints. When at home, he was passive, quiet, and rather solitary. Ms. Jackson tried to escape from her unhappy family situation at age 17 when she ran away with an unemployed soldier who had recently returned from service in the Korean War, whom she had met on an expedition into a nearby major city with her friends. She eloped with this man—who was unemployed, uneducated, and from a working-class background—against her parent's wishes after knowing him for only a few months. The couple moved into a small apartment in a rural New England town, where they lived a relatively isolated and impoverished existence.

Ms. Jackson's parents disowned her after her marriage, and the husband had difficulty holding a job because of his chronic drinking. The couple soon became the object of ridicule and gossip, however, as the husband's alcoholism became increasingly flamboyant. He was continually insecure and anxious about the discrepancy in social class between himself and his wife, and he coped with these feelings by carousing in local bars with women and causing violent scenes. After about 6 months, he became frankly psychotic, with paranoid delusions and increasingly violent behavior. Ms. Jackson, 4 months pregnant, decided to divorce him. She left New England and began a new life in San Francisco, where she met and married her current husband, a successful upper-middle-class business-man.

Ms. Jackson's relationship with her daughter from the first marriage, Katy, was difficult from the start: Katy was not a very responsive baby, and she was unable to make Ms. Jackson feel as if she were a successful mother or nurturer. As Katy grew older, her mother became increasingly preoccupied with her work as an advertising executive and with her twin daughters from her second marriage. Katy was quiet and avoidant in school; she had few friends and was somewhat of an outsider among her peers. She felt that she did not fit in anywhere, and Ms. Jackson found this annoying. At age 18, Katy suffered her first schizophrenic episode. One year later she relapsed, this time into a severely regressed state: she would stand for hours staring into the mirror, asking people around her, "Who am I?" She became disheveled and overweight. She was referred to the Yale Psychiatric Institute (YPI) for long-term hospitalization, during which she presented as a shy, frightened, profoundly sad young woman.

Ms. Jackson was openly hostile and rejecting of Katy in the initial family meeting. She was particularly disgusted by Katy's physical appearance, her sloppy dress, and especially her lack of social graces. Ms. Jackson experienced Katy's psychotic retreat into isolation as one more example of her self-centered stance toward her family. Katy was selfish, cold, and demanding, according to Ms. Jackson.

Mr. Jackson was a friendly, gregarious man. He was approximately 11 years older than Ms. Jackson and he seemed to have some genuine compassion for Katy. He attempted to make peace between the warring mother and daughter by encouraging them to sit down, talk, and learn how to compromise. However, his attempts at reconciling mother and daughter were highly ineffectual.

The projective process in this family had begun before Katy's birth. The mere image of this child was for Ms. Jackson an abrasive, visual reminder of her miserable first marriage, which she had struggled to forget. This sordid past included both her disgraceful first marriage to an abusive alcoholic, and her disappointing childhood that was characterized by an incessant, unfulfilled longing for affection and interest from her own self-involved, emotionally unavailable, and chronically ill mother. While the feelings themselves were conscious, the intergenerational origins of these feelings were not. In fact, the vague, hidden, and disguised quality of these unresolved painful affects made them more acute.

When Katy began to become visibly psychotic, Ms. Jackson became overtly enraged and narcissistically wounded. During visits to the hospital, she would criticize Katy for her unacceptable attitudes and behavior, and then she would leave in a huff because her daughter was so unrespon-sive. At each visit the two of them would go out for lunch and shopping, typically the tension would become unbearable, and they would return early and withdraw into silence. Katy denied her longings for acceptance and love from her mother. Instead, she included her mother in the long list of people who were untrustworthy, rejecting, or unempathic. Katy's need for emotional support and connectedness to her mother persisted, how-ever, and her mother was exquisitely sensitive to this neediness. Ms. Jack-son elicited it in order to feel needed as a mother, but then became con-temptuous of it and Katy because it so closely mirrored her own unexpressed internal state. In the interim, Ms. Jackson was labeled by the staff as "unavailable," too busy for her daughter, and emotionally distant.

The focus of Katy's family therapy involved helping her to accept and cope with her mother's limitations; and after many attempts at family therapy sessions with mother, father, sisters, and patient, the therapist decided that in-depth family treatment was not feasible for this family. Instead, she began working in a psychoeducational mode with the family to help them understand the nature of Katy's disorder and to help them to cope with their guilt feelings about their daughter. The therapist validated how disturbed the patient was and helped Ms. Jackson accept the severity of her daughter's condition. Katy's twin sisters came to several sessions as well, and they were educated about Katy's illness. Katy, in turn, was helped to accept her mother's limitations and to get on with her life. The therapist worked with Katy on communication skills and tried to help her accept her psychotic illness.

After a year and a half of therapy, Katy was placed in a halfway house, which she left against medical advice a few months after admission. She met a boyfriend at her day-treatment center and went to live with him in a neighboring city.

In the following section of this chapter the intergenerational FMSS data for this family are presented, and an alternative strategy for family treat-ment that might have been considered is discussed, along with additional examples of disconnected family configurations, and their associated treatment issues. We then present four types of disconnected families, all of which are characterized by a negative, weak, or disturbed attachment pattern forged in the family of origin, and recreated in the current family, albeit in different ways: (1) those in which there is strong, unrelenting neg-ative attachment in the family of origin that is the legacy of projection from a parental family-of-origin figure about whom the parent continues to have unresolved issues; (2) those in which parentification in the family of origin makes the parent contemptuous of or unable to meet the child's dependency needs; (3) those in which there has been an emotional by-pass through which the parents have avoided the hurt and rejection from their family of origin, only to have those feelings awakened by their own child's problems; (4) those in which a veneer of surface idealization both of the parents of origin and of the patient masks a weak or nonexistent attachment.

Negative Attachment as an Intergenerational Projection Process

The FMSS samples from Katy's mother, Ms. Jackson, provide extremely dramatic examples of how a very negative relationship between parent and child can be reactivated when a child presents the parent with diffi-cult problems that evoke painful affects associated with the family of ori-gin. In the following FMSS, Ms. Jackson talks about her disappointment with Katy:

> It's not easy to get along with Katy. It never has been. She was an adorable little kid, cute, nice—you know, when they're small, 2, 3, 4 years old. At the age of about 8 she became very difficult. She started to fight with her younger sisters, and she became very obstinate. When she was with me, she would do the opposite of what I asked. It made me so mad. I've never for-given her for this. Everything revolves around her. She doesn't care about me or her sisters. She expects her sisters to call every week, but she never calls them. I try to be patient with her, but I get nowhere.

During the family interaction task shortly after Katy's admission to the hospital, Ms. Jackson expressed her resentment toward her daughter:

MS. JACKSON: It annoys me when you say you feel useless. There's no need to say that.
KATY: I know, I just feel bad. Dad says the same thing.
MS. JACKSON: You don't like criticism. You don't like it when I tell you what to do to feel better. You can't always do what you want.
KATY: I didn't like it when you were always walking in my room without knocking. You would say do this, and that has to be done. And I felt it was constant criticizing, and you did it more to me than to Marjorie or Amy [sisters]. I don't think you ever accepted me as your daughter.
MS. JACKSON: I still think you don't have a lot of respect for yourself. And you think of yourself first.

A family in which the anger is this close to the surface and where the anger is so overtly expressed evokes some anxiety in the therapist, who feels a need to quell the intensity and curtail some of the destructive things being said. After this initial phase of curbing or dampening the negative affect, however, the therapist can proceed with exploring its roots. The FMSS data from Ms. Jackson provided some clues about what might be fueling the anger at Katy:

> My mother was always a sore spot in my life. She criticized everything I did. You name it. She was always furious at me because my room was messy, and she was always criticizing the way I dressed or combed my hair or talked. But if I ever asked her to do anything for me—like drive me and my friends someplace, she would fume and glare at me, and treat me as it I was bothering her. She played on my emotions. She always felt sorry for herself, and she complained a lot about her physical problems. She knew how to take care of us in terms of material things, but she basically gave up being a mother to me, you know listening to my problems or caring about what was important to me. Whenever I did anything that didn't please her, she would let me know how unhappy she was right away.

Ms. Jackson spent considerable energy repressing her feelings toward her mother, who had died shortly after Ms. Jackson's remarriage. When Katy was present, however, it was nearly impossible for Ms. Jackson to ward off the reminder of her childhood and past marriage; and when confronted with this material, she felt enraged, guilty, resentful, cheated, abandoned, and inadequate both as a daughter and as a mother. The bitter fights that inevitably ensued masked Ms. Jackson's feelings of failure and lingering sense of abandonment by her own mother, who had disowned her after her first marriage and had reestablished only sporadic contact with Ms. Jackson and her children after her second marriage.

Intergenerational interviews with this mother and daughter would not necessarily have repaired this deeply disrupted mother-child attachment bond, but they would have deepened the participants' understanding of the intergenerational issues that fueled the attachment difficulties. In turn, this deepened understanding might have formed the bedrock for a revised attachment between mother and daughter.

Such was the case with the Liebert family, another family characterized by unrelenting negative parent-child attachments that appeared to be rooted in parental family-of-origin issues. However, in the Liebert family, family treatment led to enhanced understanding between mother and daughter, and to a more benign course of treatment for the daughter, Marsha, the patient in our study. Marsha was a 27-year-old bipolar patient who, when not in acute manic episodes, functioned reasonably well. She had lived in communal homes with peers and had pursued a counterculture existence that her parents disapproved of. However, the extent of the parents' condemnation of their daughter's lifestyle appeared disproportionate and appeared to reflect some projection from Ms. Liebert's unresolved issues with her own psychiatrically impaired mother, who was described as follows on the FMSS:

> My earliest recollection of her is being shaken while I was asleep. She was afraid that airplanes flying overhead were coming to hurt us. I was afraid of her. My years with her were not pleasant. I never knew when she was going to act strange. I knew she was not normal, but I felt resentful because she was sometimes cruel and violent and she would threaten us.

In this excerpt, Ms. Liebert's mother is described as a neglectful, extremely impaired woman who was unable to care for her daughter. We have found threads of remarkable continuity in the relationships between parent and child in the previous generation, but have also found that the internal working model of attachment, as it is consciously expressed in the parent's description of the patient, may in fact show some attenuation of the attachment disturbance. In fact, our research findings have indicated that there is little transgenerational correlation among FMSS negative attachment codes (Diamond & Doane, in press). Thus, the sense of negative attachment conveyed in the preceding excerpt is somewhat ameliorated when the mother talks about her daughter, as is often the case with disconnected families. The negative feelings may be somewhat ameliorated, yet they come through.

The attenuation of unrelenting negative attachment toward the child in the context of the persistence of attachment problems that devolve from previous generation are evident in the mother's description of her daughter, Marsha, on the FMSS:

> My daughter has always been a handful. When she was little she, had very cute ways of getting attention. She would entertain us with stories and songs that she made up. But when she became older, she got more belligerent and demanding. She seemed to want to go her merry way, disregarding the rest of the family. She would come in at all hours of the night, slam her bedroom door shut, and get angry and defensive if we questioned her. She often used to smirk at me when I would tell her to do something. Her problems are a mystery to me. Nothing we did would work. She has been a problem for many years. My husband and I didn't have this problem with our other children, just with her. We've spent an enormous amount of time and money on therapy for her, but we've really gotten nowhere. No matter how much I try to understand, it doesn't lead to anything.

One can also see that the mother seems unaware of the link between her own past and her current frustrations with her daughter. But when Ms. Liebert was confronted by her psychiatrically impaired daughter, the anger, guilt, resentment, and bitterness about her own childhood broke through. Ironically, the daughter did recognize that her mother's negative attachment and overinvolved attitudes toward her devolved from her mother's lingering resentments and internal burdens stemming from family-of-origin experiences. In the daughter's FMSS on her mother, which was done at the 1-year follow-up visit, she said:

> My mother has never been able to deal with me. She's not interested in what I want or what I think. She's had a hard life. She tries to make me behave and look a certain way. She tries to control me. But I'm stubborn, just like her, and we don't get along. She just wants me to be a perfect lady and dress and act a certain way. She's always marching me into my room and lecturing me about how ill-mannered and sloppy I am. I remember once when she did that, I lost my temper and threw things around the room, and that really seemed to upset her to the point where she refused to speak to me for days. She never seemed to be able to tolerate my feelings, and I know that I didn't always express them in ways that she could deal with, but she gets upset so easily, and I just can't talk to her. She can't talk to her mother, either. In fact, she almost never even mentions her mother. I find that very hard. I'm trying to accept my mother, but she can't accept her own mother.

In the FMSSs of both mother and daughter, we see the merging or blending of issues of control, blame, and overinvolvement that is often found in the parent-child interactions in disconnected families. Obviously, this family was ripe for intergenerational interviewing in which the mother, in the presence of her daughter, could explore and refocus her own disappointment, rage, and frustration on her relationship with her own impaired mother, rather than on her daughter. In families such as the two just presented, the temptation for the family therapist would be to address only the negative affect or high expressed emotion attitudes without exploring their source in intergenerational projective processes.

Negative Attachment as the Intergenerational Consequence of Parentification

In the next group of family illustrations, disturbed attachment and negative style of affective relating are part of the intergenerational consequence of parentification in the family of origin. The identified patient, Miranda, was a 28-year-old borderline woman who drank heavily and was sexually promiscuous, paranoid, intermittently psychotic, and extremely belligerent. After the second hospitalization, her parents, Mr. and Ms. Phillips, were frustrated and openly resentful of her inability to comply with treatment recommendations, and especially the recommendation that she stop drinking. Both parents saw the patient as manipulative, impulsive, and too dependent. The father particularly was unable to form a close attachment with his daughter. He had grown up with a very impaired parent whom he had had to take care of, and his daughter's dependency evoked a set of negative affects in him that resulted in his shutting down emotionally, which is evident in the following FMSS in which Mr. Phillips described his father:

> My father was a man who worked all the time. I didn't see much of him as a child. He was alcoholic by the time I was in high school and by then I had a full-time job taking care of my brothers and sisters. My mom would send me to find him when he was drunk. My relationship with him was not a happy one. I felt drained. He was a victim of sorts, I guess. I think he suffered because he wasn't able to deal with raising kids. But I paid a price. I became the dad. Now I'm having a lot of difficulties at work, and I feel kind of burnt out and tired, and I don't have much patience for my own kids.

This disengaged and rejecting attitude was reflected in the way in which Mr. Phillips described his daughter in the FMSS:

> Miranda, since her illness, has become much more secretive. She confides in my wife, but she's not honest with me about what's going on in her life. From what I gather from the hints she drops about her life, she's not doing too good a job at managing her life right now. She seems to have difficulty finding a direction and keeps looking to us to provide it for her, and that bothers me because it's time for her to be on her own. She doesn't seem to have much ambition, and she's started drinking again, and that bothers me because I think it's an escape from being on her own.

The striking feature of this FMSS is the contradiction between the father's expressed desire to know more about his child and his anger that he often learns about important aspects of her life from his wife (which represents an example of triangulation) and his resentment of Miranda's dependency on him. He seems unaware of this contradiction or of the ways his resentment toward her neediness might contribute to her secretiveness and avoidance of communication with him.

Miranda, on the other hand, was painfully aware of what was missing for her with her father, and she conveyed the realization that her father saw her as a burden, as someone who depleted his resources.

> My father never did much with me. He used to notice every little thing— he'd yell when we didn't get all the snow shoveled off of the driveway. When I was older, he really began to avoid me. He gave my brother money for college, but not me. But I always respected him. He's very intelligent. I've never seen love from him. It's always seemed fake, not real. And it feels fake when I tell him that I love him. I think he thinks that his kids have never been anything but problems, that he would have been better off without them.

The themes of dependency and burden recur in the family interaction task that occurred at the beginning of treatment. Although Miranda is clearly placing a burden on her parents by virtue of her psychotic and act-ing-out behaviors, the links between the father's current frustrations and his relationship with his own father are evident:

MIRANDA: I'm trying not to depend on anyone.

Ms. PHILLIPS: Well, you see we are tired of seeing your getting into trouble, spending all your money, and cutting yourself. It's time-consuming, aggravating, and frustrating.

MR. PHILLIPS: Up to now, it hasn't turned out too good with you.

MIRANDA: Well, now I'm here getting treatment, so it's starting to turn out real good.

MR. PHILLIPS: Well, we'll see. I resent the time it's taken—it's interfered a whole lot with what goes on in my life. But we do love you. All I ask of you is to be independent, that's all I've ever wanted.

It is clear that Miranda's normal dependency needs to lean on her par-ents, to be nurtured by them, or to be intimate with them were thwarted in this family, in which both parents, and especially the father, were depleted by the intergenerational burdens of caring for dysfunctional parents. In the family interaction Ms. Phillips was observed to stiffen and pull away and Mr. Phillips, to become agitated and sarcastic when the patient expressed her desire to be cared for and connected to her parents. The therapist in this case first worked on strengthening the attachment between the patient and her mother, because she was the more available parent, despite an impaired mother-daughter attachment. The father-daughter relationship, however, was very slow to change. The longer-term consequences of this ruptured relationship with the father seemed evident at follow-up when Miranda reported considerable distress in her relation-ship with him, as well as with other men in her life, and talked about how she needed to stay "nearly perfect" in order to keep her father's approval.

Negative Attachment as a Result of an Emotional Bypass in the Family of Origin

In some disconnected families, the parents are not as forthcoming about their disturbed attachment to their own parents as those in the examples just described. Rather, they appear to have bypassed the anger, neglect, and rejection that they experienced. However, this bypass of the full impact of the disturbed attachment relationships in their own families of origin is replicated in their distant, lukewarm relationship with one or more of their own children. Such was the case for one patient in our study,

Daniel, a 17-year-old who had been diagnosed as borderline and who was using cocaine heavily, drinking heavily, skipping school, and refusing to abide by any of the household rules his family would apply. His mother and father, Mr. and Ms. Bollas, were fed up with the patient's behavior and felt that they could not handle him at home anymore. He was often depressed and irritable. It was recommended that he have long-term treatment to help consolidate his chaotic internal world and to stabilize and resocialize his behavior patterns.

As the following excerpts from the FMSSs in this family illustrate, however, Daniel's difficulties with his parents were anchored in a developmentally early attachment phase. Daniel felt that his mother neither wanted to form nor could form a strong positive attachment to him, despite her adequate caretaking, as evidenced in the following FMSS about his mother:

> She's nice. When I was young she was pretty helpful. When I was in trouble or I just needed someone, she always helped me out. She stood up for me about school, or if I needed help with something. But as I got older, she wanted me to do things on my own. She still helped me a little, but it wasn't the same. I was older, so I guess it was the right thing, but we never did much together, we never went out and did anything. We didn't really get along. She didn't like to sit around. She would get frustrated at me if I sat around watching TV. She was gone a lot, too. She was real busy with work, and she thought I should do things on my own and not lean on them so much. I used to talk all the time to her, and she never used to say much back. She thought I talked too much.

Ms. Bollas was quiet and fairly low-key during the family discussions. She was not an overly critical woman, and she was never intrusive with her son. In her FMSS description of Daniel, she revealed that her lack of critical or intrusive (negative affective style attitudes) devolved from indifference toward him; she revealed that she and Daniel shared no relationship:

> He was real hyperactive as a kid and was always testing the limits. He was the baby, and he always seemed to need more attention than my other son. He never got really big, but I couldn't seem to control him for some reason. His older brother used to help me control him, but after his brother went to college, he really became a problem. I don't think he wanted to be close. And there was no communication between us. Basically, I would say that there's been a breakdown in communication, and neither of us tries anymore. He looks more to his father for a relationship.

This description of a mother-son relationship is strikingly devoid of positive feelings. Ms. Bollas seems to view Daniel as a burden, but she does not appear to be angry or hurt about that. Rather, she appears to be shutdown, indifferent, and detached.

Her description of her relationship with her own mother and father shows some fascinating parallels in terms of how lack of emotion or affect was typical of her experience with them.

> My mother was quite quiet and didn't say much. She didn't get upset. I never saw her cry. She worked and took care of four children. She never seemed really tuned in to what was really going on. She never expressed affection toward any of us. We got along pretty well as I was growing up. She was never mean or nasty. She and my father used to sit on the sofa, but she would always seem to be off by herself. She loved her garden. She spent a lot of time in her garden and with her dogs. She was a nice person, but I suppose we may have missed out on some things.

This passage reveals that Ms. Bollas was not conscious of any feelings of regret, disappointment, or hurt about her lack of affection from her mother. Instead, she described her mother in emotionless, dull terms. One might wonder whether Ms. Bollas in fact had more intense feelings about her mother, feelings that might be hard to express. Ms. Bollas's relationship with her father was equally devoid of depth or emotional intensity:

> We didn't talk much. We had a superficial relationship. He took more of an interest in me than my mother did—like when I bought a car. He used to belittle my mother. I was never close to him. I sometimes thought about wishing things could change, but I don't think people really change. He was just the way he was. And that's that.

One gets the picture of a woman who experienced emotional neglect from both parents and who, furthermore, was conscious of being powerless to change anything. This tone of resignation characterized her attitudes about Daniel; she was not optimistic about the relationship improving. She did not view herself as capable of constructing or repairing the relationship in a way that would be mutually enhancing. When Daniel began to withdraw from her, she accepted this as inevitable and became more emotionally detached herself. It would be easy to attribute the mother's behavior to depression, as she clearly was quite characterologically depressed.

But Ms. Bollas's low-level dysthymia (formerly called neurotic depression) did not explain the relational dynamics with Daniel. In fact, Ms. Bollas did not seem depressed at all around her husband when they were alone. The depression and detachment appeared to be activated in relation to the Daniel. In particular, the patient's needs to be dependent threatened Ms. Bollas very much. She had grown up learning to deny her dependent longings, and she felt a secret contempt for Daniel when he began to show neediness and clinginess as a child, and particularly as an adolescent. The patient's tendency to pull away when he felt rejected by his mother fueled another of Ms. Bollas's secret fears—that she was not a very good mother.

Daniel talked to his individual therapist about feeling rejected and unloved by his mother, but he was never able to talk about these issues in the family therapy sessions. He felt too humiliated. Ms. Bollas, in the same way, would not talk about feelings of inadequacy evoked in her by her son. Mr. Bollas idealized Ms. Bollas, and Ms. Bollas felt too threatened by the thought of this sole source of approval and esteem being diminished. Since nobody in the family talked much about longing, pain, or disappointment, the family therapist did not focus much on these issues either. One might wonder whether Daniel was expressing an unspoken wish on the part of the mother—that he would move out of the family home and be on his own—when he left treatment prematurely to go and live with his older brother in northern California.

In sum, the FMSS data from the Bollas family suggests that this was a disconnected family that had mother-child attachment problems with intergenerational origins. Our model of treatment would have suggested a series of dyadic sessions between the patient and his mother fairly early during the treatment. In these sessions the mother's own problematic family relationships would have been explored in depth in front of the patient. As it turns out, the mother's own emotional experience in her family of origin was not terribly different from the patient's experience with his parents.

Mr. Bollas was a warm, friendly person who seemed very positively attached to the patient. Because his strengths were readily visible, a family therapist might be tempted to do conjoint work with both parents and the patient, and to focus on consolidating the father-son attachment, rather than fostering the mother-son attachment, especially since Ms. Bollas was quiet and withdrawn. In addition, the therapist might be tempted to focus on the patient's inability to follow limits set by the parents and on their maladaptive communication and problem-solving skills, rather than on the developmentally earlier attachment ruptures.

Ms. Kelley and her 17-year-old daughter, Tina—a depressed, labile, angry, unmanageable, and sexually acting-out adolescent—constituted a single-parent family where an emotional bypass in the family of origin led to negative attachment patterns in the family of procreation. In the hospital, Tina began a trial of lithium, her behavior soon quieted down, and she became more openly dysphoric and depressed. Ms. Kelley did not understand why her daughter was so depressed or so disrespectful. In fact, she did not understand much at all about her daughter—in some ways she felt she hardly knew her:

> Tina always gave me aggravation at home. She always seemed to be demanding something or complaining about something. She can be loving and cute, but sometimes she flies into a rage at me. She never shows affec-

tion, doesn't ever hug or kiss me. When she's angry, she sulks in her room and shows no cooperation. It's like she doesn't care to be part of our home. I don't know why she's the way she is.

Ms. Kelley described her relationship with her own mother in this way:

> My mother was a good mother—she was always there—I mean she cleaned, she fed us. She went out a lot, but she took us along. She always liked children. She disciplined us, too. There were eight of us; we all were treated fairly. I was a pretty good kid. She talks to me more now that I'm older. As far as being close to her, I guess the way that I was close to her was that she was always around. I could always go to her for help with something.

Although Ms. Kelley described her relationship with her mother as close, her description of her mother was remarkably devoid of any emotion. It seemed as though Ms. Kelley had grown up without much affection from her mother but did not really experience this as a deprivation. Rather, it seemed normal to Ms. Kelley to have minimal emotional contact with one's mother. One might speculate that Ms. Kelley had difficulty relating to her emotionally labile daughter because she herself had never received much care or attention from her own mother. She may have experienced the daughter as overwhelming, or she may have resented or envied her daughter's tendencies to demand attention and to become angry when she did not get it. One might further speculate that Ms. Kelley bypassed her own feelings about the emptiness of her own early emotional experience in her family of origin, and that these feelings fueled her resentment about the demands of caring for Tina and about Tina's indifference.

Tina saw right through her mother's repressed issues:

> I think that a lot of the stuff that went on in her life, she took out on me. She never really wanted to get married. She said that she never held it against me, but I think that's bullshit. When I would go out with my boyfriend, Mom would interrogate me when I got home, "What did he buy you?" "What did he say?" I always felt my mother tried to live through me, but she didn't like it when I was too happy, because she wasn't so happy herself. When she's down, she tries to bring me down, but I don't like it. Most of the time I avoid talking to her about my feelings. My mother is not a very happy person.

Ms. Kelley barely thought of her daughter as a child. Instead, Ms. Kelley felt her own life was being made difficult by Tina's self-centeredness. Because of her own relationship with her parents, Ms. Kelley had very little capacity to empathize with her daughter's unmet dependent longings:

TINA: You always wanted me to take care of my brother and sister, and I didn't want to.

Ms. KELLEY: I think you didn't want to handle it. You wanted to go out with your friends. Don't you think maybe you were a little selfish?

TINA: I was looking for love.

Ms. KELLEY: Maybe you were just thinking of yourself.

TINA: Maybe I don't care about myself enough to have anybody care.

The intergenerational data from this family suggest that Ms. Kelley's inability to foster a positive, secure attachment to her daughter may have more to do with her own experience with intimate relationships than any real resentment or anger toward Tina. Ms. Kelley's seemingly competitive stance toward Tina is probably borne out of Ms. Kelley's inability to see her daughter as a dependent child, with vulnerabilities, emotional pain, and feelings of unworthiness. Ms. Kelley experienced Tina as she had experienced herself as a teenager—separate, able to survive without affection, almost like a grown-up. Tina's poignant enactment of her mother's unmet needs for deeper relatedness beyond superficial caretaking activated Ms. Kelley's own unconscious resentments about the inadequacies of her own childhood.

The family therapy in this case focused on helping Ms. Kelley be a more competent parent. Thereby, it was thought, Tina would be able to have the kind of structured, supportive family environment she needed. The FMSS samples suggest that it may have been useful to have some mother-daughter intergenerational sessions in which the focus was on the mother's own inadequate emotional experience as a child. This might have fostered some mutual empathizing. As it was, after about 3 months of treatment, Tina ran away from the hospital, met a man, and promptly got engaged, thus repeating her mother's pattern for coping with her repressed dependency needs.

Disturbed Attachment Masquerading as Idealization

Eric was a shy 27-year-old who had been hospitalized for a suicide attempt. On the surface, he barely looked disturbed. He was articulate, expressive, and open, and he showed a capacity for thoughtful reflection and good judgment. In fact, he was a profoundly depressed young man who used drugs to deaden his feeling of isolation and sadness. Just before his admission, his girlfriend had broken off their engagement. Eric's mother, Ms. Williams, was a lively, talkative, extremely intrusive woman who was focused on the patient's every word. She rarely sat quietly in a family discussion, and one of the patient's major complaints about his family was that his mother did not give him space to breathe. The therapist focused on separation-individuation in the mother-son dyad and paid relatively scant attention to the patient's feeling that he did not have a close relationship with his father.

At the end of the treatment Eric spoke eloquently about how troubled he was by the lack of a warm, close relationship with his father. Although his relationship with his mother had improved somewhat, he was still depressed and saddened by the lack of a relationship with his father, as the following excerpt from his FMSS description of his father indicates:

> The last thing I remember doing with my dad was going on a trip to New York when I was maybe 6 or 7 years old. From that point on my father just wasn't in the picture. He traveled a lot; he was gone. He'd come home from work and talk about work. He didn't really ask me how I was doing. He just wasn't there for me. He's never been there for me. He's always telling me to do my best. He expected a lot out of me. Meanwhile, as a kid, I tried to communicate with him. I tried to talk to him and all that. I would go out of my way to ask him about his life, about his work, but he would never reciprocate and ask me how I was. He once said to me, "Eric, I cannot show interest in anything you have because our interests are so different." He always had an easier time talking to my sister for some reason. It just didn't make me feel very good. It's funny you know, here I am 27 years old, and if he were to die today, I don't know if I'd feel bad. In terms of missing him, I have nothing to miss. He's just not there for me. I know that he loves me in his own way. He shows concern.

The patient's FMSS on his father indicated that he felt emotionally disconnected and uncared for by his father. But in contrast, his father saw the relationship quite differently and, in fact, idealized Eric. Information obtained from the FMSSs from Eric's father at the beginning of treatment suggest that this unintended failure in fathering had its roots in the previous generation, between Mr. Williams and his own father.

At the beginning of treatment Eric's father had this to say about his son:

> Eric is a wonderful son. He's full of energy. He loves sports. He's easy to get along with. We're alike in that he's a doer and so am I. He's always been a good student. We've always gotten along. He's never been demanding. I love the outdoors and he does too. But we have kind of a generation gap. I was 35 when Eric was born, and so I think this has been a little bit difficult. But I don't think this was a big problem.

During a family interaction task, Eric saw things somewhat differently. In this discussion he told his father:

> I've always wanted to be closer to you, and I find it hard at times to talk to you about any issue. And I'd like to work on communicating with you. It's difficult because I feel you might be too critical of me or that you really just have a hard time listening to what I have to say.

In the 10 minutes of family discussion that ensued, Ms. Williams inserted herself into the interaction between father and son in a way that precluded any real discussion by them. Ms. Williams became the interpreter of each of the two men's intentions and behavior. Gradually, almost imperceptibly, the issue became diverted away from the lack of intimacy or closeness between father and son to the issue of the father's discomfort with Eric's angry feelings.

The descriptions of their relationship that Eric and his father gave on the FMSS and in the family interactions differed so dramatically that it is difficult to imagine that these two men are talking about the same family. How could Mr. Williams be oblivious to Eric's secret disappointment?

Clues to Mr. Williams's parenting failures may lie in his FMSS about his relationship with his own father years before:

> I thought my father was a very clever man. He was sort of a perfectionist, very methodical and orderly, which I admired very much. He used to stay up until all hours of the night to finish a piece of writing he was doing. At times I did not see very much of him because he was working 12 hours a day at the newspaper in the city, and he would come home from work very tired. But when he did have free time, we did things together. He was a very loving father in certain ways—he used to get up at 5 A.M. on Sundays and drive my sister and I out to the country to ice skate. I really loved him very much. He was 42 years old when I was born, so there was a bit of an age gap. But I really don't think that really did a lot of harm, because I always enjoyed my relationship with him.

It is possible that Mr. Williams's perception of his own relationship with his father colored his view of his relationship with Eric. One might hypothesize that Mr. Williams idealized his own father, and that this idealization blinded him in a way to the potential impact of his own unavailability to Eric. Perhaps he assumed that Eric would experience a similar process in developing a son-father relationship. Because Eric's father also tended to idealize Eric, he may have assumed that Eric also idealized him somewhat. And because he identified with his son, Mr. Williams may well have believed that Eric would see him much as he had seen his own father.

The idealization evident in the FMSSs was reflected in aspects of the father-son communication. Eric expressed annoyance at his dad because he could not talk openly with him. Mr. Williams, on the other hand, felt inadequate because he had problems coping with his son's anger at him. Ms. Williams got involved in this by aligning herself with Eric about Mr. Williams's inaccessibility. In this way the issue served a useful function in the family to distract them from more primitive, vulnerable feelings that all of them may have had. Neither Eric nor his father was particularly eager to talk about such unmanly things as feeling left out or unimportant. Instead, each adopted a counterphobic stance: It did not matter so much to

Mr. Williams that his father was not available, because he was a wonderful man. Eric did not feel the pain so consciously; instead, he felt anger and bitter resentment for things he did not get.

This family situation highlights the important distinction between being idealized by a parent and having a parent show curiosity and interest in one's day-to-day childhood experiences. Eric and his father did not know how to interact playfully or spontaneously. They could debate and discuss—but the playful element of the father-son relationship was absent. The therapist, sidetracked by the intense impact of the intrusive mother, focused the work on this issue and never carried out any sessions that addressed the lack of attachment between Eric and his father. Mr. Williams, in fact, was not even aware that a problem existed.

Using an epigenetic model such as ours, the therapist would forego work on the communication problems between mother and son, and mother and husband. Instead, the therapist would have a few sessions with just Mr. Williams and Eric present. In these meetings Eric would be invited to sit with the therapist while the therapist conducted a few in-depth interviews with Mr. Williams about his own experiences with his family of origin, with a focus on the things that were missing in the father-son relationship and on how Eric's father tended to minimize this. Eric might then develop some compassion for his father's lack of experience with an empathic father figure. This, in turn, might lead to a series of interventions designed to teach Eric and his father how to develop some genuine contact with and curiosity about each other.

The Low-Key Disconnected Family

Ann was a 23-year-old schizophrenic patient with a history of multiple hospitalizations, plus serious drug and alcohol abuse, and she had been unable to function outside of a hospital setting for eight years. When she suffered an episode of psychosis, she was wildly out of control and often did frightening things such as wandering off with strangers. In her individual therapy sessions, she talked repeatedly of feeling a lack of attachment to her mother, whom she tended to idealize. With her mother, however, she alternated between an antagonistic, argumentative manner and a cloying clinginess. Ms. Kravis was an educated, articulate woman who cared very deeply for her daughter but who also felt overwhelmed by her. As a result, Ms. Kravis often avoided visits or weekend passes because of heavy work commitments. Ann wanted closeness; Ms. Kravis responded by gushing over her, and sometimes by hugging her and kissing her during visits. Ann could not deal with this and complained about her mother's behaviors. Ms. Kravis felt rejected, and she accused Ann of being inconsistent.

Mr. Kravis's issues with her own parents were not so problematic, and she seemed motivated and cooperative about trying out new ways to relate to her daughter. Clearly from a disconnected family herself, Ms. Kravis tried to change the situation with Ann but had no clue about how to do so; everything she tried failed. An excerpt from a family discussion task sheds some light on why this might have been true:

ANN: When you come and you expect a hug, I don't want to hug you—if we just sat next to each other and watched TV, I'd feel soothed.

Ms. KRAVIS: I can't understand that at all. I have a hard time with it.

ANN: Sometimes you come to visit and you say, "I'm exhausted," and I think, Oh, I want to boost her energy and give her a big hug and show her that I love her and that I'm happy that she made it here alive. And then there's other times you come and you seem so interested in your own self. And I think, Why aren't you interested in me—I'm the one in the hospital? I'm so different, I don't know what to do. And you're different, and it's confusing.

Ms. KRAVIS: So it's important for you to tell me when I should hug you and when I shouldn't.

ANN: I'd rather just be next to you and feel supported without so much talking. I'm scared to say this to you because so many people reject me, and I don't want you to reject me, too.

Ms. KRAVIS: Have I ever rejected you?

ANN: And I don't like it when you feel all sympathetic. I like it when people are—not cold—just straightforward.

Ann was trying to express something important to her mother about the quality of their relationship, but her point came across rather abruptly. The therapist noted that Ms. Kravis heard and understood her daughter's request for a more comfortable relationship. But when Ann expressed this, Ms. Kravis felt criticized and inadequate.

The therapist in this situation had the opportunity to intervene and reframe this kind of problem for the family. Ann was asking for a very simple, low-key time to be spent with her mother. Because of her illness, she was especially vulnerable to stimulation from interaction, which she found overwhelming. She was enormously pleased and happy just to be with her mother, doing almost nothing. The therapist began prescribing small tasks for them to do together, which were designed to provide some doses of mutually pleasant time together. The idea was to have this mother and daughter begin to enjoy each other's company, rather than pretending to do so just to placate the other.

The visits started out with 1-hour card games during which Ann and Ms. Kravis were instructed not to discuss their relationship at all. Instead, they were just to play cards, and then Ms. Kravis was to leave. This went on for three visits, and Ann began talking to nursing staff about how much fun she was having with her mother. At the same time, Ms. Kravis began feeling less anxious and inadequate at the thought of visiting her psychotic daughter. She began to enjoy their time together too.

The card games led to lunches outside the hospital, again with the prohibition against discussing problems, family issues, or their relationship. And the visits were kept short to reduce the chances that the playtime might turn into a chore for either of them.

The visits continued, and after several months of this, Ann and her mother wanted to take a weekend vacation to the city together. The vacation was not without problems. Ann showed some psychotic symptoms when she was out on buses and in crowds, but because she felt comfortable with her mother, she was able to request and get several hours of her choosing alone, away from her mother, and with the help of prn neuroleptics to stabilize herself without incident.

Ms. Kravis was easy to work with in treatment, partly because she did not have a lot of unresolved attachment issues with her own parents. Her description of her mother on the FMSS did reveal, however, that her tendency to distance herself from Ann through retreating into her work might have roots in her family-of-origin experience:

> She always wanted me to look right and be right and act right—in short, to be a perfect lady, and I just kind of went along with it. I think as a child I thought my mother was sweet and warm. But now I realize that I've never been able to share with my mother at all. She's never talked to me at all about feelings, hers or mine. She's never really talked about my feelings about Ann. She's never asked me how I feel about having a daughter who's been hospitalized so many times. And I think part of it is her own inability to talk about feelings, which bothers me a great deal.

Some disconnected families such as this one appear to have simple communication problems. They are often able to articulate an awareness that they do not talk to each other as much as they should. Sometimes it can be a mistake, however, for the family therapist to focus on this communication problem as if it were some kind of skill deficit. In the Stein family, for example, the family members were fairly insightful and able to express themselves clearly. Bill, the 25-year-old borderline patient in the family, however, experienced this lack of communication more in terms of distance, remoteness, and disconnectedness. In his FMSS, he described his relationship with his mother as follows:

> I don't know how to describe my mother—she's sort of quiet. Up until age 8 or 9 I was pretty close to my mother. Then my sister was born, and she kind of switched to her. And I wasn't that close to her anymore. She was always depressed a lot. She always used to check up on me, track me down, sort of. In adolescence I didn't get along with her too well. It's hard for me to talk much about my mother because I really don't know too much about her because I never really talked to her that much. I don't really know who she is.

Ms. Stein described her relationship with her own mother in a similar way:

> My mother was very moody. Sometimes she was very outgoing, but other times she would withdraw—so you never knew what to expect. I helped a lot taking care of the house. Her parents lived with us, and there was a lot to do. But I always felt that whatever I did it wasn't good enough. We didn't really have mother-daughter talks or disagreements. I don't think our relationship was close—we never really talked about things. She was a good mother—she just wasn't into talking.

Ms. Stein seems to have experienced her childhood as devoid of much emotional contact, fun, or connectedness to other members of the family. In fact, her description of her mother is characterized by a sense of emptiness and lack; her mother did not talk to her about her inner life, her feelings, or her needs. Ms. Stein may have had an inadequate foundation for establishing and maintaining an intimate relationship. She was not angry or bitter about this; rather, she felt a vague kind of depression, and she often felt terribly inadequate.

Ms. Stein minimized her need to feel connected and part of someone's life. In the following excerpt from a family interaction task, she talked about why she found it so difficult to communicate well with her son:

Ms. STEIN: I feel like I'm kind of cut out from your life. And I know part of that is that I'm always so busy with work. Sometimes, though, I think you and I understand each other quite well without talking. I think you know me pretty well.

BILL: Hm.

Ms. STEIN: Because we don't talk, I have insecurities because I don't really know what's happening in your life. Not only do I feel left out, but I feel anxious too. I feel like a failure. This makes me feel bad and I withdraw.

BILL: Why do you have to withdraw then? This must be where the problem is.

Ms. STEIN: I know I need to work on this.

MR. STEIN: Yes, that sounds good. Let's bring this up in our family therapy session. Maybe you do it to manipulate, too.

Ms. STEIN: Yes, but I think I do it more often because I'm hurt.

BILL: I don't know what to say. I just don't know how to deal with it.

A family therapist working with the Steins would have faced a choice at that point about what to do next. He or she could have picked up on Mr. Stein's suggestions to focus on this issue in the family therapy sessions by inviting all three of them to come in next time.

Or, the therapist could have chosen to have an intergenerational meeting between the mother and son, during which the focus would have been on Ms. Stein's early history with her own mother. The hypothesis here would be that Ms. Stein's inadequacies activated by her son were first developed in the context of her parentified relationship with her own mother. In the session the therapist could model for Bill how to show interest in his mother, and how to bring her out without threatening her and pushing her into withdrawing emotionally. And, when Ms. Stein inevitably did withdraw in the session, the therapist could model how to gently and supportively reengage her in the discussion. In the course of this dyadic meeting it would become clear to both mother and son that when Bill began speaking to her in monosyllables, this reminded her of her own lonely childhood. She not been able to connect with her own mother or father, and she was still inadequate to the task with her son.

Bill would come to recognize that, by helping out, he could have a positive impact on how the communication with his mother went. When he learned about the historical dynamics of his mother's habit of withdrawing, he began to see that it was not really about him. This permitted Bill to empathize with his mother rather than resent her. A second dyadic session focused on these same issues. Conjoint work with the father present also then resumed. Ms. Stein's behavior toward her son would change dramatically, becoming visibly warm, more engaged, and more interested in him. Although Bill did not fully reciprocate this warmth, his behavior with his peers improved dramatically, and his suicidal ideation ceased.

Ms. Stein continued to criticize Bill periodically, but the therapist chose not to focus on such behavior during this phase of treatment, because the qualitative change in the mother-son relationship was dramatically affecting the patient. The therapist waited until this new, closer relating was solidified before beginning to work with Ms. Stein about her tendency to criticize.

Treatment Issues in the Disconnected Family

If learning to listen and react less intensely is the goal of the treatment of the high-intensity family, then learning to *play* and to *empathize* is the task for the disconnected family. This is, of course, a gross oversimplification. However, in some ways it is a useful oversimplification because it represents a distillation of what is usually a great deal of complex and sometimes confusing work that goes on during the treatment of these families.

Because we are working with an epigenetic model, treatment of the disconnected family is by definition a more difficult task in some ways than working with the most chaotic high-intensity family. This is because in the high-intensity family the attachments between the parents and the patient are relatively intact. Treatment time does not need to be devoted to working through buried resentments, projections, distortions, disappointments about whether the two individuals involved care deeply about each other as separate, albeit related, people. In the same vein, in the most affectively benign and low-key disconnected family, the level of disturbance in the relationships in the family is located at the base of everything else that goes on.

If this most basic level is not addressed, then the clear, controlled, modulated communication that occurs may have little meaning—in fact, it may even be experienced as superficial or irrelevant.

Fostering an Attachment

To understand what has gone wrong in the formulation of an attachment or bond between a parent and a child, one must first establish a forum and an atmosphere in which issues can be explored without fear. In most cases this will likely entail several dyadic sessions between the parent with the disturbed attachment and the child. Keeping these sessions focused, somewhat structured, and undestructive ensures that both parties will experience this kind of exploratory work as beneficial. In chapter 9, guidelines for conducting an intergenerational attachment interview are presented to assist the family therapist in structuring these dyadic sessions.

When the interviews work well, the intense affect comes from the parent when he or she is self-disclosing about family-of-origin material. The patient is generally discouraged from intervening to express his or her feelings about the parent's past. The tone of the session is set by the therapist, who is curious, empathic, not afraid to ask tough questions, and able to tolerate the painful material that may come up without becoming anxious, cutting off discussion prematurely, or failing to explore something in depth. The therapist models for the patient ways to show empathy for and interest in the parent's experience. The patient, in listening to the parent's history, is not overwhelmed, because the parent is sharing his or her experience as a listener with the therapist. The therapist should not be overreacting to the material or overidentifying with the parent, but empathizing with some parts of the parent's experience. In a very real sense, then, the therapist is also modeling for the patient how to react emotionally to the material. In our experience, when these kinds of dyadic interviews are done well, they often dramatically affect the treatment of the entire family in ways that will be further described in chapter 9.

It is sometimes tempting to analyze a particularly productive parent-child intergenerational interviewing session. However, we have found it best not to process these sessions exhaustively. The therapist can co-opt away the fledgling feelings that may be developing between parent and child by talking about their feelings too much. The evolution of a positive attachment between a previously estranged parent and child is often a powerful, if slow and subtle, process. Once the process has begun, it grows of its own accord, with minimal therapeutic intervention or analysis.

So what should the therapist do as a next step? Basically, the therapist continues to provide a forum and an atmosphere in which the mutual exploring and the deepening of awareness of the differences between parental issues and child issues can emerge. The therapist ensures such a forum through regular contact and containment of the work in the sessions; that is, the family is instructed not to do this work on their own. In various ways the therapist also makes sure that the spouse is not threatened by the work that is going on. For example, the therapist can meet with the spouse on alternate weeks to discuss different issues or to get additional information. The therapist also can plan for the spouse to meet alone with the patient after the therapist and the first parent have finished their session. The spouse can be given a specific therapeutic task.

Therapeutic "Experiences"

When intergenerational interviewing is part of the treatment, this is usually done fairly early on in the work, but often after a couple of conjoint sessions where other family members are present. The introduction of dyadic interviews is done after the therapist has obtained the spouse's trust, thus minimizing resistance or sabotage caused by the spouse's feeling left out or threatened. After the intergenerational interviewing phase, the therapist can focus on assigning low-key, enjoyable, playful experiences for the dyad to do together. The idea is to start with small interactions and gradually expand these only as the dyad indicates a readiness for more prolonged or intense contact.

To start with, the task can be playing a card game for an hour, eating lunch together, going on a brief shopping trip, taking a walk, cooking a small meal together, baking a cake, or riding bikes. The task ought to be interactive (e.g., no watching TV or movies), mutually enjoyable, and low-pressure. Talking about the relationship is forbidden at first; later, brief discussions can be allowed. This minimizes not only the possibility of the family members' reversion to verbal interchanges about their difficulties, but also the probability that tempers will flare or that boredom and anxiety will take over. This approach also maximizes the probability that family members can relax with one another and just be themselves briefly. The ensuing tasks should be equally brief.

Later, as an in-depth attachment begins to develop, the two family members will often actively express a desire to spend longer periods of time together. As this happens, the rules about what can be discussed are relaxed somewhat, and interaction becomes more natural and spontaneous. When the therapist is attuned to the feelings of both members of the dyad, he or she will be able to adjust and fine tune the play tasks in ways that facilitate the development or deepening of an attachment between the two.

Daniel Stern's notion of optimal mismatch is useful here (Stern, 1985). This concept, from his experimental investigations of mother-infant interactions, refers to the fact that an infant is most comfortable being with his or her mother when the mother is attuned to the baby's gaze and movements in ways that are slightly out of synch with the baby's rhythms but not so far away from where the baby is that the baby feels a break between them in their interaction. A mother, for example, can expand an infant's emotional experience by introducing variations on their mutual play, thereby expanding the child's affective and interactional repertoire. Too much affect or too much distance makes the infant turn away or start crying.

The therapist who is attuned to each member of the dyad's needs in terms of stimulation, emotional space, shyness, and fearfulness will be better able to create experiences or therapeutic tasks that fit the needs of each. Also, such a therapist will observe and create the conditions under which both synchrony and expansion of the relationship can occur.

Later Phases of Treatment

After the attachment issues have been addressed, the therapist can focus on issues such as hostile communication, intrusiveness, inability to listen, and excessive criticism. These issues are never easy to deal with in family treatment, but it is much easier to work with family members who have a fundamental attachment that provides a basis for their joint addressing of these problems.

In contrast to high-intensity and low-intensity families, disconnected families require the therapist to be alert constantly to the likelihood of intergenerational disappointment as the driving force behind a critical or hostile remark to the patient. Because these issues have already been explored in depth during the intergenerational interviewing phase, the therapist probably will recognize the appearance of this issue as soon as it arises.

Psychoeducation for the parents as well as the patient may also be a focus of treatment at this point. Treatment planning and problem solving may be conjoint efforts during this phase. Many of the treatment techniques used for both high-intensity and low-intensity families can be introduced in this later phase of treatment. When regressions occur or family members revert to negative ways of relating, the therapist intervenes at the developmental level that best fits the situation.

CHAPTER 7

Treatment of the High-Intensity Family: A Model of Teaching Affect Regulation

T HE LABEL "high-intensity" was chosen for this group of families because it captures both the families' volatile style of affective relating and the overall feeling evoked in family therapists as they work with such families. Typically, the therapist becomes rapidly absorbed in the family's affect and may feel intensely engaged with the parents almost immediately. At the end of the initial contact, family therapists typically feel exhausted and drained by the intensity of the emotional reactions of the parents and the patient. A mutually engaging *affect spiral* seems to operate in these families. However, high-intensity families can display very different kinds of affect, even within one family. A verbal, demanding mother might be matched with a rigidly closed and silently angry son. Or, an angry, accusatory father might have a disorganized, psychotic son who is intrusive, inappropriate, and agitated. Another family might be characterized by a bizarre and verbally overwhelming schizophrenic daughter and a mother who is frozen in disorganized silence but reacts to every syllable spoken by the daughter.

In thinking about treatment for these kinds of families, we might first ask what underlying matrix of dynamics would drive the intense affective family interaction. Our research data provided us with some insight into family dynamics and allowed us to generate some hypotheses about what drives these systems. First, regardless of the type of negative affective displays they might exhibit in interactions with their disturbed child, the parents in these families have an attachment to their disturbed child that is neither negative nor attenuated. The inevitable stresses and strains of severe psychopathology do not rupture the characteristically secure, strong attachment bonds in such families; nor do such strains lead to disturbed attachments. There is typically a strong, positive attachment between parents and child that has endured the relational rampages and stresses of severe psychiatric conditions, such as schizophrenia. (Approximately 80% of the high-intensity families have a son or daughter with schizophrenia.)

The tenacity and power of attachment bonds in high-intensity families may represent both the strength and the weakness of such families. The stresses inherent in coping with a severely disturbed and disturbing child are buffered by a strong attachment bond between the parents and the child. Since the parents are often denying or minimizing the nature and severity of their child's disorder, an inevitable first question is, Should the therapist tamper with this denial process, which may be sustaining a positive bond? We argue yes, as long as the therapist tampers lightly and gradually. The therapeutic challenge then becomes how to address this denial in the context of a very powerful family dynamic and to rechannel maladaptive behavior in a more helpful direction, without damaging the underlying positive attachment bonds between family members. The core of work with high-intensity families involves first entering and becoming accepted by these difficult families, and then working from within to teach the family that less emotional reactivity, and less intense and entangled attachments, are often more conducive to a patient's recovery. The therapist is incessantly challenged by the emotional reactivity of the parents in the same way that the patient is. He or she is constantly invited to join in with family dramas or scenarios where the issues or meaning often become blurred and insignificant in the face of strong affect.

For example, at the beginning of one high-intensity family's treatment, the patient began by complaining that his hospital room was too hot and that the nurse was not helpful because she would not help him get an air conditioner. The father, reacting to his son's affective intensity, responded with equally intense affect by vociferously demanding that the therapist intervene immediately to investigate this situation. The therapist at this moment was tempted to react to the father's intensity by perpetuating the discussion about room temperature, thereby getting off the track of important family issues.

The affect in high-intensity families is particularly seductive because it is often direct, seems to stem from parental concern and caring, and has an inviting, inclusive quality. In contrast, the disengaged family's affect is often of a type that makes the therapist feel shut out, pushed away, or rejected.

The high-intensity family needs to be stabilized and educated, which often involves first reframing their overinvolvement as a maladaptive variant of attachment. Such reframing facilitates the reshaping of intrusive, critical behaviors into modes of relating that are more conductive to the patient's recovery. Typically, these families have major communication problems—they are often angry, critical, hostile, intrusive, or guilt-inducing. Confrontations designed to challenge or restructure family patterns are less successful with these families and are neither necessary nor effective. In the case just presented, for example, confronting the father and son about their tendency to go off on tangents would likely provoke another intense and defensive discussion with the therapist. Instead, a calm, neutral but firm insistence that the family remain focused on the topic at hand gently coaxes them back on track without further escalating their affect. Because the primary attachments between parents and children are basically secure and not layered with ambivalence and conflict (as is often the case for families in which buried, unresolved intergenerational issues exist), the motivation, if not the capacity, to change for the better is typically present.

In the remainder of this chapter we present several clinical problems typically evident in these families, and we illustrate ways of dealing with them, based on actual treatment cases. Such typical problems include parental intrusiveness, parental feelings of helplessness, parental over-helpfulness, family enmeshment, and perfectionism.

Stages of Treatment

The Roberts were a prototypical high-intensity family. Both parents were positively attached to their son, and during the first family meeting both parents clearly showed their emotional overinvolvement with him. Although they would become frustrated with their son at times, they did not have critical or rejecting or hostile attitudes toward him when they were interviewed with the Kreisman Scale for Rejecting Attitudes. Like many other high-intensity families, however, they were critical of the patient during a highly charged family discussion. In interviews about their families of origin, both parents were found to be emotionally overinvolved with their own parents, whom they tended to idealize, as well.

The parents in the Roberts family came to their first meeting with the therapist full of anxiety and eagerness to get some answers about how to cope with the chronic schizophrenic disorder of their son, Jimmy. He had just been hospitalized for a schizophrenic episode, his fourth psychiatric admission in three years. He had become increasingly paranoid, had insulted neighbors, and had threatened his elderly grandfather with bodily harm. Psychotic and threatening on the ward, Jimmy was not happy about being given neuroleptic medication. Jimmy did not like psychiatrists or psychiatric hospitals, and he pleaded with his parents to take him home. Mr. and Ms. Roberts were confused, anxious, and frightened. They did not want their son to be put in seclusion for the weekend, and they felt torn about taking him home when they knew he should stay in the hospital.

When they met Dr. Onegin, their family therapist, Mr. and Ms. Roberts began the session by flooding her with their anxiety, both of them speaking at once. The therapist wondered whether she should allow them the entire 45 minutes just to ventilate. After all, they seemed overwhelmed, and better that they overwhelm her rather than Jimmy, Dr. Onegin reasoned. Ms. Roberts began to cry and to demand advice about what to do next. Mr. Roberts was frustrated and agitated about a number of vaguely defined issues having to do with Jimmy's treatment plan. Mr. Roberts's preoccupation with and suspicion about the adequacy of Jimmy's treatment plan appeared to stem in part from his strong identification with his son, and particularly with his son's humiliation at being locked up and being forced to submit to authority. He felt the urge to protect his son, and he acted this out by lashing out at Dr. Onegin's competence and credibility.

Dr. Onegin felt pressured to accomplish several initial tasks, such as taking a family history. But she also felt flooded with Mr. and Ms. Roberts's affect. She had only 45 minutes to meet with them. It was Friday, and the parents had plans to visit Jimmy on Friday evening, Saturday afternoon, and Sunday afternoon. The therapist had several choices: she could meet with Jimmy alone, meet with the parents alone, meet with all three of them together, or some combination of these.

Following the dictum that in high-intensity families the first task is to dampen affective display—even while affirming, if reframing, the strong, positive attachment bonds that fuel them—in this case the therapist first focused on interventions that would not only reduce the stimulation for the patient but also reduce the parents' anxiety and reframe their anxiety-driven overprotectiveness and overinvolvement with his treatment plan. The parents met with the therapist alone for the first half of the session; Jimmy was invited to join in for the last half of the meeting. During the first half, the therapist chose not to allow the parents free rein to ventilate their anxiety. Instead, she spoke calmly to the parents about Jimmy's current state, the severity of his psychotic symptoms, and the plan to get these under control. She validated the positive attachments in the family by focusing on how appropriate it was for the parents to get Jimmy to the hospital, and she acknowledged the struggles they went through with their son to get him to the hospital against his will. The therapist inquired about Jimmy's prepsychotic state and helped the parents see that they had no choice but to act accordingly, as their son's clinical state had changed over the last two weeks. Mr. and Ms. Roberts were visibly relieved by this brief but focused discussion.

Dr. Onegin then educated Mr. and Ms. Roberts about the notion of reducing emotional stimulation for psychotic patients. She explained to them that schizophrenia was a stress-related biological disorder that is exacerbated by emotional overstimulation. She explained to them that even well-intentioned interactions with family members could sometimes be stressful for patients with this disorder. She also explained how psychotic patients are often frightened and overwhelmed by emotional stimulation, but do not necessarily accept any revision of their relationships and activities. She reframed their overinvolvement as care and concern for his best interest, and told them that affectionate restraint over the weekend visits would be a clear message of support and concern that would help Jimmy. They were advised not to engage in arguments and discussions about taking Jimmy out of the hospital. When Jimmy would bring this up, they would both agree that this would be discussed again on Monday, with Jimmy's psychiatrist. For the time being, the issue of Jimmy's hospitalization would be put aside.

Dr. Onegin helped the parents anticipate what kinds of topics or issues might emerge that would lead to intense discussions or arguments. She then helped the parents construct "miniplans" for how to divert attention away from these issues and get on to something less stimulating, and hence, less stressful for Jimmy. The parents decided that talk of Jimmy's future career was another issue that would spiral the family into an intense scene. Jimmy would talk of his desires to become a pilot and travel around the world, which would send his parents into an anxious state because this activated their fears that he might leave and get into a job where he would be out of control. They were not able to see and understand that the motivations behind Jimmy's lofty aspirations were to restore a sense of self-worth. They responded with intense anxiety to the content of Jimmy's proclamations, and not to the feelings Jimmy might be having about being insecure, inadequate, humiliated, and ashamed of his impairments. Mr. and Ms. Roberts were thus instructed to ask Jimmy to postpone this discussion when he brought it up, and to instead reassure him that when he was feeling better and in more control, it would be a better time to talk about his future plans. They were advised not to say things to provoke Jimmy like, "No this isn't a good idea," but rather, "Let's talk about that later, after you're feeling better. You will have some time to decide what to do next for work."

The therapist also helped the parents cut down their visit to an hour on each of the weekend days, instead of the four to five hours they had planned. This shortening of the visits, the therapist explained, would reduce stimulation, which in turn would lessen the biological stress associated with the disorder. By making this change, the parents could reassure the patient of their commitment and love for him, but not create a situation where he could become overstimulated and stressed by prolonged contact with his emotionally engaging parents.

The following week, they reported to Dr. Onegin that their visits had gone well. They felt good about the way they handled the weekend, and felt like competent parents. They also reported that they had enjoyed having some time alone at home without being wrapped up in Jimmy's problems, that this was the first such weekend they had like this in eight or nine months.

The Intrusive Parent in the High-Intensity Family

In many high-intensity families, one encounters a pattern of parent-child relating that involves one or both parents' obsessional preoccupation with the internal life of the child. The parent may relentlessly intrude into all aspects of the child's life, including his or her day-to-day existence, inner world, and emotional life. In our sample of families, many of the parents exhibited this kind of intrusive behavior with their children. Some parents desperately and futilely sought to be included in their child's world by inserting themselves into situations in a way that left the child feeling intruded upon, violated, or invaded. The following quote from a discussion between Ms. Bonner and her schizophrenic son, Joshua, illustrates the general quality of this kind of relationship:

JOSHUA: Everybody has to have some privacy.

MS. BONNER: I don't understand that. I'm your mother. You're not well. Why would you want to hide things from me. I mean it's not like I'm following you to the shower! You used to get so angry just because I would ask you where you and your friend went.

JOSHUA: No, you wanted to know every single place we went.

MS. BONNER: But it wasn't to criticize you; it was just nice to know what you did and what kind of things you do that are fun.

Ms. Bonner's inquisitiveness and intrusiveness are rooted in her basic feeling of being excluded from emotional contact, not just from her son, but from everyone else in her life. Her own mother had been an angry, cold woman who had little interest in her daughter. Ms. Bonner, now a mother herself, still had unmet needs for connection with her parents, which she was able to gratify through an overly close and enmeshed relationship with her son. However, as her son, Joshua, matured, she discovered to her dismay that a mutually dependent and enmeshed relationship was less and less possible.

Increasingly, Ms. Bonner and Joshua fought about autonomy, secrecy, and space, and about her controlling behavior. What they were really fighting about, however, was Ms. Bonner's need for close emotional contact with her son, which he increasingly found burdensome and oppressive. Ms. Bonner sought reaffirmation of her strong positive attachment to her son, and when he did not respond accordingly, her own anxiety escalated. She then became intrusive and controlling in response to her own anxiety about separation, which in turn caused him to become angry at almost everything his mother said and to withdraw further. These responses fueled her feelings of inadequacy, and she covered the shame and humiliation with sarcasm, anger, and outrage at his need for secrecy.

Thus, in contrast to the disconnected family, in which intrusion often masks a lack of emotional connectedness, parental intrusiveness in the high-intensity family becomes a vehicle to recement an overinvolved attachment.

The therapist in this case might have been tempted to work on communication skills training with this family. However, such skills training would not have effected any lasting change unless the therapist had focused on the underlying intergenerational themes of isolation and being cut off in this family. The therapist in this case first interviewed Ms. Bonner, in front of the patient, about her early experiences with her own mother. As she recounted painful scenes in which she was left feeling rebuffed by her aloof, uninterested mother, the patient began to have empathy for his mother for the first time. He, as well as she, began to see her need to intrude as at least partially the result of this lifelong feeling of being left out, unconnected, and not part of what was going on in the family. Her incessant inquiries about his life represented bungled efforts to share something with him. The therapist helped this very angry, volatile, defensive woman talk about these feelings instead of acting out the frustration by intruding into her son's inner world. Since Joshua was sitting there in the room with the therapist and his mother, he had a chance to observe how someone could respond to his mother's needs without being invaded by her. The therapist helped the patient not to overreact to his mother's desperate intrusiveness when she would talk with him. Rather than just advising the mother to cease her intrusions into her son's life and psyche, the therapist chose to address this problem from an intergenerational perspective.

The intergenerational focus resulted in a very dramatic drop in the intensity of the mother's intrusive forays. The patient was able to begin seeing his mother as a separate person, distinct from himself, with her own problems, issues, and needs, many of which had little to do with him. This decreased his rage and allowed him to be less emotionally reactive when she would intrude. This kind of intervention is often extremely powerful and produces very rapid and dramatic change in the way that people relate to one another. In this case, these changes occurred after only five sessions.

The struggle in this family appeared on the surface to be between mother and son. The therapist here conceptualized it another way: it was a struggle within the self of the mother—a lifelong struggle that was always failing to provide relief, and one that the mother herself emotionally reacted to. By thus reframing the problem, the therapist was able to address the intergenerational origins of this intrapsychic and ultimately intrafamilial problem.

Parental Feelings of Helplessness in the High-Intensity Family

Laura was an engaging and intense 25-year-old with schizophrenia, and she was alcoholic. She would walk right up to people she liked and involve them in intense, often intimate discussions about herself. However, she was extremely emotionally fragile and reactive, and would quickly make paranoid constructions of interactions with others that could lead her to attack others verbally and to become incoherent. Her mother, Ms. Seidenberg, was a quiet, understated woman with a master's degree in library science who was completely overwhelmed by her daughter's reactivity and changeability. When Laura would become symptomatic, Ms. Seidenberg would freeze up, become tongue-tied, get increasingly anxious, and begin to react to every nuance of feeling Laura expressed. Ms. Seidenberg would try to sort through Laura's affect logically, but would become confused herself, which led to more anxiety. Ms. Seidenberg's silence and confusion made Laura more anxious, and she interpreted her mother's silence as rejection or a lack of interest. Consequently,

Laura would try harder to get her mother to respond, which made Ms. Seidenberg withdraw further, and so on.

The family therapist knew from the Five Minute Speech Sample (FMSS) data, and from her interview with Laura's mother, that Ms. Seidenberg was attached to her daughter in a positive, if low-key, way. She accepted her daughter's profound deficits and tried to help her daughter by anticipating what she was feeling or thinking, but these deficits did not elicit hostility. However, because Laura was so disorganized, her mother's attempts to paraphrase her internal world were usually doomed. Although Laura had periods where she seemed lucid and coherent in her thinking, her coherence would deteriorate rapidly during periods when Laura was actively psychotic.

In the initial family therapy session, the therapist invited mother and daughter into her office, and let them talk with each other for 10 minutes or so at the beginning of the meeting. She observed patterns of mutually frustrating interaction. Laura would try to communicate with her mother in metaphors and fragmented allusions, and Ms. Seidenberg would become confused and would try to understand by saying things like, "Oh, you mean you're. . . " or "You must be saying that you feel I'm ignoring you" or "I think you're confused now, dear." Since, the family therapist knew from the family assessment that the mother-daughter attachment was largely positive and that Ms. Seidenberg did not have major unresolved attachment issues with her family of origin, she hypothesized, first, that the frustrating and intrusive mother-daughter interactions devolved from the mother's attempts to counter her feelings of helplessness in the face of the daughter's psychosis. The therapist hypothesized, second, that Ms. Seidenberg needed help and direction in how to respond to her severely disturbed and bizarre daughter without becoming immobilized. The therapist hypothesized, last, that Laura was seeking contact with and reassurance from her mother and needed help in how to do this without flooding her mother.

The therapist decided to end the conjoint part of the family session by telling Laura that she was going to be talking with Ms. Seidenberg alone for a while alone, and that she would meet again with Ms. Seidenberg and Laura together in three days. For the next 30 minutes the therapist helped Ms. Seidenberg understand what was happening with her daughter's thinking when the two of them would interact. The therapist shared with Ms. Seidenberg that she too had trouble dealing with Laura's intensity when Laura was disorganized, and she shared with Ms. Seidenberg her own ways of dealing with this. She encouraged Ms. Seidenberg to set aside very brief periods for regular visits and phone contact. Laura wanted to talk to her mother every night for 30 to 45 minutes, sometimes two or three times a night. Ms. Seidenberg was advised to approach Laura herself about phone calls and to set up a plan for regular 10-minute calls. This accomplished the following: it helped to decrease Laura's spirals of disorganization, which appeared to be exacerbated by contact with her mother; it gave the mother a way of being there for her daughter without getting overwhelmed in the process; and it reassured Laura that her mother's interest and attention were intact, while at the same time fostering increased differentiation between Laura and her mother.

In Ms. Seidenberg's phone calls to Laura, she inquired about very basic issues. She noticed immediately that the conversations with her psychotic daughter proceeded better when the questions came from her, and when they were simple, direct, and nonemotional. Ms. Seidenberg was advised that asking open-ended questions about her daughter's thoughts or feelings was likely to elicit a lot of disorganized thinking, incoherent speech, and debilitating anxiety. The mother was reassured that after her daughter's medications began to take hold, more meaningful discussions would resume. In effect, Ms. Seidenberg was directed to dramatically lower her expectations and hopes about what would transpire as she interacted with her daughter when Laura was in a florid psychotic state. The therapist helped Ms. Seidenberg carve out a way to stay in close contact with Laura, without getting flooded and overwhelmed.

Later the same day, the therapist sat and chatted with Laura for a few minutes. The therapist shared her thought with Laura that Ms. Seidenberg was very concerned and caring about Laura, but that she got easily overwhelmed with Laura sometimes. She wondered whether Laura noticed this too? The patient agreed and eagerly asked the therapist whether this was because her mother was mentally unstable. Dr. Onegin assured the patient that Ms. Seidenberg was indeed stable, but that Laura could contribute to making things easier for herself. First, Laura could come to Dr. Onegin with her concerns about how she was feeling. Also, she could save her most problematic issues involving her mother for times when she and her mother were meeting with Dr. Onegin. Laura was encouraged to try to keep her conversations with her mother on "day-to-day" topics for the time being, to see if this helped Laura feel better. The patient seemed to like this idea, because it was a chance for her to try her competence. It also meant that she had to worry about less, and the suggestion was made that Laura might be able to keep some of her feelings for herself, bring them to Dr. Onegin, and not spill them onto her mother. This idea intrigued her.

As treatment progressed with Laura, Ms. Seidenberg began attending psychoeducation meetings for parents and learned about her daughter's illness. She learned about how stress makes the symptoms worse. Dr. One-gin helped her translate this into her regular interactions with Laura, and the therapist discussed similar information with Laura. Then, when Dr. Onegin restricted the amount of time Laura's mother would spend together, she invoked the issue of stress management as a reason why. Both the mother and the daughter began to organize around competently managing their stress rather than trying to manage each other's thoughts and feelings. When Laura would begin to disorganize, unravel, and start raging at her mother, Ms. Seidenberg would stop trying to understand what her daughter was saying and would calmly step back and assess what was going on.

How did Ms. Steinberg terminate this spiral of affect? She would not react to Laura's invitations to argue and instead would say, for example, "I don't want to argue with you about this now." She would try to gently distract her daughter onto a more benign topic, or ask her if she would like to go for a walk. She would ask Laura whether she thought it was time for her mother to leave, or whether they should have a 5-minute break, during which her mother would leave and but then come right back. If these interventions failed to quell the affect spiral, then Ms. Seidenberg would end the visit, telling Laura that she would call her later that evening and would see her at the next visit, at a specific time. This tended to reduce Laura's panic about having driven her mother away forever, and it pre-vented a scene from developing. And Ms. Seidenberg intervened without feeling bad, rejected, or confused. Laura was given the message that her mother was not going to get involved in an intense argument, but that she would still be available when Laura was feeling more in control. Ms. Sei-denberg learned to practice this way of regulating herself and her daugh-ter so that when the time for discharge came, this was an accepted routine for both of them.

The patient developed increased self-esteem because she learned how to be with her mother without feeling out of control and without feeling terrible guilt and anxiety for exploding at her mother. Ms. Seidenberg felt like a competent parent for the first time since her daughter was diag-nosed. Laura and her mother still had many more issues to explore, but these were shelved until after Laura was settled in an aftercare day hospi-tal and she and mother had stabilized a visiting routine. Because the thera-pist could assume that the underlying attachment between them was not predominantly damaged or disturbed, she could put these other issues on hold for several months and help them cope with the immediate stresses of the illness, knowing that hidden negative affect from Ms. Seidenberg was not the driving force behind the pair's affect spirals.

In essence, Dr. Onegin taught the mother how not to react to her daughter's affect and provocative behavior. But how is it that the mother was able to relearn such a basic thing as emotional reactivity to her own child? D. W. Winnicott (1960) has written about the holding environment as a way of conceptualizing the necessary emotional nutrients required for the developing child to experiment and grow and try out risky new behaviors.

Ira Levine and Arnold Wilson (1985) have extended this use of the holding environment to the hospital milieu. They argue that the hospital ward has a wide variety of professionals available to the patient within the context of a protected, structured setting, and this plethora of treatment contacts enables the disturbed psychiatric inpatient to make use of significant others in this therapeutic world to grow and recover.

The notion of a holding environment is a useful way of conceptualizing what it is that the therapist seeks to provide for the parents in the high-intensity family. The therapist functions as a container for the affect in the family, but he or she does more than this. The therapist functions as a container in a special way—by holding the intense *reaction* of the parent without dismissing it or minimizing it. The therapist "holds" it, as it were, in a way that gives the parent a few minutes breathing space to regroup, stop and think, and *then* react to the situation. The therapist holds the parent's intense disappointment, frustration, or anger, while helping the parent lower expectations about what the patient can do. As parental expectations fall into line with the patient's true capabilities, intense overreactions to things the patient says and does begin to diminish *gradually*. Change is subtle and occurs in small steps. Like the patients he or she is treating, the therapist must have realistic expectations, too.

Failures of Affective Attunement in the High-Intensity Family

Daniel Stern (1985), in his groundbreaking book on infants' interpersonal world, writes about the importance of attunement between mother and child to the development of an infant's stable affective life. A mother is attuned to her infant when she slightly deviates from his or her affective state to raise or lower the child's emotional temperature, or to expand or enlarge on the child's emotional repertoire. Because the mother is slightly more intense or reactive, or is less vivid and more restricted than her child, the child will learn to expand his or her repertoire of affective experience in ways that might not happen solely through personal struggle with frustrations of the external world. Mother-infant research (Stern, 1985) has shown, however, that when the mother misreads or misinterprets the infant's emotional experience and consequently responds in a much too intense or indifferent manner, the baby becomes distressed. If her rhythm or tone of voice, eye contact, or other paraverbal communications are too discrepant from those of the baby, a mismatch occurs, which truncates the possibilities for the infant to expand his or her emotional repertoire. Thus, ideally, the mother does not attempt to impose her own needs on the situation, nor does she try to refocus the child's experience. Rather than being intrusive, she augments the child's own experience.

In a sense, the parent stretches the child's world. Many times in high-intensity families the parent seems to be trying—unsuccessfully—to share an affective experience with the child. Usually the parents rush in to match the patient's affect quickly, often missing it altogether in their frantic attempts to make contact. Consequently, the patient often feels misunderstood. The parent becomes exasperated at the repeated failures to have an empathic connection with the child and then becomes critical or hostile.

Case Illustrations

Ms. Wilmet was, by all accounts, an extraordinarily devoted mother to her 21-year-old daughter, Anna, who had had her first bipolar episode only one month before. Anna was going through a period of severe depression after her manic break, and her mother had become caught up in it also. Ms. Wilmet understood the biological component of the manic episode, as Anna was visibly disorganized, paranoid, and psychotic during this time. However, Ms. Wilmet intuitively felt that Anna's depressed face and eyes were caused by Anna's thinking depressing, negative thoughts. If Ms. Wilmet could somehow get Anna to see this, to grasp it, struggle with it, then Anna could be less depressed—and, consequently, so could Ms. Wilmet, or so she thought.

Mr. Wilmet, Anna's father, was also affected by her moods. Like his wife, he would feel despondent, inadequate, and helpless when his daughter would express how despondent, hopeless, and isolated she felt. The parents were quite attached to Anna, and they felt validated as parents when they could see Anna's face light up with smiles or laughter.

Visits and passes with parents were usually stressful experiences for Anna, who, according to the nursing staff, returned from visits crying, withdrawing, or feeling depressed. However, Anna told her therapist that she felt very loved by her parents, that nothing at all was problematic for her regarding her family. Similarly, the family presented themselves as having little to work on, with no real problems or conflicts, and family therapy came to a stalemate.

The following interchange was observed by Anna's therapist one evening, which led to a formulation of Anna's case as involving a high-intensity family:

> The parents walked onto the ward, and sat down in the lounge. Anna soon walked in and sat down. She looked glum, quiet and avoided eye contact. Her mother inquired how she was, and Anna replied "fine." Mother seemed dissatisfied with this and went on to ask a series of questions about why the patient seemed depressed when she visited the family home over the weekend. The mother said, "You know, when you're down like that, it hurts me, I try to cheer you up and I can't. And you won't talk to me and it really bothers me." "Maybe it's because you're really angry with us and don't want to come home." (Anna says "no.") "Or maybe you worry that you'll never get well again; well, we worry about that too of course. Couldn't you come up to me and at least say, "'Hi mom, what's for dinner?'" "Instead, you just walked away from me when I was talking with you and I felt terrible. I just didn't know what to do. I felt your pain and I didn't know what was wrong and I couldn't fix it" "Are you depressed? Are you suicidal? Do you think you're always going to be sick? Because you're not, you know, you're going to be fine pretty soon—get right back on track, back to college, back to boys, you'll see. Soon it'll happen. In fact right now, you're making progress already, I can see it." "Can't you, Daddy?" Anna's father gets tearful and says, "Yes, Mom's right, it's not so bad, you can beat this thing."

At this point Anna felt flooded with anxiety, and she began to cry, saying, "I've always tried to do what you want me to do, always." She then got up, ran off to her room, and asked that her parents leave. Anna's parents felt frustrated and helpless. Privately, they also felt convinced of their inadequacy as parents—they could not reach out and help their daughter. Perhaps they had something to do with causing her illness as well, they thought.

Anna's mother and father needed to learn how to deal with their own emotional reactions to Anna's moods. The family therapist arranged a session with just the couple during which she explored with each of the parents individually (but in front of the other) exactly what kinds of feelings were evoked during the previous scenario she had witnessed on the unit. The therapist reviewed the entire situation from the time the parents got into the car to drive down to New Haven from Boston to visit. She started with having Anna's mother talk about the thoughts, feelings, and fantasies she had when she got into the car and started heading toward Connecticut. The therapist went over the incident step by step, exploring with each parent, at each step, the feelings and fantasies each was having. At moments when the parent clearly was overreacting, the therapist stopped the parent and questioned the validity of the parent's experience. In this way the therapist began to teach the parents about which of their emotional reactions were within normal limits and which might have been overactive.

The therapist was clearly aligned with the parents during this exploratory session and used support, humor, and empathy for them to quietly challenge the necessity of the parents' overreaction to Anna's despondency. The therapist was able to point out, for example, that the parents visited Anna twice weekly and had never missed a family session; that they called her at least once per night; and that they were in fact very attentive parents and did not necessarily need to question their adequacy just because their daughter had little interest in talking to them. This lead directly into psychoeducation about their daughter's mood states and how those interacted with Anna's personality traits. The therapist suggested that when the parents allowed themselves to become upset when Anna was depressed, that Anna became overwhelmed with their reactions, which then led her to shut down as a means of protecting herself. The therapist helped the parents make a list of things they could say when they came to visit and Anna was feeling down. The suggestions the parents raised were often well intentioned but too intrusive or intense. The therapist helped the parents edit these remarks and phrases so that they would prevent affect flooding of the patient.

This was just one step in this family's treatment, but it set the tone for subsequent sessions. Mr. and Ms. Wilmet's emotional reactions were accepted by the therapist, but then explored, and sometimes reframed or even dropped. The family therapist had a meeting with Anna's individual therapist as well to share this treatment strategy. The individual therapist was able to help the patient develop some resiliency to her emotionally expressive parents so that she did not have intense emotional reactions to them, for such reactions on the part of the patient might in turn only escalate the parents' emotional reactions.

Overidentification in the High-Intensity Family

In the FMSS administered to Gina's mother, Ms. Giordano at the beginning of Gina's hospitalization, she revealed many of the issues that troubled her about her relationship with her daughter.

> As far as Gina and I are concerned we're very close but she always likes to argue with me when she's off her medication. When she's on it she's fine, she

doesn't argue. She used to be a fun-loving person. She still is, but she's so confused. She doesn't know half the time what to do. And that's why she's here in the hospital. She used to be very clean and then she turned to being very sloppy. As far as loving us, she loves us too much. I mean it's good. I like it, but I want her to be a little independent too. She doesn't seem to know how to handle herself in the outside world. Basically she's a good person. She's capable of working, but she doesn't seem to know how to handle it. She tries very much to have a relationship with the family, but she seems to make it worse. I just want her to get better. She cries one minute and laughs the next. When she's so sick, I get overwhelmed.

Gina's mother was so overwhelmed with her daughter's psychotic symptoms that she focused on the stress of the moment and on ways of finding relief from the immediate burden. When Gina was stable, her mother was stable; when Gina was symptomatic, her mother felt stressed, anxious, and irritable. Ms. Giordano's goal was to find relief from this situation. Although she vaguely longed for her daughter to be more independent, she lacked the vision or know-how needed to help Gina develop some autonomy. Ms. Giordano quietly hoped for a miracle cure for her daughter, but she did not believe there was much she could do to change the course of her daughter's illness.

Gina's father similarly felt overwhelmed by his daughter. Mr. Giordano also felt somewhat powerless, because he was physically disabled from an accident and therefore could not do things with Gina as he once had. Gina's mother was also feeling overwhelmed by taking care of her ill husband.

Psychoeducation about schizophrenia helped Gina's parents enormously, but they had no clue about how to translate some of this information into their interactions with Gina. The therapist in this case became a coach for these parents and helped them with very basic skills, such as how to curb their reactivity to Gina, how to solve problems with her, and how best to communicate their feelings in a way that was not overstimulating. The longer-term goal was to help the patient tolerate moving out of the family home into a halfway house where she would have a chance to live independently and make friends. In the beginning phases of treatment, however, this idea was far too drastic a change: Gina associated moving away from her parents with literally dying; and Mr. and Ms. Giordano, who loved Gina, were keenly aware of how gravely impaired she was and wanted to care for her. In fact, they saw Gina's care as a natural part of their family life, and the family value of taking care of one's own had been embedded in generations of this family.

To call these parents pathologically overinvolved was to miss the point in many respects. Gina's parents lacked the cognitive capacity to think about their daughter and her disorder as separate and distinct from themselves. Their developmental sense of Gina was arrested as well. They remembered the responsive, loving girl she had been before her sickness, and they saw her now a severely disturbed psychotic who could not function outside of the home; but they could not see her as continuing to grow and develop, or as being someone who could gradually develop the skills needed to live a relatively autonomous existence. Furthermore, they felt that Gina's departure from their home would signal the end of their relationship with her. Ms. Giordano, for example, could not fathom the idea that Gina was attached to her mother as a person, and that Gina wanted to come and visit her simply because she enjoyed Ms. Giordano's company. Instead, Ms. Giordano had defined her own relationship with Gina exclusively in terms of a mother caring for her disturbed child; she did not know any other way of relating to Gina.

The therapist in this family was flooded with problems he could have chosen to deal with. He thought Gina would be much better off in a day hospital and halfway house because she was so dependent on her parents, but he realized very quickly that this would be a major upheaval in the family. He chose, therefore, to invest some time early in the treatment to begin to change Gina's parents' conceptualization of their daughter's life and disturbance from a developmental perspective. A 6-month timeline was made for the parents in which Gina would first become stabilized on her medication, then would move home. However, instead of having Gina merely stay at home during the day, the plan was for her to begin day treatment while living at home. Ms. Giordano's anxiety and tendency to overprotect were rechanneled by having her take charge of the interviewing procedures for day programs. She agreed to drive Gina to and from these interviews and to help Gina think over which day program she wanted to go into.

Because the therapist did not pressure Gina to move out of the house immediately, Gina was able to get involved in the treatment plan. Although she was not really enthusiastic about day treatment, it was within the range of change that she could tolerate. After 6 months, the patient and her family were to reevaluate Gina's course and progress and make plans from there regarding her living situation. In effect, this delay gave Gina's mother time to cope with the anticipated loss of her daughter. It gave her several months to prepare herself cognitively for this event, and it allowed the therapist to work with the mother to establish new rituals and routines between mother and daughter that were more appropriate to Gina's ultimate goal of partial differentiation. For example, Gina and Ms. Giordano began a weekly routine of preparing a meal together. Gina would help her mother plan, shop for, and prepare a family dinner. This gave Gina and Ms. Giordano a new way to be close together, which permitted the strong attachment between them to continue but began to loosen the somewhat stifling overinvolvement between them.

As Gina began to attend the day program, her anxiety accelerated dramatically. At this point, the therapist worked directly with the patient to absorb this anxiety and prevent her from dumping it onto her parents. He firmly reassured the patient that she could learn to tolerate the day program. The parents' task was to continue facilitating their daughter's attendance at the day program. The therapist reassured them of the important function this behavior had in their daughter's longer-term picture. They were reassured that their handling of things was not only appropriate but "just right." When the patient began to complain and made threats about regression, the therapist helped the parents resist succumbing to her pleas to let her drop the program. No other goals or moves toward independence were discussed by anyone in the treatment. All of the rest of the tasks Gina needed to accomplish were put on hold. The effect of this was to break up the enormous task facing both the patient and the parents of this very severely disturbed young woman. By helping the patient's family develop a concept of movement, the therapist paved the way for small, steady, gradual change to occur.

The Perfect Family

Alan had a bipolar disorder and had recently been arrested for disorderly conduct while on a manic episode. Although both parents, and his brothers and sisters, were shaken, they showed a consistent desire to work in family sessions to try to help Alan. They insisted that Alan's disorder was the one problematic area in a family they all defined as nearly perfect. As they saw it, they could discuss any topic, and there was little evidence of hostility in their interactions. Ms. Tolman, Alan's mother, described her son as an extraordinarily kind, loving, giving person who was always generous to everyone. Alan's father, who was very identified with his son, thought that they shared many attributes; they were both extremely sensitive to what was going on in the emotional world around them. Alan's father, a retired military man, was devoted to his family as well as to several community volunteer projects. He saw his son as special and in need of special attention. However, their sense of him as special and unique had an overinvolved quality, as the following FMSS of Ms. Tolman describing Alan indicates:

Alan has been a very warm, loving, sensitive person. . . . And I always wanted to protect him. . . because he was always gentle and loving. He was always there for his friends. . . and for his sisters. He never complained. He never said when he was angry; he just took everything. . . . We have a very close relationship. He's always been very open, very open with me. We just had a very giving, good relationship.

When the family therapist met with this family, she found them to be open, verbal, and courageous in confronting their current situation. Yet, she did not feel that everything was in fact wonderful. A close look revealed that everyone in Alan's family, including Alan, was overly preoccupied with the affective state of everybody else in the family. One somehow got the feeling when sitting with the family that Alan was the victim of emotional theft. It was not possible for Alan to have a strong feeling about anything without someone in the family overempathizing with him about it, or commenting endlessly on his feeling. This hypercontrolling mode of relating co-opted or took away Alan's emotional experience. The mother's FMSS on her own mother indicated that such a hypercontrolling, possessive mode of relating had its roots in the family-of-origin experience.

My mother, she loves her family to death. She liked to control everything about me, including my friends. She used to get up early on school mornings and come into my room and help me choose what to wear. She wanted me to look pretty. This was fun for her. She always told me I was her best friend. Whenever I was unhappy, I learned not to tell her because she would ask a million questions and I would feel overwhelmed by it. If I ever got angry with her, she would sometimes stop talking to me for days, so it wasn't worth it. Sometimes she would climb into bed with me and cuddle with me even when I was a teenager, and I remember thinking that I didn't like it anymore, and wishing that she could give me more space.

This passage indicates that the tendency to express caring through overcontrol was part of Ms. Tolman's relational legacy from her family of origin, which she was unwittingly reenacting with her son. However well-intentioned, Ms. Tolman's compulsive caring through overcontrol encouraged Alan's already strong tendency to isolate. He had trouble articulating what was wrong. The therapist guessed that it was hard for Alan to have angry feelings toward his seemingly wonderful parents.

A very powerful intervention for this family was for the therapist to block the empathic response of family members when the patient began to be more forthcoming about his affective experience. In the initial stages of treatment, the therapist would counsel the parents not to jump in to try to rescue Alan, to anticipate his every need and feeling, and to ease his pain. "You don't need to fix this Ms. Tolman." "Don't help him figure this out;

let him struggle with it a little bit." Family discussions became more awkward and sometimes uncomfortable. As the patient's family life became more real, the patient was gradually able to begin showing some of the less pleasant aspects of his inner world to his family. When the patient began to criticize his father for being self-centered, the therapist intervened to contain the father's emotional reaction to Alan so that Alan's feelings could be vented in their full intensity. This work led to a series of sessions in which the father talked about his own life with an emotionally controlling father and how these experiences caused him to go overboard in trying to make sure that his son's life was "nearly perfect."

The Overly Helpful Family

Mr. and Ms. Hall had seven children, one of whom was schizophrenic. Lea, age 23, was a bright, verbal, talkative girl who was devoted to her parents. Mr. and Ms. Hall knew that their daughter suffered from a severe psychiatric disorder, but they felt it their duty to give their best guidance to her just as if she were one of their normal children. During one of the family discussion tasks, they brought up the issue of Lea's not speaking up for herself with other people. The following discussion illustrates how in this family the parents were so tuned in to Lea's feelings that their reactions became too intense for Lea to handle. Despite Mr. and Ms. Hall's good intentions, Lea felt overwhelmed by her parents' suggestions and guidance.

Ms. HALL: You should learn to speak up for yourself.
LEA: I've got to work on that while I'm here.
Ms. HALL: That's right, because people don't say things to hurt you—you take it the wrong way, as an insult. Like the other day your sister said to you, "You never wear nail polish anymore." I imagine that you thought, "I don't look so good today."
LEA: Yeah.
Ms. HALL: But that's not what she was saying. She was just commenting on it. You should say something like, "Yeah, I just don't have time." I think that when you don't say something back, you just swallow it and it starts to bother you.

At this point in the discussion, the patient turned the tables in the family and turned the issue around into Ms. Hall's problem.

LEA: Well, Mom, I worry about you and your self-esteem. Sometimes I wonder whether you're as assertive as I'd like you to be.

Ms. HALL: I'm me.

MR. HALL: What do you mean, like you want her to be?

LEA: I'm just saying, you should feel better about yourself.

Ms. HALL: But why do I need to go out and do that?

LEA: Just to feel good. Just to have something to do. I like pastels, bright colors.

Ms. HALL: I would never wear green.

LEA: But see, you're wrong, you can't know how things are going to be until you do it.

At this point, the entire family was confused, and the discussion was derailed. The discussion continued for another several minutes and became increasingly tangential.

The therapist in this case decided that the parents needed more specific education about the nature of their daughter's illness. She helped the parents understand the role of stress in their daughter's illness and how their efforts to help their daughter live a more productive life were sometimes experienced as unmanageable demands. Also, they learned how to tolerate their daughter's eccentric interpersonal behaviors. They stopped being so tuned in to her comfort level and reminded her about looking for a job. They began to realize that certain of Lea's habitual ways of dealing with people were fairly adaptive for Lea, given her illness. As the patient began to feel less pressured, her tendency to argue and escalate the intensity during family discussions diminished.

Eventually, Lea entered a day program in which her case manager began working with her on interpersonal skills. Because Lea was able to feel less intruded upon by her parents, she was able to tolerate living at home while she went to the day program. Mr. and Ms. Hall's strong attachment to their daughter made it easier for them to modify their attitude toward her behavior, and the family intervention was a fairly brief treatment.

The Affectively Overwhelmed Family

Mr. and Ms. Borus are the parents of Danny, a profoundly disturbed schizophrenic 27-year-old man who had been hospitalized many times for serious suicide attempts and florid psychotic relapses. Both parents were positively attached to Danny—as Mr. Borus put it, "There is nothing that we wouldn't do for Danny." Danny was an extremely labile person and cried very easily. Any sign of suffering on Danny's part upset both parents very much. They felt that Danny had suffered his entire life, since birth, and that they had suffered along with him.

Danny was intensely dependent and unable to survive outside of a hospital setting for more than a few months. In the following discussion, Ms. Borus was intensely reactive to her son's emotional state. In this high-intensity family, an affect spiral ensued when any one of the three family members experienced sadness, guilt, hopelessness, or other similar emotions.

Ms. Borus: When I'm talking to you on the phone and you start to cry, I say try not to do it, because I'm still going to be there for you. I know in your own way you're trying to get sympathy from me. And believe me, I do understand what you feel.

Danny: No.

Ms. Borus: No?

Danny: No.

Ms. Borus: What do you mean, no? Well, why are you doing it then?

Danny: I don't know.

Mr. Borus: He just hates to leave us. There's nothing wrong with that. It's part of growing up.

Ms. Borus: But as you grow older, you will become less dependent on us.

Mr. Borus: I can see in your face that this stresses you, Danny.

Ms. Borus: I know it makes you sad.

Mr. Borus: It's hard for us too, but we can't just start crying, because we have to show strength and be together about the situation for you.

Ms. Borus: What's making you cry now?

Danny: I'm sick.

Ms. Borus: No.

Danny: What do you mean, no? I'm sick, Ma; I have mental problems. And you don't understand them, you really don't. Nobody does. None of these doctors understand them either, you know. And I'm trying hard.

Ms. Borus: If you were that sick, do you think you'd be able to sit here and talk in reality like you are now?

Danny: Sometimes I'm not in reality, Mom (cries).

In this passage, the patient was reacting to his parents' emotional reaction to his affect. No one in the family knew why Danny was crying, not even Danny. The family therapist needed to start by asking, simply and directly, what kinds of thoughts Danny was having. Had he been able to, Danny probably would have said that he felt terribly inadequate, especially compared to his father, and that he despised his own neediness. The therapist might have helped the parents to accept this, to listen to Danny, and to try to understand how Danny felt, without jumping in to change his feelings.

These parents were afraid of their own emotional reactions. They feared that the pain—both Danny's and their own—would be unbearable. Danny's parents needed to learn that their son would be able to tolerate his own pain and that when he would cry, he would soon stop. As the parents began to learn to tolerate their own affective reaction to their son, Danny himself became less labile. He still had many problems in dealing with his schizophrenia, but the decrease in emotional reactivity in Danny and in his parents permitted him to live at home without making suicide gestures.

Conclusion

In our experience, treatment with high-intensity families is often a fairly lengthy process. The positive attachments in these families may be one of the reasons that they do not drop out of treatment. The family's commitment to their disturbed child leads them to stay with treatment even during periods of little or no progress in the patient. The patients in these families often verbalize a sense of being cared for by their family. In our sample, some of the patients in these families had good outcomes, despite being profoundly disturbed for many years. It is possible that the families' positive, secure attachment bonds buffer these patients and thereby keep them in treatment, keep them interested in their own recovery, and allow them to survive stressful events without relapsing.

In the best-case scenario, the patient stabilizes and develops some autonomy after an extended period of treatment. Such was the case of Mr. and Ms. Roberts and Jimmy, discussed at the beginning of this chapter. When the parents came to visit with us for the research study, Mr. Roberts sat down and began an intense discussion with one of us. He was his usual heated self, shouting and getting excited—but this time, about his vegetable garden. His basic nature had not changed much, but the things he chose to get excited about had changed a great deal. This represents, in essence, the approach to working with the high-intensity family: fostering a few, carefully selected changes that have a high payoff in the patient's life. Other aspects of the family are left untouched. The two parents will probably always be rather confusing people to listen to, because their communication style is rather vague and amorphous. They have learned to listen, however, and to modulate their emotional reactivity to their son in ways that have facilitated and helped sustain his partial recovery and stabilization.

CHAPTER 8

Treatment of the Low-Intensity Family

I N THE YPIFS we classified 18% to 20% of the families as low-intensity ones; that is, families who combine positive attachment bonds with low levels of negative affect. Perhaps it was because we were studying patients with serious psychiatric disorder that so few families fit this category. However, even in other treatment settings, we have found that the number of families who initially have minimal problems with either attachment or negative affect is relatively low. In our work with patients who have psychotic disorders as well as personality disorders, we have found that the majority of families present with problems similar to those described for the high-intensity families or the disconnected ones. In previous chapters we pointed out that treatment approaches that focus on straightforward behavioral or problem-solving methods have not been well suited to high-intensity or disconnected families. Consequently, considerable preparatory work was often needed before the family could use interventions such as management techniques, skills training, and so on.

The low-intensity family enters therapy more emotionally available and ready to participate in the treatment immediately. The members of the family seem to be less angry, less anxious, and more easygoing. As indicated in chapter 4, the parents in these families appear to have more differentiated, balanced views of their own parents. They do not idealize their own parents, but rather express their appreciation for certain qualities or attributes of their parents. The low-intensity parents are less critical and hostile toward the patient in the family interactions. If they are excessively critical as treatment begins, they usually deescalate the level of criticism very rapidly after treatment begins, and they are not likely to revert to criticism or hostility later if the patient's course worsens.

When the parents speak about their own parents, they do not deny the negative aspects or difficulties in their relationship. Despite the fact that many low-intensity parents endured significant hardships of one kind or another with their parents, they seem to have emerged from their families with a sense of mastery over their experience rather than a sense of depletion from caring for impaired parents. To some extent, the parents in this group appear more mature and integrated, but their individual personality characteristics alone would not explain the difference entirely. Low-intensity parents were not more likely than other parents to have been in individual psychotherapy. Yet, they often seemed to have more ego strength, coping capacity, and personal resiliency.

For all of these reasons, working with low-intensity families in treatment is less taxing than working with the other two types of families. Typically, treatment can be less intense, less frequent, or less lengthy, or all three. In general, we have found that an education-oriented consultation approach to treating these families works well. It is often possible to begin discussing with the parents from the onset of treatment what the therapeutic tasks are and what aspects of the family transactions need to be changed. Simple requests for more or less visiting, for example, are often easy to implement without elaborate discussion or disruptive feelings. Soon after treatment begins the therapist can also encourage the patient to begin expressing his or her needs to the parent. The therapist has less fear that the parents will be narcissistically injured or will act out angry feelings when the patient makes demands or criticizes them.

As with the high-intensity family, the therapist does not have to spend time helping the family members repair or build an attachment. And with low-intensity families the therapist does not have to spend several sessions helping the family members learn how to react less intensely to each other. Bouts of criticism or hostility that occur during intense family discussions are infrequent, and this frees up the family and the therapist to address other issues.

We have identified a number of issues or themes that commonly arise during the treatment of low-intensity families. The case vignettes that follow illuminate some of the treatment issues that emerge in working with the low-intensity family.

Acceptance Versus Idealization
in the Low-Intensity Family

The difference between the idealization typically found in high-intensity families and the balanced acceptance of the other typically found in low-intensity families is illustrated in the following clinical example. Sally was one of the most disturbed patients in our study. She had been hospitalized over a dozen times for her schizophrenic disorder, which she refused to accept. Whenever the patient became stable, she left the hospital, stopped her neuroleptic medication, and relapsed. It was impressive to see how tolerant, patient, and calm her parents, Mr. and Ms. Thomas, could be in the midst of all of this chaos and stress in the family. Mr. and Ms. Thomas visited regularly, and they were never overly emotional or visibly upset. During the family interactions, Ms. Thomas occasionally expressed frustration with her daughter's pattern of denial of her problems. Both parents were supportive of their daughter and tried to reassure her that once she was well, she could get back to her life and do the things she wanted to do, such as go to school.

Ms. Thomas's thoughts and attitudes about her daughter, as expressed in the Five Minute Speech Sample (FMSS), were consistent with her behavior toward Sally:

> Aside from this illness, Sally has always been enthusiastic, outgoing, and talented in many ways. She's been good at school, and had lots of friends. She's got a wonderful sense of humor, and the entire family enjoys it. She makes every situation a happy one. It's been very hard for me to realize she's sick. When she's not sick, she's a wonderful cook, and I admire her, I suppose. We've always gotten along. There's been no friction between us. She doesn't tell me everything she's thinking—no reason she should. Generally, I have very high hopes for my daughter—that she will bring herself through this illness and have a good life ahead.

Note that Ms. Thomas stops short of saying that her daughter will be cured of her severe disturbance. She does not idealize her in a way that suggests denial; rather, she is clearly recognizes the severity of Sally's plight. There is a sense from the passage that Ms. Thomas likes her daughter as a person. And her fantasies about Sally's future life are not clouded with anxiety or doubt, or ambivalence.

Mr. Thomas is also openly fond of Sally, as the following statement indicates:

> From the day she was born, she was a special person because she was such a beautiful baby and such a beautiful little girl. In fact, she's always been special, right up to this very day.

In the family therapy sessions with Sally and her parents, it became clear that Sally had strong desires to deny the fact she that had schizophrenia. Sally concentrated her energies and defenses on getting out of the hospital so that she could get back to her normal life, which meant getting back to her job as an assistant editor. After all, she reasoned, this is what people in her family did: they worked hard and succeeded. Although Sally's father acknowledged that his daughter was seriously disturbed, he nevertheless assumed that at some point she would go back to work and resume a stimulating lifestyle like the one she had had growing up. Mr. and Ms. Thomas did not pressure their daughter. In fact, they were the epitome of moderation and patience. Despite this low-key style, however, the subtle message came through: Sally would recover from this illness and return to a full life.

Although some patients with schizophrenia eventually return to a demanding job after a schizophrenic break, many cannot, and Sally clearly was not one of these people for whom it would be an easily achievable goal. She was completely overwhelmed by the stimulation and pressure of the outside community. Despite protection from neuroleptic medication, she became paranoid and disorganized when she was riding on the subway or dining out. When the paranoia set in, Sally's anxiety escalated and she stopped taking her medication in an effort to regain control. She reasoned that the medication was making her feel less vigilant, less able to defend herself, and, because she was becoming so anxious, that it was not working.

Eventually, the therapist focused this family's treatment on helping the parents accept how profoundly disturbed their daughter was and how vulnerable she remained to psychotic recurrences in the face of stressors such as a return to work. As the parents began to understand and accept these realities, the patient also began to accept them. She got a part-time job that she could tolerate and focused on staying on her medication. She was rehospitalized during the first year out of the study, but the need for rehospitalization gradually diminished after that.

One factor that set the family tone for coping with a disturbed member may have been Sally's father's own experience of dealing with a depressed parent, as reflected in Mr. Thomas's FMSS about his father:

> Early on, I took the role of supporting father and trying to get him through his depression when his sister died unexpectedly. I stuck close to him and didn't get upset myself. And of course, that made us close because he appreciated that.

This experience of coping with a depressed father enabled Mr. Thomas to tolerate dealing with his psychotic daughter, although Sally's problems involved more than riding out a rough period and then returning to life as usual.

Sally had a history of unstable periods in the course of her psychiatric disorder, and these were expected to continue, although in less intense forms. Yet her parents were able to sustain a positive, secure attachment relationship with her, despite the vicissitudes of her illness. This solid attachment base enabled the therapist then to address more problematic issues around roles and boundaries, communication style, and modes of expressing affect.

Parentification as a Mastery Experience in the Low-Intensity Family

Rachel, an adolescent who was decidedly out of control, had run away numerous times from school. She also abused drugs, showed incessant oppositional behavior at home and at school, often sullenly refused to talk, and threw temper tantrums in which she became physically out of control and threatening. Rachel's mother, Ms. Wolf, was a remarkably calm woman who sat in the room with her agitated daughter and never lost control by becoming overly critical or making her daughter feel guilty.

Ms. Wolf's own family life has been difficult. Her alcoholic mother had abdicated parental responsibility when Ms. Wolf was about 7 years old. After that time, Ms. Wolf became the surrogate mother in the house for her two brothers and two sisters. When Ms. Wolf was 16, her mother came home from the hospital after having her last child, walked over to Ms. Wolf, and presented her with the newborn baby. In her FMSS on her mother, Ms. Wolf remarked:

> She didn't want the baby. But she had it. It's kind of sad. And I've been taking care of babies and people's problems ever since. Everybody depends on me. And I can't depend on anybody. It's kind of sad. But then I always thought, Well, maybe that's the way I was meant to be—taking care of everybody.

Ms. Wolf clearly met the *DSM III-R* criteria for dysthymia. A family therapist could easily have focused on helping the mother with her depression. Instead, however, the therapist chose to capitalize on the mother's strengths and counseled her in how to set limits with her daughter and how to resist debating with her daughter about drugs. The therapist was able to count on Ms. Wolf's consistent, warm attachment toward Rachel. Thus, when Ms. Wolf began to confront her daughter and set limits, the therapist could be fairly certain that this would occur in the context of a secure attachment relationship. Rachel's treatment was fairly brief. She left the hospital to return home to live with her mother. After a rather rocky transition, in which Ms. Wolf received telephone crisis counseling in how to manage her daughter, Rachel settled down and attended school. A year later Rachel and her mother were getting along well. Rachel was not using drugs and had not been rehospitalized, and Ms. Wolf was less depressed.

A case with this outcome was not typical in our study. One might expect that, given her own troubled childhood, Ms. Wolf would have had significant difficulties as a parent. The FMSS in which she speaks about her father provides some clues about how Ms. Wolf viewed her family life:

> My father was always there when you needed him. He used to say, "Momma's got problems and there's nothing I can do to help, so we'll just leave her alone." He saw that I was always helping like a mother to the other kids. But he said I should go to school. Later he said it was time for me to have a life of my own. He said I couldn't just keep taking care of the family, that I had to have a life of my own. He was sad a lot, but even when he was sad, he always found time to stop and make me laugh. I know I missed out on my childhood. My mother drank so much. I don't know why she did it. Maybe he understood her better than I did.

One gets the impression here that although the patient's father did not like the mother's drinking, he tolerated it in a way that seemed empathic and caring, from the patient's point of view. Similarly, when Ms. Wolf reflected on why her mother was alcoholic, she did not implicate herself in any way for the mother's problems. Perhaps the father helped to keep the patient free from the web of the mother's alcoholism in a way that left Ms. Wolf burdened, but with a sense of her own efficacy and competence unscathed. In the same vein, perhaps Ms. Wolf carried this template for coping with upsetting and mystifying behavior in a loved one to the situation with her daughter. Instead of becoming angry, anxious, and helpless, she was able to remain calm, empathic, and supportive while her daughter received assistance in stabilizing her behavior.

Perhaps the stable, positive attachment to the father helped buffer Ms. Wolf from the stress she had endured while growing up. In the context of a warm, positive attachment, the father was able to separate out the child's role and protect that to some extent. Perhaps this positive and nonparentified attachment bond with the father, enabled Ms. Wolf to ultimately experience her caretaking role in the family as a mastery experience. In her family of origin, Ms. Wolf clearly functioned as a surrogate parent, but it seems as though this was made explicit by the father as exceptional and temporary. Furthermore, she was not recruited into a surrogate wife's duties or role vis-à-vis the father.

Generosity of Spirit in the Low-Intensity Family

The low-intensity parents exhibited what we called a generosity of spirit—an attitude of reaching out to hold, or tolerate, some aspect of the other person that is difficult or painful to accept. The person does this without a sense of sacrifice or righteousness. Instead, it seems as if it is part of life, part of the way things are in the family, part of one's role as a human being.

Mr. Bach was the father of Karen, age 25, who was schizophrenic. After three hospitalizations, Karen had only partial remission of her symptoms with standard neuroleptic treatment. Mr. Bach was positively attached to his daughter, and he and his wife were committed to helping her develop a life outside of the hospital. He described her this way in his FMSS at the outset of treatment:

> Well, I've always felt very affectionate towards Karen because she had a hard start in life. She was sick as a baby and had trouble with her ears. And she had a lot of anxiety too. We always called her "worrywart" because she worried about everything. But of course that was her nature, and if you're like that, it's very difficult to change. But she did well in school, she made friends. She took a long time to walk, and she had trouble with reading. She had a hard time, but she was a good child.

Mr. Bach grew up with a mother who was diagnosed with schizophrenia. His FMSS about his own parents revealed that his experiences with his own severely disturbed mother may have helped him cope empathically with his daughter's illness. About his mentally ill mother he said:

> She was always a very caring person. She always looked out for my welfare. I was protected, clothed, schooled. She was always available. We traveled a lot, my mother and father and me. I enjoyed their company. The only problem was her mental problem. She had this feeling that she was being manipulated by TV or radio waves—that things were done to us that she had no control over. She thought it was a conspiracy. She accused my father of being involved. And my father put up with this and was hearing it constantly. It got worse with age. It's a shame, because she worked hard all her life, and they saved money, but she can't enjoy life. She can't enjoy life because she has all these preoccupations, and I know they're not real. But she believes they are real. It's been impossible to get her to get help. She doesn't want it.

Notably absent from this FMSS is a focus on the son's deprivations. He did not experience himself as having been deprived by the circumstances of his mother's illness, and he seemed remarkably tolerant and unfrightened of her symptoms. And like many of the other parents in the low-intensity group, he noticed the accepting and tolerant attitude and behavior of the other parent toward the disturbed parent's problematic behavior. Perhaps this man identified with his father and had internalized his father's style of coping with the provocative behavior of his psychotic mother. In the father's FMSS about his own father, this explanation receives some support:

> My father was a very hard working individual. And he was always kind towards me. I always thought of him as quietly suffering my mother's eccentric behavior. And I really couldn't understand it, and I can't understand it now except that they were very close and they did everything together. He was always there for me. One time I was stuck on the freeway at 4 A.M., and I called him and he came and got me and he wasn't angry. He did things out of the ordinary for me. And I appreciated all the things he did for me.

Perhaps Mr. Bach's experience with a father who was consistently emotionally available, supportive, and empathic helped him tolerate a number of personal stresses in life, including not only having a daughter with schizophrenia, but having lost his first wife in a car accident when Karen was 7. In addition, Karen suffered two relapses in the first year after she left the study. Yet Mr. Bach's consistently empathic tone and tolerant attitude never changed. He remained very supportive and committed to his daughter's treatment, and he acknowledged frustration but did not overly or harshly criticize Karen.

However, as is often true in low-intensity families, the family members were so cooperative, empathic, and emotionally available that the therapist assumed that this calm acceptance of the illness and its implications was true also for the patient. Karen's placid smile and nonconfrontational manner in the family meetings led the therapist to conclude that Karen had accepted the fact that she had schizophrenia, that her condition necessitated an indefinite period of taking neuroleptic medication, and that she would have to make major lifestyle changes to survive the disorder's episodic nature.

In actuality, Karen only partially accepted her schizophrenia. She did not fully understand the disorder or its implications, and she did not believe all of the things that her family was saying about her condition. When beginning to recover from a psychotic episode, many schizophrenic patients want to seal over the experience. If the family appears readily available to talk directly about the episode, using medical terminology and their new-found psychoeducational knowledge, the therapist may be tempted to see the patient's quiet, nonconfrontational stance as reflecting consensus with the parents. The fragility of these patients is often obvious to the clinician. Collusion with the patient's denial of what is going on may seem appealing to the clinician, who may fear damaging the patient further by presenting too much difficult information about the disorder. The price for benign neglect here is high, however, because many of these patients unilaterally decide to stop taking their medication shortly after they leave the hospital.

In our experience, patients in these kinds of families often deal better with psychoeducation about their disorder when the family is absent. This strategy permits the patient to face emotionally the material being presented. When the therapist or the parents are "too supportive," they can sometimes prevent the patient from emotionally experiencing the impact of what is being said. Thus, with these families, clinicians must be careful not to judge the patient's perspective about the disorder too favorably because of the parents' high-level responses when interacting with their child.

Curiosity Instead of Anger

In low-intensity families, the family members often express frustration or intense affect in terms of curiosity or lack of understanding, instead of resentment or anger, and they often describe the patient-child as kind. Ms. Miller, the parent in the following FMSS sees her daughter, Becky, a 16-year-old with a diagnosis of borderline personality disorder, as kind, bright, and competent.

> I've always admired Becky. She's able to speak her mind. We've always been close, and she's been able to confide in me. Sometimes she would ask me for advice. When she started having problems she would shut down a little, but generally we've been able to talk. She likes people. She's very kind. Sometimes she's a little impatient. But, we all have that (laughs). She's very bright and has ability but rarely is able to finish things. That's always been hard for her. Sometimes she does things just to get attention. She needs a lot of attention. I'm glad she knows that we aren't going to give up on her.

Similarly, Becky's father depicts his daughter as kind and considerate, and he expresses concern and puzzlement about her reckless behavior.

> Basically, I feel she is a very kind person, very considerate. She gets very emotional at times, and she was physically abusive. But she's very family minded, even though she doesn't sometimes treat her family very well. We're very concerned about her running away; we don't understand why she keeps doing it. We asked her, she said "It's boring at home. It's just exciting to be on the streets." We're concerned about her and we don't understand this. Her self-esteem is low, and she feels like she's not worth anything. We just don't really understand it.

In the family interaction task, these parents talked with Becky in a tone that suggested curiosity. The absence of anger was quite apparent, particularly given the nature of Becky's acting-out behavior.

Mr. Miller: Well, we love you very much and we don't understand why you want to run away. If there is something we could do to help you with the problem, we would be happy to do it.

Becky: I don't think there's anything you can do. Only I could do it. The reason why I've been running away is so I can have freedom.

Mr. Miller: But what about the chances you're taking with it?

Becky: I don't know what to say. I think I learned my lesson this time.

Ms. Miller: What can we do to help you?

Becky: I don't know.

Ms. Miller: It's a serious issue. Everybody has to work under some kind of authority, Becky. That's why we have rules and laws—so that everybody isn't running all over the place doing anything they want.

Mr. Miller: Well, we have to do everything we can to help you, everything we can to protect you from risky behavior. That's what we have to do.

In this interaction the parents' ability to stay close to the issue of their daughter's reckless behavior without either generalizing to a host of other problematic issues or engaging in critical attacks or guilt-inducing comments is noteworthy.

Empathy and a Cooperative Spirit in Problem Solving

One treatment goal for families of patients with a major psychiatric disorder is to increase the family members' empathy and tolerance for the patient's difficulties by providing them with education about the nature of the disorder. In the high-intensity families, parents too readily express a need to be involved and a sense of concern, but clearly exhibit empathy for the patient's plight. In the disconnected families, empathy for the patient and his or her problems, which may be pronounced, is often clouded by other issues or is missing. In our study the low-intensity parents had not had psychotherapy themselves, nor had they had prior education or therapy about their child's illness. We do not fully understand why some of these parents appear to have empathy for their child and to be able to convey it effectively.

In the following FMSS a mother speaks about her schizophrenic son in ways that suggest tolerance, empathy, and a capacity for reflecting on her own role in causing problems for him:

Well, Jack is just a real nice person. I'm upset because he has this disease that he's really not aware of. He wasn't much trouble until he began getting sicker and sicker over the last few years. There was also a lot of turmoil in our house with other kids, and I know that this affected him, too. People were never really settled, and I wasn't aware of a lot of Jack's emotional needs. While he was growing up, he should have had somebody else around besides me. It was difficult because I had to work and I didn't have a lot of time for him. I didn't put a lot of demands on him either. I wish that he were not angry at me for having been instrumental in having him hospitalized. I don't blame anyone. In future years I would like him to understand his illness and accept it and realize there is a lot he can still do even with the illness, and that there will be a lot of people around him who will support him through this.

As this mother's FMSS excerpt shows, she seems to have a developmental time perspective about her son's situation that is not typical of parents in the other two groups. Jack's mother easily moves back and forth from the remote past to the recent past to the current situation and to future goals. More typically, parents have a more cross-sectional time perspective when talking about the patient and their situation with him or her. Many emotions associated with different time periods and perhaps different phases of the disorder are compressed into a single slice of time—the present—and the parent is often flooded with contradictory and inconsistent feelings about the patient and the problems that the illness poses or threatens to pose.

During treatment with these families, clinicians can help by acknowledging this kind of developmental perspective and helping the parents expand and solidify it. By integrating a developmental time perspective into their attitudes and thoughts about the patient, themselves, and all of the problems posed by the illness, the parents can manage more effectively, as well as tolerate and integrate many seemingly contradictory, intense emotions.

The following example from a family interaction task between Jack and his mother, Ms. Eagle, shows how one mother was able to express her empathic attitude and capacity for self-reflection during a face-to-face discussion with her son:

Ms. EAGLE: I often feel I would like to more about you, and what you think and feel, but I'm afraid to intrude. You seem so distant.

JACK: I wish I could confide in you more but I'm always afraid to upset you or tell you things that will make you worry—like when I feel like I'm not going to make itoutside the hospital.

Ms. EAGLE: I know that sometimes I must give you the message that I can't tolerate what you're feeling, so I shut off communication. I so want you to be back in the swing of things that if you give me the message that you're despairing, I can't bear it. I know that's not fair to you, because even though you're doing so much better, you have days when you feel awful inside.

JACK: Right. I can't face that feeling, so I have trouble talking to other people about it, especially to you.

MS. EAGLE: Well, maybe I need to learn to tolerate all of your feelings better, including your awful feelings. I know that it must be frightening to think about leaving the hospital and going back to school, even though you're eager to get on with your life.

JACK: Yes. I wonder if I'm going to be able to make it, and worry that if and when I go back to school, no one will understand what I've been through here, so it's kind of a lonely feeling.

In another discussion task, Ms. Eagle was able to set small, step-by-step goals to help her son solve a problem.

JACK: I know you want me to go back to school and I want to go too, but these discussions make me feel like a failure.

MS. EAGLE: I believe that if you take one step at a time, you'll be able to do it, because there were times when you did so well in school. . . when you were feeling okay.

JACK: Yes, but I have so much trouble finishing assignments, and I always end up feeling overwhelmed by it all

MS. EAGLE: The last time you took a class you did well in the beginning, but then you got frustrated with one assignment and wouldn't go for help. I know that if you take it slowly, and do your assignments every week, you'll make it through. Also, it probably doesn't make sense to take a full load first semester and to take courses in areas where you've done well before, and not try anything too difficult.

JACK: I think that if I could take one or two courses, I wouldn't feel so overwhelmed in the beginning. It's just that I always feel like people expect me to go back full time.

MS. EAGLE: Not necessarily. It's possible to attain the things you want. But you've got to go through the steps, not fly right in like you have in the past.

Conclusion

In many instances we found that low-intensity families responded to family treatment rapidly. They quickly learned and adopted new ways of working with their child and the problems his or her disorder posed for the family. It was not unusual, after a period of stabilized improvement had occurred in the patient, for the clinician not to see the family for a month or so between sessions. A brief phonecall would often be made during the month to touch base and update the parent on any changes in the basic treatment plan, or to alert the parent to impending crises. During the middle and later phases of treatment, the family therapist functioned more as a consultant or coach than a therapist per se. As the psychotherapy work with the patient continued and many times deepened or intensified, this liaison relationship with the family became vital and allowed the individual therapist to consult with the family therapist to intervene periodically and prevent problems from escalating into major crises.

CHAPTER 9

Intergenerational Interviewing and Parent-Child Rapprochement: General Principles

W HILE THE INTERGENERATIONAL family interview is a technique that has been developed and utilized by previous family theorists and therapists, most notably, Boszormenyi-Nagy and Spark (1973), Framo (1992), and Stierlin (1974, 1977), the focus of such interviews in previous work has been on the processes of unbinding homeostatically enmeshed families, rather than on reconnecting unattached or relationally fragmented families. As Stierlin (1977) points out, most refinements of multigenerational family therapy techniques have revolved around binding, or in our system, high-intensity families, because it is often easier to treat families that have a transgenerational bedrock of attachments, regardless of how enmeshed, than to treat families that have a legacy of ruptured or disrupted attachments. Because "primary binding seems an even more difficult therapeutic task than unbinding" (p. 330), we will focus our discussion of the intergenerational interview on techniques with the disconnected family. However, although the intergenerational interview as described in this chapter is usually most appropriate for treatment of disconnected families, the general principles outlined would be, with some modifications perhaps, for any family in which there are severe conflicts around attachment and separation. Since the goal of therapy with disconnected families is to achieve parent-child rapprochement, the crux of the interview is a dyadic session between parent and child, in which the therapist interviews the parent about his or her early attachment experiences in the family of origin, and thereby fosters the development of mutuality and empathy in the dyadic.

The Purpose and Structure of the Interview

The epigenetic model outlined in chapter 2 stipulates that if attachment problems exist, they ought to be addressed first before moving on to other higher-level forms of dysfunction in the family system. Our own clinical experience dictates that when intergenerational interviewing is done well, it can dramatically influence the family because it catalyzes intense emotional reactions among family members that can make them more accessible to each other. Therefore, conducting such interviews during the earlier stages of treatment is usually beneficial, although the optimal time may vary. As is generally true of clinical work, the therapist's timing and good judgment are crucial. We have found, however, that the earlier such sessions occur in the treatment, the better.

At the same time, it is important not to push the family to explore intergenerational issues before they are ready. Some families, particularly those in which the parents have displaced onto the family of procreation unconscious wishes for revenge toward their own parents for real or imagined past hurts and neglect, may become extremely threatened by exploration of family-of-origin issues. Such efforts challenge their mode of adaptation and their family-based defenses so much that they may become disorganized and, hence, may drop out of treatment. With very suspicious or narcissistically fragile parents, the therapist may want to wait several months before suggesting this kind of intervention. Other families who are emotionally ready or perhaps even eager for such an opportunity can begin after two or three sessions.

The intergenerational interview provides a forum in which the parent can disclose and explore without fear the early attachment history with his or her parents. Furthermore, the presence of the child with whom he or she has an impaired attachment provides an opportunity for the child to develop an empathic understanding of the parent's relationship history without the pressure of having to interact directly with the parent. The tone of this interview is set by the therapist, who, above all, is curious and empathic, but also unflinching in catalyzing revelation and exploration of the most painful or difficult aspects of the multigenerational family history. The therapist needs to be able to ask tough questions and to tolerate the painful material that may come up without becoming anxious, short-circuiting the exploration of problematic issues, or coming to a premature resolution or closure before the family has faced and worked through difficult multigenerational material.

First, the patient is asked to sit with the therapist, who talks with the mother or father about personal experiences with his or her own parents. The patient's task is to listen and watch. The focus ought to be on the parents' reactions, rather than the often intense affect that parental revelations or feelings may generate in the patient. This is not the arena for the patient to vent his or her frustrations and complaints, and if the patient begins criticizing the parent or inducing guilt, the therapist firmly blocks this. The task is for the parent to tell his or her story. The sharing of vulnerable, painful, and even traumatic memories is meant to form the basis for a deepened understanding between parent and child, not to serve as a vehicle for solving problems or airing differences. The anxious or volatile parent may very well try to provoke the therapist into a conflictual discussion with the patient around problematic issues as a means of avoiding discussing some painful or difficult aspect of his or her history. The therapist must not succumb to such pressures during this aspect of treatment, because a negative experience in this phase can sometimes result in an emotional retreat by the parent to the safer, less emotionally difficult route of focusing on the patient's difficulties.

The Therapist Models Interest in the Parent's Experience

Many parents and children alike fail to notice a distinction between superficial attention and deeper interest or involvement in the internal world of another. Particularly in severely disturbed families there has often been a radical breakdown in what Daniel Stern (1985) refers to as intersubjective relatedness; that is, the capacity to engage in reciprocal and mutually enriching emotional exchanges with another person. Parents who lack the capacity for intersubjectivity are often completely absorbed by problematic aspects of the disturbed child's behavior or by the child's appearance, talents, or skills (or lack of them), but have little interest in or understanding of the child's inner life, or the world of subjective meanings and intentions, affect, fantasy, and motivation.

Severely disturbed patients whose parents tend either to overreact emotionally or to disengage from them often have learned to adopt a defensive stance in family interactions for fear of being criticized, invalidated, or neglected. Neither parents nor children may feel free to explore with others the subtleties of their experience or the interpersonal implications of their own experiences for the current parent-child relationship. The child may be too much on-guard emotionally to sit back in quiet curiosity, and the parent may have long since given up any hope that the disturbed offspring might be able to empathize with his or her experience. If such is the case, the therapist can help by using a tone of openness and receptivity that contrasts with one of scrutiny and evaluation or defensiveness.

Gathering a multigenerational history in such a context involves a focus not on facts but on the nuances and complexities of the parent's feelings about personal experiences while growing up. Whatever the parent experienced is what counts, not whether what happened or failed to happen was justifiable or wrong.

Exploring Early Attachment Bonds

The following examples are offered as suggestions for how to begin asking questions about the parent's early attachment history with his or her mother and father. Generally speaking, we have found it easier to start with questions about one parent first, finish this series of questions, and then move to the relationship with the other parent.

What was your experience like, growing up with your parents?

What about, specifically, with your mother?

Were you close to your mother?

Was she someone who was able to anticipate your needs? Could you give a specific example of her responsivity or lack of it.

What happened when you were upset or hurt? Could you discuss it with her?

Was she someone who was critical of you? In what ways?

Did you get the sense that she was someone who was interested in you?

Did you get the sense that your mother was in tune with you?

What was missing in your relationship with her?

Were you someone who grew up fast?

Do you remember times when you felt rejected by her?

The Consequences of Suppressed Attachment Needs

Parents who have had to deny or suppress their own attachment needs either because their parents were not emotionally responsive or available, or because they were parentified and grew up in caretaking roles that deprived them of much of their childhood, often are oblivious to the consequences of such experiences. Sometimes a parent gains a sense of mastery; more commonly, however, the parent has buried resentments and unmet yearnings for attachment after a childhood oriented around meeting the attachment needs of self and others.

Thus, suppressed, unmet attachment needs inevitably come up for discussion in these interviews. Descriptions of early attachment experiences often elicit raw, painful feelings, and a skilled therapist will create an atmosphere in which the person feels safe to talk openly about these feelings. John Bowlby (1980) and his followers (Cassidy, in press) have hypothesized that when caretakers respond either inconsistently or minimally to the attachment overtures and needs of their child, the child will adopt a defensive pattern in which feelings are minimized and in which attachment needs are excluded from awareness or denied altogether. Dysfunctional behavioral patterns of attachment then become crystallized into working models that exclude attachment needs from awareness.

Parents whose own attachment longings have been submerged for years may need some help recognizing the consequences of never having had their own yearnings for relatedness adequately met. The original purpose of such attachment patterns and their concomitant working models, in which attachment information is excluded or denied, is to protect the individual from the pain associated with the early experiences of rejection, loss, and neglect. However, before these original painful feelings can be exhumed, the parent often expresses anxiety, contempt, resentment, and even disgust for their child's dependency longings. Sometimes a parent attempts to ward off painful feelings by projecting the attachment needs and dependent feelings onto the child ("He is so needy, but it's time for him to grow up!"). Alternatively, the parent may be blind to the child's need to be dependent ("He's old enough to do this on his own now. He should be out there doing it, without my help!").

The parent also often maintains the defensive stance of denying any attachment needs or related feelings. Indeed, Arietta Slade (1993) has recently commented that adults who tend to be dismissing of attachment (that is, tend to belittle the importance of attachment experiences in their lives) also often express contempt and disgust in the face of others' attachment strivings. Slade interprets such reactions as an indication of the

> tremendous need dismissing people have to create distance from their feelings. . . . Contempt and disgust are used to create distance between oneself and another. . . . They are also rather cold and contained ways of expressing rage. . . . Belittling and mocking the feelings of others is a strategy common to dismissing individuals, who keep themselves far away from the messy world of emotions. (p. 4)

When the therapist senses that further exploration will be pointless and may even bring on more resistance, he or she can look for alternative words that the parent can tolerate, such as "frustration" or "always having to be on your toes." These parents may have difficulty recognizing both their own and their children's needs, and many times they do not even recognize their own lack of understanding. Instead, they feel martyred or depleted. The parent may have limited tolerance for the child's problems, and he or she often has inappropriate expectations of self-sufficiency and responsibility for the child.

When the attachment needs are defensively excluded and denied, the therapist must not only make the parent aware of them but also explore empathically with the parent and the child the origins of these attitudes. After seeing how he or she came to have such blind spots or distorted ideas, the parent can develop some compassion for himself or herself and for the disturbed child, as well as an appreciation for the generational repetition involved in the parent's inability to tolerate the burdens of caring for a disturbed child. Such a multigenerational perspective on the problem then permits the development of compensatory relational patterns that permit both the parent and the child to express attachment-related needs and feelings.

Case Example 1: Disguised Attachment Longings

Jane and her mother, Ms. Stein, came to the attention of the mental health system when Jane, at the age of 28, suffered a major depressive episode that led to a brief inpatient hospitalization and that remitted only partially with medication. Ms. Stein was raised by two narcissistic parents, both of whom were accomplished, successful, professionals who rarely had time to spend with her. Ms. Stein spent most of her own childhood mastering new talents and skills in order to keep her parents interested in her. By the time Ms. Stein was 30, she was remarkably self-sufficient, opinionated, and known by her friends and husband as having a sharp tongue. Jane recalls her mother always having been critical, aloof, and unloving. Ms. Stein remains a profoundly insecure person, and she feels inadequate and tentative as a mother. Jane's capacity to evoke feelings of inadequacy and inferiority in her mother made Ms. Stein feel alternately idealizing and rageful toward her daughter.

During Jane's brief inpatient stay, the family therapist had done a brief family assessment, which consisted of several sessions with Jane and her mother. Struck by the intense negative feelings between this mother and daughter—particularly the high level of criticism and guilt-inducing remarks—the family therapist had recommended family treatment for Jane and her extended family, including her mother. However, a previous trial of family therapy aimed at helping the family learn how to resolve conflict and to solve problems had not decreased the intense hostility and bitterness that characterized the mother-daughter dyad. Subsequently, Jane and her family embarked on another trial of family treatment, which utilized the multigenerational family assessment model described in the foregoing chapters.

The initial multigenerational family assessment indicated that this was a typical disconnected family in which intrusiveness and criticism in the parent-child relationship masked a deep emotional estrangement. It quickly became apparent that Ms. Stein felt rejected by her daughter, as she had by her own mother. Ms. Stein had hoped to develop a close mother-daughter relationship with Jane, in part, to compensate for what she had never experienced with her own mother. But she was unable to express this desire directly, and instead expressed it in terms of vague demands and expectations that Jane felt she could never meet. Then Jane, feeling that she had been rejected, spurned her mother. The more Ms. Stein would push and try to get Jane to confide in her or tell her intimate things, the more Jane would withdraw and evade her mother.

Jane felt sure that her mother would disappoint her, and Ms. Stein felt the same about her daughter. These views represented a projection of blame for their own inadequacies. Ms. Stein could not reveal to Jane any sadness or sense of loss about the lack of intimacy and trust either in her relationship with Jane or in her relationship with her own mother. Instead, she was defensive and concerned with appearing strong, in control, and competent. Feelings of dependency evoked so much shame and self-contempt in Ms. Stein, that she presented herself as someone who had no needs. In turn, Jane experienced her mother as someone to be tolerated at best, and at worst, as an intrusive, critical person who needed to be warded off. Jane experienced her mother as wanting to get closer to her in order to criticize her or find fault, and she felt that her mother was controlling and guilt-inducing.

The family therapist was able to help Jane see beyond her mother's surface characteristics. After a series of five intergenerational interviews, Jane was gradually able to see that at the core, her mother had felt excluded, emotionally neglected, and unloved by her own mother and, in turn, felt the same about Jane. Also, Jane became aware that her mother, unable to express these feelings directly, reverted to intrusive, critical behaviors and remarks to engage Jane and to punish her for not being able to repair her mother's history. The recognition of this dynamic enabled Jane to be more tolerant and forgiving of her mother's behavior, as well as to begin to diffuse it by changing her own responses. Whenever her mother began doing or saying things that enraged her, Jane looked through the behavior and saw how her mother might be feeling left out and excluded. Jane began reinterpreting her mother's sarcasm as reflecting insecurity; and instead of challenging her mother about personal issues or limitations, Jane learned to accept them and to calibrate her own responses so that the negative interactional pattern could be transformed into a more authentic dialogue.

The therapist encouraged Jane to explore with her mother in the family sessions exactly how her mother was feeling. She also helped Jane to lower her expectations about how rapidly or smoothly the work would proceed. When Ms. Stein would retreat and become defensive about a remark Jane made, the therapist would help Jane understand that such defensive maneuvers represented her mother's attempts at self-protection. Understanding that her mother lashed out at her in order to protect herself, rather than to hurt Jane, enabled Jane to gradually develop some tolerance for her mother's attitudes.

The family repeatedly threatened to drop out of family therapy, especially as the most severe and debilitating symptoms of Jane's depression disappeared and she began to resume her usual level of functioning. The therapist was able to help keep the treatment alive by working with Jane's fears that nothing would ever change or that trying to have a relationship with her mother was impossible. Gradually, Ms. Stein and Jane began going out for lunch. The therapist contracted with them that they would not discuss their relationship or their difficulties with each other while on these outings. At first the lunches were extremely tense and superficial, but the therapist reassured Jane that such contact was indeed sufficient. After several months and several such outings, Jane and her mother began to enjoy each other, and a new phase of relationship development began. This involved the gradual strengthening of an attachment bond that had been negatively tinged. During this phase of the work the therapist provided an important function of helping Jane to modulate both the actual development of the relationship—that is, to prevent Jane from connecting very intensely, as was her usual pattern—and her expectations of what was going to come next. In individual treatment, Jane was proceeding with an exploration of her own development, self-worth, and desires for the future, which helped her both to separate from her mother and to begin a more differentiated relationship with her.

As the treatment continued, a shift occurred whereby Jane began to address problems she was having with her own daughter. Jane was painfully aware of how she was recapitulating with her oldest daughter, 8-year-old Elsa, issues from her own relationship with her mother. Elsa was an unhappy child, like Jane had been, and Jane found it difficult to get close to her. She attributed to her daughter many of the traits she had assigned to her mother—rigid, stubborn, emotionally withdrawn, and remote. Because of the work Jane had done with her own mother, however, her work on her relationship with her daughter went rather smoothly and quickly.

Discovering the Parental Triggers for Emotional Reactivity

After two or three sessions with the parent and the child, the therapist will have identified the two or three triggers that catalyze negative affective displays in the parent-child dyad. It is critical for the therapist to spend time identifying the intergenerational aspects of these triggers and exploring in depth the subtleties of how they get activated for the parent. The central goal here is to identify those triggers that activate unresolved representations in the parent. Once the therapist has identified the triggers and understands how they activate key representational structures in the parent, he or she can recognize instantly when these issues begin to get enacted in a cycle of projection that leads to maladaptive parent-child interactional patterns. The therapist can then intervene in the session and help the parent and the child understand the process of projection itself, interrupt it, and assess what is really going on—a problem generated solely by the child, or an unresolved issue within the parent that is being activated by the child's irritating or annoying behavior. Perhaps an example of this process is the best way to illustrate how this works.

In the case just presented, Ms. Stein, Jane's mother, was an accomplished and self-sufficient woman. As a single parent, she had raised three children for most of their lives, and she had simultaneously developed a new career for herself as well. She was quite successful in her career in advertising, an accomplishment that Jane admired. However, Jane was openly bitter and saddened by her relationship with her mother, and during an initial consultation, she wept profusely when she spoke of the years she felt "completely alone" and of the incessant criticism she received from her mother about nearly everything she did. One area that was especially sensitive for Jane was her relationship with Elsa, which reminded her of her relationship with her own mother. Ms. Stein believed that Jane was too harsh with her granddaughter, that Jane did not understand Elsa, and that Jane was verbally abusive to Elsa (in the same way that Ms. Stein had been toward Jane).

Ms. Stein was openly reluctant to participate in family treatment. She felt things were hopeless with Jane, whom she saw as an insensitive, selfish girl who hated her mother. Ms. Stein had agreed to a brief period of family therapy only because her daughter was depressed and sometimes suicidal, and she drank heavily.

During an intergenerational interview with Ms. Stein about her history as a young wife and mother, she revealed that at age 18 she was confronted with an unplanned pregnancy. Despite apprehensions that she might not be ready, she went ahead and had the baby. Her husband became ill with terminal cancer 5 months after the baby was born. Ms. Stein went to stay with her parents for a month during this time, because she felt terribly inadequate about her ability to mother Jane. Ms. Stein felt criticized but was also secretly pleased that she had a break from child care and could resume working while her mother struggled with child-care duties. Ms. Stein began to feel that her mother was taking over and surpassing her in the care and raising of Jane, whom Ms. Stein came to associate with these negative feelings and with a sense of guilt.

When Jane became a teenager, she rebelled and became antagonistic with her mother. She reminded her mother about how much time she, Ms. Stein, had been away from home because of work, and about how Ms. Stein had expected her own mother to care for Jane. When Ms. Stein tried to explain her actions, Jane became sarcastic and hostile. Jane began acting out, becoming openly rebellious and disrespectful. Each of them became angry and resentful of the other.

In later years, certain expressions on Jane's face or certain tones of voice could evoke strong guilt feelings in Ms. Stein. These guilt feelings generated self-contempt in Ms. Stein because she felt inadequate as a mother. After all, she reasoned privately, a competent, loving mother would never have raised a child as angry and belligerent as Jane.

Ms. Stein described herself as the special one in her own family. She was favored over both of her brothers by both parents and usually had her way. She often set her own rules in the family home. She was proud of her ability to please her parents; it meant she was competent, able to cope, and a winner. Ms. Stein studied music and dance, and she glowed as she spoke about her numerous childhood accomplishments. However, she had more difficulty talking about the emotional side of life with her parents. She quietly described her father as easier to get along with than her mother. She denied any feelings of sadness or neglect when she spoke about her mother, but her face darkened when she spoke, and her voice became soft and distant. The Five Minute Speech Sample (FMSS) data indicated that on a conscious level, Ms. Stein idealized her mother and actively resented any suggestion that her mother was anything less than an ideal mother.

One of Ms. Stein's triggers was the sight of Jane crying. This evoked unconscious memories of her own sadness regarding her mother's emotional distance. When Jane cried, Ms. Stein became argumentative and hostile, primarily as a defense against the unmet dependent longings she still had, but secretly despised. When Ms. Stein would stiffen and become angry at her daughter, Jane in turn would lash out at her mother about how she was "always so critical." Ms. Stein would then feel vindicated because her daughter was showing her selfish, ungrateful, disrespectful side. And so on.

A second trigger for Ms. Stein occurred when Jane would indicate during a conversation that she did not want to discuss some issue, or that she was reluctant to share some piece of information with her mother. This enraged Ms. Stein because it reminded her of childhood feelings of never belonging, never fitting in. Although she had felt privileged in her house in terms of feeling special, her mother or father had had little interest in spending special time with her. Her mother never had private mother-daughter talks with her. In fact, Ms. Stein could not recall her mother ever sitting down with her and talking about how she herself felt about anything. Ms. Stein's mother was aloof and concerned with how Ms. Stein performed in her school, dance, and dramatic arts activities. Ms. Stein grew up being strong, a "fighter" of sorts, someone who prided herself on surviving the struggle, a person who did not make too many emotional demands on anyone. In fact, she was a woman who really did not have too many emotional needs. Or so she thought, until Jane evoked them in her.

When Jane and her mother talked, the therapist noticed when Ms. Stein's triggers would get activated and intervened by making this process conscious and visible for both the mother and the daughter. Gradually, as treatment progressed, both of them became more adept at recognizing this process as it began, and then stopping and pausing to reflect on what might be going on inside of them besides the surface issue being discussed. Additionally, Ms. Stein was unable to respond to Jane in a fully parental and caring manner because she felt that her own mother had favored Jane over her, and had provided Jane with the love, attention, and genuine acceptance that she (Ms. Stein) had never experienced. Hence she perceived Jane more as a rival for her own mother's affection than as a child who needed her total unconditional caring.

Some of the more common emotional reactions parents have when intergenerational issues are activated are the following:

- becoming icy or shutting down emotionally
- becoming defensive
- becoming rigid
- becoming anxious and intrusive
- becoming demanding
- becoming critical

Common Intergenerational Triggers
for Parents' Negative Affect

The following represent some of the common triggers that parents have articulated and that we have observed as clinicians during family treatment:

- feelings of inadequacy, particularly around parenting roles
- recollections of unmet yearnings for attachment
- memories of not belonging, feeling left out, or ignored
- memories of feeling powerless to get one's needs met
- facial expressions that reflect neglect and dislike
- voice tone that expresses disapproval, impatience, or rejection
- physical characteristics of the patient that remind the parent of a primary object
- dyadic interaction patterns that reproduce old negative relational patterns
- feelings of loss
- complaints of feeling bored by the patient

Although similar triggers probably exist for the child, these are not the focus of treatment, as our assumption is that the force or intensity of intractable criticism and negative affect in the parent toward the child devolves from unresolved issues in the previous generation. Hence, our treatment model stipulates that we focus our attention on the source of the disappointment, resentment, or anger that drives the parent to express criticism, hostility, or intrusiveness toward the child. This is not to say that the child never does or says irritating or provocative things. Rather, however, we are addressing the parent's inability to cope with these things in nondestructive ways. Later, after the parent and child have begun to consolidate a more positive attachment bond, the ways in which their communication skills need improvement can be addressed.

The effectiveness of intergenerational interviewing necessitates that the family therapist be sensitive to the impact of parental revelations on the severely disturbed adolescent or young adult, titrating the degree of emotional stimulation and monitoring the patient's reactions carefully so that he or she is not unduly or traumatically burdened by the parent's feelings. In addition, it is often advisable, particularly with severely disturbed adolescent patients, for the family therapist to work closely with the patient's individual therapist during the intergenerational interviewing phase of treatment in order to monitor shifts in sense of self and parental objects that may occur as a result of the intergenerational interview process. In any case, intergenerational interviewing is often only the beginning of a long process of continually working through on increasingly deeper levels, often in both the individual and family therapy contexts, the multigenerational dynamic conflicts and relational deficits that have contributed to the maladaptive interactional patterns between the parents and the disturbed child. Especially in situations where there is no coexisting individual psychotherapy, the family therapist must review again and again the ways in which intergenerational patterns have been projected into and deformed the current parent-child interaction.

The Therapist as a Container of the Affect

The therapist in the intergenerational interview functions as a container for the affect in the family—for the parent's affect as well as the patient's—and in so doing creates a holding environment that enables the family to express and explore a range of primitive and difficult feelings and attitudes (Levine & Wilson, 1985). The therapist must not overreact to the material being presented by the parent and must maintain a stance balanced between the parent and the patient, without overidentifying with either. The therapist needs to maintain a neutral position and react empathetically while also confronting the patient and the parent when appropriate. Such a neutral stance models for the severely disturbed patient the capacity to experience the affect of the moment in ways that are not overwhelming or that hinder the flow of the parent's story. The patient who cannot do this on his or her own borrows the ego strength, so to speak, from the therapist. Thus, the patient can reflect on what is being said, as well as take in what is being said with minimal defensiveness or distortion and integrate it into his or her own mental representation, or internal working model, of daily parent-child transactions.

The therapist employs strategies such as the following to interact with the parent while the parent discusses the difficulties he or she had while growing up: asking probing but gentle questions to draw the parent out gradually, expressing curiosity and empathy for the parent's plight, and bringing the discussion to an end without coming to premature resolutions or summary statements. Many patients reported to us that they learned a great deal from these interviews about how to talk to their parents without the parent becoming angry or withdrawing from the discussion.

The Development of a Parent-Child Rapprochement

As the patient in the disconnected family begins to enter a phase of exploring possibilities for connecting with a previously emotionally estranged parent, he or she may go through protracted periods of feeling very unstable, shaky, and agitated. The patient in these situations often appears blasé and defensive, as if expecting just one more disappointment. However, if the patient feels neglected or emotionally damaged in some way, he or she may express intense anger.

If some genuine closeness—however limited—with the parent begins to develop, the patient may become extremely anxious. In this situation, the individual therapist can anticipate this and help the patient tolerate the anxiety and refrain from acting in ways that might jeopardize the growing attachment with the parent. For example, the patient may feel tempted to cancel an impending play-task date with the parent because he or she fears another major disappointment. Or the patient may pressure the parent into a more intense, prolonged visit, against the therapist's instructions, as a means of sabotaging the treatment. Anticipating this anxiety and helping the patient talk about it before it actually happens can help the patient get through this difficult period.

Structurally, what may be occurring during this phase of treatment is that the patient does not yet have a consistent or coherent internal working model of the attachment figures. That is, he or she may not yet have a working model of attachment that fortifies the expectation of a stable, consistent, caring presence. During the period of carrying out play tasks, the patient may experience transient states during which he or she feels connected to the parent, but these may be unstable, tenuous states. As the treatment progresses and the members of the dyad continue to interact in ways that are mutually gratifying and reciprocal, if not totally conflict free, the representation of the parent may gradually begin to take shape, and then solidify. The therapist can assist in this process by helping the patient avoid idealizing the parent, developing unrealistic expectations of the parent, and engaging in other potentially disappointing maneuvers.

The therapist provides a holding environment or container for the counterpoint development not only of the patient's representation of the parents but also of the family members' real-life relationship. The representation of the parental attachment bond is targeted fairly directly in this approach to treatment. The therapist comments on the patient's evolving descriptions of the parent—for example, "Maybe your mother is really someone who wants to be included in your life" or, "Perhaps your father is not very good at showing affection when he feels inadequate as a father" or, "Perhaps your mother has no clue how to be warm toward you because nobody was with her." As the real relationship between the parent and child begins to change, a parallel shift often occurs in the internal representational world. In the next section the ways in which these shifts in representations and patterns of relating may occur are discussed.

A Shifting Dialectic

In virtually all forms of psychodynamically oriented individual treatment the therapist facilitates the development or modification of representations in the patient's internal world. For example, aspects of the therapeutic relationship, especially the convergence of gratifying involvement and experienced incompatibilities, together with well-timed interpretations will catalyze the development of more integrated, cohesive, and differentiated internal images of the parental objects (Blatt & Behrends, 1987). Such modifications of the representational world typically take place in the context of a therapeutic transference relationship that develops gradually between the patient and the individual psychotherapist. The patient relates to the therapist as a professional, as a parental object, and as a person. The blending and gradual integration of these aspects results in the internalization of the new object (the therapist) and of the functions that the new object carries out for the patient, such as nurturance, soothing, self-reflectiveness, and acceptance (Blatt & Behrends, 1987).

The points just made necessarily represent an oversimplification of the extremely complex process of shifts in the representational world of the patient that occurs in individual psychodynamic psychotherapy. Until recently, family therapists have overlooked the significance of such shifts in attachment representations. The family treatment approach outlined here is one of the first to emphasize that similar shifts in the attachment representations may be occurring in the family arena. The family therapist may be facilitating an ongoing dialectic between such internal shifts in working models of attachment and the ongoing interpersonal transactions in the family.

In such a treatment model, the therapist creates a forum in which representations are targeted, and in which shifts in such representations may be expressed and explored as family members try out new images of each other. The therapist supports and fosters this constant dialectic between the internal world of attachment representations and the actual family transactions in many ways.

We want to emphasize that we do not hypothesize nor observe in our clinical practice a one-to-one correspondence between changes in the actual parent-child rapport and shifts in the representations of the parents. Indeed, it is important to recollect that internalization of the self in relation to attachment figures devolves from a matrix of both actual parent-child transactions and the internal world of fantasy, drive, wish, and affect that is evoked both through such transactions and through the press of maturation (for example, shifts in psychosexual stages and in stages of separation-individuation). In addition, with severely disturbed patients the internal representational world is often characterized by polarized, unintegrated, phantasmagoric, and primitive images of the self and significant others that bear little correspondence to the actual parental figures (Kernberg, 1975, 1980). However, regardless of how primitive and polarized the parental representations may be, it is thought that reviewing the parent's own life history contextualizes the current parent-child relationship in the flux of generations, and thus provides an opportunity for the patient to recognize the extent to which he or she may hold distorted or exaggerated images of the parent, whose shortcomings as a parent might in turn reflect his or her own past experiences. The following case example further illustrates how this process may occur.

Case Example 2: Changes in the Parental Attachment Representations

Brian was admitted to the hospital after he became increasingly out of control. One of his friends informed the family that Brian had purchased a gun and that he was talking about shooting his parents. He was persuaded to enter the hospital. At admission, he was disorganized and emotionally volatile, but he soon collapsed into a depressed, hopeless stance and complained that he felt dead and empty inside. This was Brian's fourth psychiatric admission, and he felt bitter, angry, and hopeless about his ability to live a stable or productive life.

When Brian was 5, his parents divorced and he went to live with his mother in Utah. Brian's eyes would glaze over when he talked about his life with her. Brian's mother was a religious fanatic of sorts who often left him alone or with strangers while she attended religious events. She would often not feed him for several days, and when she would take care of him, she would often be preoccupied with her own religious concerns. Nonetheless, Brian was very attached to her, and when she sent him away at age 11 to live with his father in Rhode Island so that she could devote herself to her religious sect, he was devastated.

Brian felt neglected by his busy father, with whom he had only sporadic and largely unsatisfactory contact after his parents' divorce. In addition, Brian's father had recently started a new business and had remarried when Brian first came to live with him, and Brian inevitably felt left out of his father's busy life and began to act out in increasingly drastic ways as he grew older, engaging in drug and alcohol abuse, truancy, and vandalism to gain parental attention. These behaviors led to further rejection and opprobrium on the part of Mr. James, and Brian began to perceive his father as a manipulative, critical person who did not care about him. When first hospitalized, Brian expressed the conviction that he was in the hospital because of his parents, particularly because of his father, whom he described as abusive, cold, and cruel toward him.

Initially, Brian refused to meet with his father for family therapy sessions, but he did allow the therapist to meet with his father. Brian had not seen his father in several months. Mr. James told the therapist that he in fact had been a good father and that his son's problems were due to a neglectful and inadequate mother.

Brian was unable to sustain close friendships because he would become unrealistically demanding and infantile in relationships with others. He was also easily frightened by his own overwhelming needs, which realization would then cause him to withdraw from others. He avoided most social contacts and spent a good deal of time listening to heavy metal music. The only strong feeling that Brian was aware of or able to articulate was rage, and even this was expressed in an inchoate and largely preverbal way. He related in a sullen, angry, menacing manner most of the time, driving away potential friends as well as therapists. In fact, Brian's rage served to protect him from his underlying desires for and fears of interpersonal contact.

The family treatment in this case was focused on Brian and his father. It took several weeks of overt persuasion to get Brian to agree to a family meeting. Mr. James was reluctant as well, and he asked the same questions of the therapist that Brian did—"What is the point? What good will dredging up the past do? What good will possibly come out of this?"

Whereas Brian's defensive style was organized around hostile bravado and rejection of his father, his father's tendency was to be equally uninterested, but in a cool, aloof way. Initially, he came across as calm, rational, uninterested, and overcontrolled. Both of them were afraid to admit that they wanted more of a relationship.

In the first family meeting Brian began to accuse his father, in a tone that was overtly hostile and angry, of rejecting and neglecting him. Mr. James in turn expressed contempt for his son's neediness and disgust about his unruly and unlawful behavior. The therapist immediately intervened and told Mr. James that he knew how what feelings must be arising from Brian's intense attacks. The therapist said that Brian's anger had confused him at first because he thought it meant that Brian did not have any positive feelings at all—that he was all anger and hostility. The therapist said he came to realize, however, that Brian talked like this whenever he felt any strong emotion of any kind, and the therapist suggested somewhat indirectly that the father might consider not reacting to this anger and that he might examine the sources of his own contempt toward Brian. Although furious about his father's contemptuous remarks, Brian stayed in the room because he felt some trust in the therapist, whom he had come to experience as a person he could count on as accepting and available.

Brian's level of anxiety about contacting his father was so intense that the therapist decided to pace the treatment for every other week. This worked well because it gave the patient a significant period of time after each session to integrate the events of the previous session and to experience a break from the emotional intensity. These breaks helped Brian tolerate and metabolize on an internal level problematic issues that were emerging in the family treatment. As Brian began to realize that he could have a more positive relationship with his father, his defensive structure of rigid, walled-off anger began to weaken. Similarly, Brian's father began to examine the ways in which his contempt for and aloofness from Brian devolved from his feelings about his own alcoholic father, who had drained the family's emotional and financial resources. At this juncture, a critical element in the treatment was the therapist's active encouragement of the development of new relational patterns. The therapist began to help Brian develop a new sense of himself as a young man whocould verbalize and share his feelings, instead of encouraging him to keep his distance from his father, to intellectualize about the experience, and so on.

Before each of the subsequent meetings Brian would become intensely anxious and would pressure the therapist to cancel the meeting. The therapist would resist these pressures and would tell him that he should wait and think it over first before canceling. Inevitably, this resulted in the session being carried out as planned. Many of the ensuing father-son meetings were emotionally intense. Brian was capable of rapidly escalating rage, and his father was quick to criticize. Brian's father could not understand why his son was so angry with him. In Mr. James's view, it was his ex-wife who emotionally abused Brian, so he was baffled by Brian's sullen, demanding, and bitter stance toward him.

Of course, Brian longed for a deeper connection with his father but felt helpless to make this happen. The therapist understood that Brian and his

father were at cross-purposes: Brian was totally unable to foster a relationship with his father because he overwhelmed and immobilized him with
his overt rage, whereas Mr. James was almost incapable of expressing such
rage directly, and he could not tolerate his son's affect. Mr. James had been
raised by two alcoholic parents who had provided little in the way of
guidance or caretaking, and consequently he had little understanding of
how to be a parent. He had no idea how to respond to his son's feelings,
and he felt helpless and powerless whenever his son vented negative
affects. The therapist's crucial role in this treatment was to help the father,
in pari passu, accept, cope with, and integrate Brian's rage as it came up
intermittently throughout the initial sessions of family treatment.

Because Brian was shy and introverted by nature, having a busy, aloof,
and emotionally unavailable father was traumatic for him, and traumatic
in a chronic way. As treatment progressed, Brian reluctantly began to see
that, in fact, his father cared for him in ways that he had been unaware of.
His father acknowledged regret at having been closed off to Brian's feelings as a child. During the intergenerational interview, Mr. James began to
realize that he never felt truly cared for by his own parents, especially by
his alcoholic father. He came to recognize that all of his life, he had sealed
off the part of him that was hurt by his father in order to avoid the pain of
recollecting the early experiences of neglect. As a father, he had turned to
focusing on Brian's problematic behaviors instead of Brian's feelings. As
he reflected on his mistakes with his son, Mr. James commented on
how he had believed that his emotionless demeanor was appropriate for
having a son, because men were not supposed to show affect anyway. As
an angry young adult, Brian began to challenge his father's belief that he
was such a competent father. Instead, Brian's hostile withdrawal evoked
feelings of inadequacy in his father, and these feelings ignited painful
remembrances of his fruitless efforts to gain his own father's interest and
attention. As treatment continued, Brian's father gradually became less
contemptuous of his son's emotional needs.

After the sixth meeting, Brian and his father began to go on walks
together. The family work continued, and they gradually began to build a
father-son relationship. The therapist insisted that they do this very
slowly. Both Brian and his father were probably relieved about this,
because each was terrified of failure and rejection. At this point the individual therapy began to focus on other issues such as Brian's self-sabotag-
ing behavior with peers. Discussion of Brian's relationship with his
mother was postponed until much later. The therapist also worked with
Brian to develop his new and very shaky sense of self, which included seeing himself as a man with feelings and desires, a man who wanted things

from people and who could trust another human being. Brian also began to modify his representation of his father in parallel ways, as one who is trustworthy, caring, and emotionally available.

Extending the Intergenerational Interview

After helping the patient work through the relationship with the parent from whom he or she is estranged, the therapist can expand the work by exploring the patient's experience with the other parent. For many parents the relationship with the same-sex parent is particularly significant, but the relationship with the opposite-sex parent is usually also very important. In some cases the therapist may want to involve another generation and bring grandparents into the family therapy.

Another strategy is to focus on the sons' or daughters' relationships with their own children vis-à-vis the attachment issues with their own mothers or fathers. This is particularly valuable for assisting parents in breaking the chain of negative relationships between parent and child that often occurs in disconnected families.

When these interviews are carried out in depth, the results are often powerful in terms of changing the quality of the family's affectional ties. The intergenerational interview provides the matrix for the development of revised representations of parent figures. For many severely disturbed patients, the experience of perceiving parental figures as vulnerable vis-à-vis their own parents may modify internal working models of attachment in ways that profoundly influence the individual's perception of and experience of the self and others. Rather than perceiving the self as unworthy and the parent as all-powerful and rejecting, the disturbed patient may gradually begin to perceive that the parent's rejecting behaviors stem from his or her own sense of unworthiness and neglect vis-à-vis his or her own parents. Such a perception may loosen rigid defenses and revise maladaptive relational patterns. The patient may begin to make alternative attributions of intent to the parent's remarks and behaviors. Most important, the patient may recognize that the parent's experience was indeed so painful that he or she could only cope with it by recreating such a disturbed pattern of relating in the family of procreation. In the case of Brian, his father's aloofness came to be seen as inadvertent ineptness stemming from his own lack of adequate fathering by an alcoholic father, rather than as a conscious rejection.

A Transitional Space

In families with pronounced attachment problems, the patient may look back over his or her life and feel dissatisfied, disappointed, or angry about perceived mild neglect or lack of interest from a parent. In some cases the patient may have experienced abuse, incessant criticism, or overt rejection. Often the patient is resentful, afraid to have any desire, not hopeful, suspicious, negativistic, and afraid. So how do we understand the change that we observe?

From the clinician's perspective, we can view the patient as developmentally arrested, damaged, or unfinished. In some cases we may view the patient as strong-willed, courageous, and sensitive; and we may see a capacity for growth, for positive change. In adolescents and adults with borderline personality disorder this underlying strength can be covered underneath layers of hostility, labile moods, irritability, demandingness, and infantile behavior. When family treatment works well, it constitutes a transitional space for the patient during the weeks or (more commonly) months while a new relationship with a previously estranged parent is being forged. This space contains the volatility of the patient and his or her internal world as it begins to shift and change. Simultaneously, the therapist contains the anxiety and other emotions that emerge in family members as connections between people shift and begin to develop along new pathways.

How does one create a holding environment or transitional space for the patient's new self to develop? Limiting expectations plays a very important role. In Brian's case, the therapist explored and assessed the potential for a relatively healthy attachment to develop between Brian and his father. The therapist then set very small, very simple goals for the work. Initially the goal was merely to have Brian and his father develop a civil relationship so that they could be in the same room together for an hour without fighting. This achievement, which was held out to be the mark of success, generated good feelings between Brian and his father, and helped to take the place of feelings of suspiciousness, uneasiness, and resentment. It gave them confidence that each could interact with the other in ways that were mutually gratifying and enriching. Most important, it allowed the patient and the parent to be themselves without any pressure to perform. Brian and his father were encouraged to just "hang out" together regularly over time. Here, the therapist worked on the assumption that nature would take its course. When an attachment bond begins to become consolidated, the therapist very soon becomes less important in family. He or she begins to take on new roles and functions that have to do with higher-level interventions. It is àt this point, for example, that work with communication skills might become the focus of treatment.

Priorities

In our approach the therapeutic priorities are organized around a down-to-earth assessment of the patient's reality in his or her family. If we ascertain that the parent cannot or will not reconnect with his or her child, then we help the patient to understand this, mourn the loss, and move on. If the parent is willing, hesitant, or ambivalent, however, then this possibility of rapprochement and reconnection becomes the priority.

In concrete terms, this means that the therapist, for example, makes the scheduling of parent-child activities or contacts a priority, thereby conveying a powerful message to the family about priorities. The therapist confronts the patient when he or she avoids discussing some important aspect of the family work. Rather than actively pushing for reconnection, the therapist is supportive of the patient's *effort* to explore the possibilities for a relationship with the parent. The patient is encouraged and helped to explore actively the *possibility* of developing a positive attachment with the parent. The therapist teaches patience, slow and easy steps, lowered expectations, and ways to control boundaries and affect in the relationship.

A New Template for Affective Relating

At some point we have to ask, Why would a parent with unresolved attachment issues in the family of origin keep interacting with a child in the same repetitive negative patterns, when no gratification ensues? Fred Pine, (1989) in his analysis of the tendency to repeat (Freud, 1955), argues that there is a universal tendency to actively repeat old internalized object relations, as they were experienced. Further, Pine contends that cumulatively, such object relational patterns have the slowly accruing quality of disturbing, irritating trauma. This "strain" trauma (in contrast to "shock" trauma) accumulates throughout life, particularly because of distressing familial relationships for the child. The person makes repeated efforts to master these archaic passive experiences by turning them into active ones—either by doing things to others or doing things to himself or herself. The "pleasure" of such efforts derives from repeating the same behaviors that are irritant-level traumas or worse, so as to rid the person of the sense of being in the passive position. The "goodness" or "badness" of such efforts, he argues, is not for the outsider to judge, because these "are the 'pleasures' of attachment to the only parents one has had, and in this sense pleasurable whether 'objectively' built around apparently good or apparently bad experience" (p. 39). Pine sees this repetition in the effort for mastery of the strain trauma in the old object relations as the "stuff" that functions as the primary motive force in the domain of object relations.

Our treatment approach emphasizes mastery over the affective domain as it relates to parental figures. The mastery is conceptualized here on the plane of actual transactions, but it is thought to occur in the representational level as well. The interactional and intrapsychic spheres are seen as interrelated and not necessarily isomorphic with one another. The therapeutic task is to help the patient develop a new *template* for relating to his or her parent, a template that may not necessarily fit his or her most pernicious or ideal fantasies, but one that matches and lets in the reality of the familial world, as it is being reconstructed through treatment.

Interactions with the parent that continue to develop without generating negative affective displays or engendering disappointments tend gradually to consolidate more positive attachment bonds, which in turn lead to modifications of the internal working models of attachment. A sense of mastery over painful feelings and trauma gradually develops. Of course, this process is interactional in that the patients with a more receptive attitude and approach to their parents in turn elicit more warmth, attention, affection, or interest from the parents. Repetitive interactions that are basically satisfying or enjoyable will modify and shape this working model for both parties, because affective memories of pleasurable *interactions* are laid down and begin to accumulate. It is the dyadic interaction itself, both with the parent and with the therapist, that is thought to lead to crucial modifications of internal working models.

The Power of Play, Habits, and Rituals

We have found that one of the most effective formulas for therapeutic work with the families of severely disturbed patients occurs when the therapist combines sensitivity with playfulness in the therapeutic work. In disconnected families especially, family members have often forgotten how to play. In the high-intensity family, family members take everything in and absorb all of it in an over-serious, overreactive way. Rituals, play tasks, and new family habits are all effective ways to begin to break up old patterns and develop healthier attachments. A small but predictable ritual between father and son, for example, can create a sense for each that they have a "father-son" relationship—or at least the beginnings of one. Each time it is performed, the ritual reaffirms the growing attachment between the two. Because of the crucial role of rituals and play, priority time is set aside for these tasks, and the individual and family therapists both actively encourage such activities. It is not the frequency or the duration of the event that is important, but the meaning of the event for the participants.

The intergenerational interviews are a prerequisite for assigning play tasks. Without the information gleaned from the intergenerational interviews, the therapist is likely to miss the target with the family because of a failure to grasp the central dynamics that prevent parent and child from having a decent time together.

The essential elements for the play-task assignments are that they be brief, low-intensity, mutually enjoyable activities that are free of discussion about the relationship. The therapist may suggest, for example, that the parent and the patient go for an hour-long walk. The mother of one teenaged girl had a makeup lesson session with her daughter. A simple excursion into the community, such as getting bagels and coffee, for example, can have very profound meaning for a mother and daughter who cannot stop fighting and arguing. The therapist reminds the two people that they must not talk about their relationship or about family problems.

Once the initial two or three "play dates" have occurred and no major problems have arisen, the therapist can lengthen the time that family members spend together or expand the activities so that they are more intense or more stressful. Typically, the attachment between parent and child starts to deepen at this point, because the dyadic relationship is gradually being strengthened.

Alternatively, the therapist may decide that turning the task into a regular ritual may be beneficial. A mother and son might start meeting for lunch every other week. Or a father and son might wash cars together each Sunday. In this case, the brief but highly predictable, regular, and pleasant activity begins to breed a kind of familiarity, tolerance, and growing fondness between parent and child.

At this point in the treatment the therapist assesses further problematic issues and makes recommendations about additional work, if any, that may be necessary. We have found that once the positive attachment begins to take hold in the parent and child, it tends to stabilize and develop on its own, without much intervention by the therapist. Often the therapist's role becomes that of a consultant, helping the family decide what, if any other problems, they would like to confront next. Families often begin to work on communication problems, issues around roles and boundaries, or problem-solving skills at this point. Such treatment goals are much easier to address when the underlying bitterness, resentment, and disappointment stemming from disturbed attachments have been diminished or resolved.

How Does Intergenerational Interviewing Lead to Change in the Family?

In the preceding case examples, we illustrated that disturbed attachment appears to go hand in hand with the individual's inability to integrate, modulate, or tolerate negative affects in their internal working models or representations of significant family members. Mary Main and colleagues (Main et al., 1985) have found that in insecurely attached individuals, discrepancies appear between the semantic and episodic attachment memories. This means that, for example, individuals assessed as dismissing of attachment appear to simultaneously hold two contradictory internal working models of attachment figures: the dominant (semantic) model, characterized by rigid idealization of the parents; and another model, characterized by episodic—but defensively dissociated or repressed—memories of rejection, abuse, or neglect by the parental objects.

Such was the case, for example, with Ms. Stein, who held to a rigidly idealized description of her mother, but who was clearly living out her own experiences of maternal rejection and neglect with her own daughter. Main and colleagues' (1985) research with the Adult Attachment Interview has shown that when higher-level generalized or semantic representations are discrepant with lower-level representations based on events, the individual can sometimes recall negative or rejecting attachment-related events, but be unable to experience the associated affects of pain and anger. Or conversely, the original generalized negative attachment experiences will be repressed altogether, so that the individual has limited access to attachment-related information. Such was the case with Brian's father, Mr. James, whose own early experiences of neglect and abuse by an alcoholic father had led him to be dismissive and contemptuous of his son's attachment yearnings.

One of the primary goals of the intergenerational family interview is to break through such maladaptive defensive patterns and find ways to reintegrate and metabolize negative affects based on past attachment experiences so that their pernicious impact on internal working models across the generations will be curtailed. The method of family treatment we have outlined gives primacy to assessment and revision of internal working models of attachment across generations, and it offers technical guidelines for targeting attachment representations within the family context. Our empirically based family typology and model of family treatment are unique in highlighting the significance of the multigenerational array of internal working models of attachment for ongoing family transactions.

Recently, a number of treatment models have been developed from a variety of theoretical perspectives, including psychoanalytic and cognitive-behavioral models, which are designed to effect relational changes through an analysis of representational structures (e.g., Sperling & Lyons, 1993). However, with few exceptions (Byng-Hall, 1991; Heard, 1982; Reiss, 1989) the significance of attachment representations for family treatment has been overlooked. In extending treatment designed to target and modify the representational world directly into the family arena, our model has contributed to the growing body of therapies designed specifically to precipitate shifts in internalized images of self and significant others. Some of these therapies have been shown empirically to be effective catalysts for change in intrapsychic and relational patterns (Cramer et al., 1990; Sperling & Lyons, 1994; Stern-Bruschweiler & Stern, 1989).

Although we have not yet conducted outcome studies based on our model of treatment, our clinical observations and experiences of supervising trainees in this model indicate that the technique of targeting the multigenerational attachment representations in the family, often in conjunction with intensive individual therapy, produces enduring individual and systemic changes. Until recently, attachment theorists (Bowlby, 1988; Main et al., 1985) have hypothesized that internal working models become consolidated in the first 3 years of life and then remain stable until the advent in adolescence of formal operations, which involves the capacity to recognize, reflect on, and thus potentially reorganize one's abstract thought processes, meaning systems, and sense of reality. However, Inge Bretherton (1990) has recently acknowledged that in addition to the acquisition of formal operations, change in internal working models may require a period of heightened emotional experience. Bretherton and other attachment theorists fail to articulate what aspects of such an emotional experience might facilitate transformation of internal working models, or what the mechanisms of new internalizations might involve. Nevertheless, the attachment literature provides many examples of dramatic shifts in attachment patterns in children after catastrophic family events (Main & Hesse, 1990), in women undergoing the transition to motherhood (Fonagy, Steele, & Steele, 1991), and in new mothers after a brief course of psychotherapy designed to target maladaptive mother-child interactional patterns (Cramer et al., 1990).

Our clinical experience suggests that family therapy that gives primacy to intergenerational interviewing provides such an arena of heightened emotional experience where attachment representations may be brought to awareness, articulated, explored, and reconfigured according to new and more mutually gratifying parent-child relational patterns, which may be established in such family sessions. Several aspects of intergenerational interviewing contribute to such a reconfiguration of parent-child attachment. First, such interviews afford both the parent and the child an opportunity to understand the ways in which aspects of the parents' attachment representations may have shaped their fantasies and attitudes about their child, and hence have contributed to shaping the child's behavior, personality, and attachment representations. Second, the mutual disclosure involved in such interviews provides a window for the parent and the child into the internal world of the other, and hence provides an opportunity for the inner mental life of both parent and child to penetrate and influence each other in mutually beneficial, rather than maladaptive, ways. Further, the moments of interface between the internal worlds of parent and child created in intergenerational interviewing deepen the capacities of both participants for intersubjective relatedness. Stern (1989) hypothesizes that in the course of development, the "complexion of the infant's growing internal representations or object world will be largely determined by which self-experiences are communed with and thus supported, and which are under parental pressure to be altered in one way or another. Also the infant's sense of self as 'reflected' by the parents will be shaped by the history of past and present attunements and misattunements" (p. 12). Intergenerational interviewing, then, offers a developmental opportunity for both the parent and the child to discover and reconfigure aspects of their own internal representational world of attachments and to explore how their own attachment histories converge or diverge. Such affectively laden exchanges may lead to a deepened capacity for intersubjective relatedness, which in turn may catalyze shifts in attachment representations.

Narrative construction—that is, the opportunity to recreate a life story or life stories of significant family members in ways that are coherent, consistent, and comprehensible, rather than fragmented, incoherent, and obfuscating—further contributes to the changes in both the intrapsychic and interactional arenas that are wrought by intergenerational interviews. Family treatment that is organized around understanding and exploring multigenerational attachment representations and narratives about those representations offers the opportunity to construct and reconstruct relational patterns and the representations of those patterns. Given this focus, our model of treatment converges with the hermeneutic-narrative model (Schafer, 1980; Spence, 1976; Stern-Bruschweiler & Stern, 1989), which stipulates that historical and objective truth attains meaning primarily through narrative construction. In reconstructing their own individual and family history narratives, families may become generative partners in the interplay of attachment representations and attachment behaviors that shape the generations, rather than static players destined to reenact and recreate a chain of disturbed attachment histories from one generation to the next.

References

Aber, L. S., & Slade, A. (1987, January). *Attachment theory and research: A framework for clinical interventions.* Paper presented at a regional scientific meeting of Childhood and Adolescence Division for Psychoanalysis of the American Psychological Association, New York.

Ainsworth, M. D. S., Blehar, M. C., Waters, E., & Wall, S. (1978). *Patterns of attachment: A psychological study of the strange situation.* Hillsdale, NJ: Erlbaum.

Albers, L. J., Doane, J. A., & Mintz, J. (1986). Social competence and family environment: 15-year follow-up of disturbed adolescents. *Family Process, 25,* 379–389.

American Psychiatric Association. (1987). *Diagnostic and statistical manual of mental disorders* (3rd ed., rev.). Washington, D.C.: American Psychiatric Association.

Armsden, G. C. & Greenberg, M. T. (1987). The inventory of parent and peer attachment: Individual differences and their relationship to psychological well-being in adolescence. *Journal of Youth and Adolescence,* 427–454.

Armsden, G. C., McCauley, E., Greenberg, M. T., Burke, P. M., & Mitchell, J. R. (1990). Parent and peer attachment in early adolescent depression. *Journal of Abnormal Child Psychology, 18,* 683–697.

Bates, J. E., Maslin, C. A., & Frankel, K. A. (1985). Attachment security, mother-child interaction, and temperament as predictors of behavior-problem ratings at age three years. In I. Bretherton, & E. Waters (Eds.), Growing points in attachment: Theory and research. *Monographs of the Society for Research in Child Development, 50*(1–2, Serial No. 209), 167–193.

Bauer, W. D., & Twentyman, C. T. (1985). Abusing, neglectful, and comparison of mothers' responses to child-related and non-child-related stressors. *Journal of Consulting and Clinical Psychology, 53,* 335–343.

Beavers, W. R., & Voeller, M. N. (1983). Family models: Comparing and contrasting the Olsen circumplex model with the Beavers systems model. *Family Process, 22,* 85–97.

Behrends, R., & Blatt, S. J. (1985). Internalization and psychological development throught the life cycle. *The psychoanalytic Study of the Child, 40,* 11–39.

Belsky, J., Rovine, M., & Taylor, D. G. (1984). The Pennsylvania infant and family development project III: The origins of individual differences in infant-mother attachment: Maternal and infant contributions. *Child Development, 55,* 718–728.

Blatt, S. J. (1991). A cognitive morphology of psychopathology. *Journal of Nervous and Mental Disease, 179,* 449–458.

Blatt, S. J. (in press). Representational structures in psychopathology. In D. Cicchetti & S. Toth (Eds.), *Representation, emotion and cognition in developmental psychopathology.* Rochester, NY: University of Rochester Press.

Blatt, S. J., & Behrends, R. S. (1987). Separation- individuation, internalization and the nature of therapeutic action. *International Journal of Psychoanalysis, 68,* 279–297.

Blatt, S. J., & Homann, E. (1992). Parent-child interaction in the etiology of depression. *Clinical Psychology Review, 12,* 47–91.

Boszormenyi-Nagy, I., & Framo, J. L. (Eds.). (1965). *Intensive family therapy.* New York: Harper & Row Medical Department. (Reprinted [1985]. New York: Brunner/Mazel)

Boszormenyi-Nagy, I., & Spark, G. M. (1973). *Invisible loyalties.* New York: Harper & Row Medical Department. (Reprinted [1984]. New York: Brunner/Mazel)

Bowen, M. (1978). *Family therapy in clinical practice.* New York: Aronson.

Bowlby, J. (1969). *Attachment and loss: Vol. 1. Attachment.* New York: Basic Books.

Bowlby, J. (1973). *Attachment and loss: Vol. 2. Separation.* New York: Basic Books.

Bowlby, J. (1977). The making and breaking of affectional bonds. I. Etiology and psychopathology in the light of attachment theory. *British Journal of Psychiatry, 30,* 201–210.

Bowlby, J. (1979). *The making and breaking of affectional bonds.* New York: Methuen.

Bowlby, J. (1980). *Attachment and loss: Vol. 3. Loss, sadness and depression.* New York: Basic Books.

Bowlby, J. (1988). *A secure base.* New York: Basic Books.

Bretherton, I. (1985). Attachment theory: Retrospect and prospect. In I. Bretherton, & E. Waters (Eds.), Growing points in attachment: Theory and research. *Monographs of the Society for Research in Child Development, 50*(1–2, Serial No. 209), 3–34.

Bretherton, I. (1987). New perspectives on attachment relations: Security, communication and internal working models. In J. D. Osofsky (Ed.), *Handbook of infant development* (2nd ed.) (pp. 1061–1100). New York: Wiley.

Bretherton, I. (1990). Communication patterns, internal working models, and the intergenerational transmission of attachment relationships. *Infant Mental Health Journal, 11,* 237–252.

Brown, G. W., Birley, J. L. T., & Wing, J. K. (1972). Influence of family life on the course of schizophrenic disorders: A replication. *British Journal of Psychiatry, 121,* 241–258.

Brown, G. W., Carstairs, G. M., & Topping, G. G. (1958). Post-hospital adjustment of chronic mental patients. *Lancet, 2,* 685–689.

Byng-Hall, J. (1988). Scripts and legends in families and family therapy. *Family Process, 27,* 167–179.

Byng-Hall, J. (1991). The application of attachment theory to understanding and treatment in family therapy. In C. M. Parkes, J. Stevenson-Hinde, & P. Marris (Eds.), *Attachment across the life cycle* (pp. 199–215). New York: Routledge.

Carlson, V., Cicchetti, D., Barnett, D., & Braunwald, K. (1989). Finding order in disorganization: Lessons from research in maltreated infants' attachments to their caregivers. In D. Cicchetti & V. Carlson (Eds.), *Child maltreatment: Theory and research on the causes and consequences of child abuse and neglect* (pp. 494–528). New York: Cambridge University Press.

Cassidy, J. (1988). Child-mother attachment and the self in 6 year olds. *Child Development, 59,* 121–134.

Cassidy, J. (in press). Emotion regulation: Influences of attachment relationships. In N. Fox (Ed.), Biological and behavioral foundations of emotional regulation. *Monographs of the Society for Research in Child Development.*

Cassidy, J., & Berlin, L. J. (in press). The insecure/ambivalent pattern of attachment: Theory and research. *Child Development.*

Cole, H. E. (1991). *Worrying about parents: The link between preoccupied attachment and depression.* Paper presented at the biennial meeting of the Society for Research in Child Development, Seattle, WA.

Cramer, B., Christiane, R. T., Stern, D. N., Serpa-Rusconi, S., Muralt, M., Besson, G., Palacio-Espase, F., Bachmann, J. P., Knauer, D., Berney, C., D'Arcis, U. (1990). Outcome evaluation in brief mother-infant psychotherapy: A preliminary report. *Infant Mental Health Journal, 11,* 278–300.

Crittenden, P. M. (1985). Maltreated infants: Vulnerability and resilience. *Journal of Child Psychology and Psychiatry, 26,* 85–96.

Crittenden, P. M. (1987). Relationships at risk. In J. Belsky & T. Negworski (Eds.), *Clinical implications of attachment* (pp. 136–176). Hillsdale, NJ: Erlbaum.

Day, R. (1982). Research on the course and outcome of schizophrenia in traditional cultures: Some potential implications for psychiatry in the developed countries. In M. J. Goldstein (Ed.), *Preventive intervention in schizophrenia: Are we ready?* Washington, D.C.: U.S. Government Printing Office.

Diamond, D. (1986a). *Attachment and separation-individuation.* Unpublished coding manual, Yale University, New Haven.

Diamond, D. (1986b). Intergenerational family attachment, bonding, and separation-individuation interview schedule, Yale University, New Haven. Unpublished interview schedules.

Diamond, D., & Blatt, S. J. (1994). Internal working models of attachment and psychoanalytic theories of the representational world: A comparison and critique. In M. B. Sperling & W. Berman (Eds.), *Attachment in adults: Clinical and developmental perspectives* (pp. 72–97). New York: Guilford.

Diamond, D., Blatt, S. J., Stayner, D., & Kaslow, N. (1992). *Differentiation-relatedness scale of self and object representations.* Unpublished manuscript, Yale University, New Haven.

Diamond, D., & Doane, J. A. (in press). Disturbed attachment and negative affective style: An intergenerational spiral. *British Journal of Psychiatry, 164.*

Doane, J. A. (1978). Family interaction and communication deviance in disturbed and normal families: A review of research. *Family Process, 17,* 357–376.

Doane, J. A., & Becher, D. F. (in press). Changes in family emotional climate and course of psychiatric illness in hospitalized young adults and adolescents. *New Trends in Experimental and Clinical Psychiatry.*

Doane, J. A. Goldstein, M. J., Falloon, I. R. H., & Mintz, J. (1985). Parental affective style and the treatment of schizophrenia: Predicting course of illness and social functioning. *Archives of General Psychiatry, 42,* 34–42.

Doane, J. A., Goldstein, M. J., Miklowitz, D., & Falloon, I. R. H. (1986). The impact of individual and family treatment on the affective climate of families of schizophrenics. *British Journal of Psychiatry, 148,* 279–287.

Doane, J. A., Hill, W. L., & Diamond, D. (1991). A developmental view of therapeutic bonding in the family: Treatment of the disconnected family. *Family Process, 30,* 155–175.

Doane, J. A., Hill, L. W., Kaslow, N., & Quinlan, D. (1988). Family systems functioning: Behavior in the laboratory and the family treatment setting. *Family Process, 27(2),* 213–227.

Doane, J. A., Johnston, R., & Becker, D. (1989). *The New Haven Recovery Index (NRI) coding manual.* Unpublished coding manual, Yale University, New Haven.

Doane, J. A., West, K. L., Goldstein, M. J., Rodnick, E. M., & Jones, J. E. (1981). Parental communication deviance and affective style—Predictors of subsequent schizophrenia-spectrum disorders in vulnerable adolescents. *Archives of General Psychiatry, 38,* 679–685.

Dozier, M. (1990). Attachment organization and treatment use for adults with serious psychopathological disorders. *Development and Psychopathology, 2,* 47–60.

Dozier, M., Stevenson, A. L., Lee, S. W., & Velligan, D. I. (1991). Attachment organization and familial overinvolvement for adults with serious psychopathological disorders. *Development and Psychopathology, 3,* 475–489.

Egeland, B., & Farber, E. A. (1984). Infant-mother attachment: Factors related to its development and changes over time. *Child Development, 55,* 753–771.

Emde, R. N. (1983). The affective self: Continuities and transformations from infancy. In J. B. Call, E. Galenson, & R. L. Tyson (Eds.), *Frontiers of infant psychiatry.* New York: Basic Books (pp. 38–54).

Emde, R. N. (1983). The prerepresentational self and its affective core. *The Psychoanalytic Study of the Child, 38,* 165–192.

Emde, R. N., Gaensbauer, T., & Harmon, R. (1976). Emotional expression in infancy: A biobehavioral study. [Monograph 37]. *Psychological Issues, 10.*

Falloon, I. R. H., Boyd, J. L., & McGill, C. W. (1984). *A problem-solving approach to the treatment of mental illness.* New York: Guilford.

Falloon, I. R. H., Boyd, J. L., McGill, C. W., Razani, J., Moss, H. B., & Gilderman, A. M. (1982). Family management in the prevention of exacerbations of schizophrenia: A controlled study. *New England Journal of Medicine, 306,* 161–164.

Falloon, I. R. H., Boyd, J. L., McGill, C. W., Williamson, M., Razani, J., Moss, H. B., Gilderman, A. M., & Simpson, G. M. (1985). Family management in the prevention of morbidity of schizophrenia: Clinical outcome of a two-year longitudinal study. *Archives of General Psychiatry, 42,* 887–896.

Fischmann-Havstad, L., & Marsden, A. R. (1984). Weight loss maintenance as an aspect of family emotion and process. *British Journal of Clinical Psychology, 23,* 265–271.

Fonagy, P., Steele, M., & Steele, M. (1991). Maternal representations of attachment during pregnancy predict the organization of infant-mother attachment at one year of age. *Child Development, 62,* 891–905.

Fonagy, P., Steele, M., Moran, G., Steele, H., & Higgitt, A. (1991). Measuring the ghost in the nursery: A summary of the main findings of the Anna Freud Center–University College London Parent-Child Study. *Bulletin of the Anna Freud Center, 14,* 115–131.

Fonagy, P., Steele, M., Steele, H., Moran, G., & Higgitt, A. (1991). The capacity for understanding mental states: The reflective self in parent and child and its significance for security of attachment. *Infant Mental Health Journal, 13,* 200–217.

Framo, J. L. (1992). *Family-of-origin therapy: An intergenerational approach.* New York: Brunner/Mazel.

Freud, S. (1955). Beyond the pleasure principle. In J. Strachey (Ed. & Trans.), *The standard edition of the complete psychological works of Sigmund Freud,* (Vol. 18, pp. 3–64). London: Hogarth Press. (Original work published 1920)

George, C., Kaplan, N., & Main, M. (1985). *The Berkeley Adult Attachment Interview.* Unpublished manuscript, Department of Psychology, University of California, Berkeley.

George, C., & Solomon, J. (1989). Internal working models of parenting and security of attachment at age six. *Infant Mental Health Journal, 10,* 222–237.

George, C., & Solomon, J. (1991). *Intergenerational transmission of the family system: Children's representations of the family in doll play.* Paper presented at the biennial meeting of the Society for Research in Child Development, Seattle, WA.

Goldstein, M. J. (1985). Family factors that antedate the onset of schizophrenia and related disorders: The results of a fifteen-year prospective longitudinal study. *Acta Psychiatrica Scandinavia, 71,* 7–18.

Goldstein, M. J., Rodnick, E. R., Evans, J. R., May, P. R., & Steinberg, M. R. (1978). Drug and family therapy in the aftercare of acute schizophrenics. *Archives of General Psychiatry, 35,* 1169–1177.

Greenberg, J., & Mitchell, S. (1983). *Object relations in psychoanalytic theory.* Cambridge, MA: Harvard University Press.

Grossmann, K., Fremmer-Bombik, E., Rudolph, J., & Grossmann, K. E. (1988). Maternal attachment representation as related to patterns of mother-infant attachment and maternal care during the first year. In R. A. Hinde & J. Stevenson-Hinde (Eds.), *Relationships within families: Mutual influences* (pp. 241–260). Oxford: Clarendon Press.

Grossmann, K., Grossmann, K. E., Spangler, G., Suess, G., & Unzner, L. (1985). Maternal sensitivity and newborns' orientation responses as related to quality of attachment in northern Germany. In I. Bretherton & E. Waters (Eds.), Growing points in attachment: Theory and research. *Monographs of the Society for Research in Child Development, 50,* (1–2, Serial No. 209), 233–256.

Haft, W., & Slade, A. (1989). Affect attunement and maternal attachment: A pilot study. *Infant Mental Health Journal, 10*(3), 157–172.

Heard, D. (1982). Family systems and the attachment dynamic. *Journal of Family Therapy, 4,* 99–116.

Heresco-Levy, U., Greenberg, D., & Dasberg, H. (1990). *Israel Journal of Psychiatry and Related Sciences, 27*(4), 205–215.

Hogarty, G. E., Anderson, C. M., Reiss, D. J., Kornblith, S. J., Greenwald, D. P., Javna, C. D, & Madonia, M. J. (1986). Family psychoeducation, social skills training, and maintenance chemotherapy in the aftercare treatment of schizophrenia: I. One-year effects of a controlled study on relapse and expressed emotion. *Archives of General Psychiatry, 43,* 633–642.

Hooley, J. M. (1985). Expressed emotion: A review of the critical literature. *Clinical Psychology Review, 5*(2), 119–139.

Hooley, J. M. (1987). The nature and origins of expressed emotion. In M. J. Goldstein, & K. Halweg (Eds.), *Understanding major mental disorder: The contributions of family interaction research* (pp. 176–194). New York: Family Process Press.

Hooley, J. M., & Hahlweg, K. (1983). Patterns of interaction in high and low expressed emotion dyads. In M. J. Goldstein, I. Hand, & K. Hahlweg (Eds.), *Treatment of schizophrenia* (pp. 85–96). Berlin: Springer.

Hooley, J. M., Orley, J., & Teasdale, J. D. (1986). Levels of expressed emotion and relapse in depressed patients. *British Journal of Psychiatry, 148,* 642–647.

Hooley, J. M., Rosen, L. R., Richters, J. E. (in press). Expressed emotion: Towards a clarification of a critical construct. In G. A. Miller (Ed.), *The behavioral high-risk paradigm in psychopathology.* New York: Springer Verlag.

Hooley, J. M., & Teasdale, J. D. (1989). Predictors of relapse in unipolar depressives: Expressed emotion, marital quality and perceived criticism. *Journal of Abnormal Psychology, 98,* 229–235.

Hughes, S. O., Francis, D. J., & Power, T. G. (1989). *The impact of attachment on adolescent alcohol use.* Paper presented at the biennial meeting of the Society for Research in Child Development, Kansas City.

Invernizzi, G., Bressi, C., Bertrando, P., Passerini, A. (1991). Emotional profiles of patients with heart operated patients: A pilot study. *Psychotherapy and Psychosomatics, 55*(1), 1–8.

Isabella, R., & Belsky, J. (1991). Interactional synchrony and the origins of mother-infant attachment: A replication study. *Child Development, 62,* 373–384.

Isabella, R., Belsky, J., & von Eyre, A. (1989). Origins of mother-infant attachment: An examination of interactional synchrony during the infant's first year. *Developmental Psychology, 25,* 12–21.

Izard, C. E. (1978). On the ontogenesis of emotions and emotion-cognition relationships in infancy. In M. Lewis & L. A. Rosenblum (Eds.), *The development of affect* (pp. 389–413). New York: Plenum.

Jacobson, E. (1964). *The self and the object world.* New York: International Universities Press.

Johnson, A. M., & Szurek, S. A. (1952). The genesis of anti-social acting out in children and adults. *Psychoanalytic Quarterly, 21,* 323–343.

Karno, M., Jenkins, J. H., de la Selva, A., Santana, F., Telles, C., Lopez, S., & Mintz, J. (1987). Expressed emotion and schizophrenia outcome among Mexican-American families. *Journal of Nervous and Mental Disease, 175*(3), 143–151.

Kernberg, O. (1980). *Internal world and external reality.* New York: Jason Aronson.

Kernberg, O. (1990). New perspectives in psychoanalytic affect theory. In R. Plutchik & H. Kellerman (Eds.), *Emotion: Theory, research and experience* (Vol. 5, pp. 115–130). New York: Academic Press.

Kernberg, O. (in press). Psychoanalytic object relations theories. In B. E. Moore & B. Fine (Eds.), *Psychoanalysis: The major concepts.*

Kobak, R. R., & Sceery, A. (1988). Attachment in later adolescence: Working models affect regulation and representations of self and others. *Child Development, 59,* 135–146.

Kobak, R. R., Sudler, N., & Gamble, W. (1991). Attachment and depressive symptoms during adolescence: A developmental pathways analysis. *Development and Psychopathology, 3,* 461–474.

Koenigsberg, H. W., Klausner, E., Pelino, D., Rosnick, P., & Campbell, R. (in press). Extending the expressed emotion construct: EE and glucose control in insulin-dependent diabetes mellitus. *American Journal of Psychiatry.*

Kriesman, D. E., Simmens, S. J., & Joy, V. D. (1979). Rejecting the patient: Preliminary validation of a self-report scale. *Schizophrenia Bulletin, 5,* 220–222.

Kropp, J. P., & Haynes, O. M. (1987). Abusive and nonabusive mothers' ability to identify general and specific emotional signals of infants. *Child Development, 58,* 187–190.

Kuipers, L., & Bebbington, P. (1988). Expressed emotion research in schizophrenia: Theoretical and clinical considerations. *Psychological Medicine, 18,* 893–909.

Kwakman, A. M., Zuiker, F. A. J. M., Schippers, G. M., & deWuffel, F. J. (1988). Drinking behavior, drinking attitudes, and attachment relationships of adolescents. *Journal of Youth and Adolescence, 17,* 247–253.

LaFreniere, P. J., & Stroufe, L. A. (1985). Profiles of peer competence in the preschool: Interrelations between measures of influences of social ecology and relation to attachment history. *Developmental Psychology, 21,* 56–66.

Lamb, M. E., Thompson, R. A., Gardner, W., & Charnow, E. L. (1985). *Infant-mother attachment: The origins and developmental significance of individual differences in strange situation behavior.* Hillsdale, N.J.: Erlbaum.

Leff, J., Kuipers, L., Berkowitz, R., & Sturgeon, D. (1985). A controlled trial of social intervention in the families of schizophrenia patients: Two-year follow-up. *British Journal of Psychiatry, 146,* 594–600.

Leff, J., & Vaughn, C. (1981). The role of maintenance therapy and relatives' expressed emotion in relapse of schizophrenia: A two-year follow-up. *British Journal of Psychiatry, 139,* 102–104.

Leff, J., & Vaughn, C. (1985). *Expressed emotion in families.* New York: Guilford.

Leff, J., Wig, N. N., Ghosh, A., Menon, D. K., Kuipers, L., Korten, A., Ernberg, G., Day, R., Sartorius, N., & Jablensky, A. (1987). Expressed emotion and schizophrenia in North India: III. Influence of relatives' expressed emotion on the course of schizophrenia in Chandigarh. *British Journal of Psychiatry, 151,* 166–173.

Lefley, H. P. (1985). Families of the mentally ill in cross-cultural perspective. *Psychosocial Rehabilitation Journal, 8*(4), 57–75.

Levine, I., & Wilson, A. (1985). Dynamic interpersonal processes and the inpatient holding environment. *Psychiatry, 48,* 341–357.

Lewis, J. M., Beavers, W. R., Gossett, J. T., & Phillips, V. A. (1976). *No single thread: Psychological health in family systems.* New York: Brunner/Mazel.

Lewis, M., & Feiring, C. (1989). Infant, mother, and mother-infant behavior and subsequent attachment. *Child Development, 60,* 831–837.

Lidz, T. (1985). Social factors and maintenance neuroleptics in schizophrenic relapse: An integrative model: Commentary. *Integrative Psychiatry, 3*(2), 82–83.

Lidz, T. (1992). *The relevance of the family to psychoanalytic theory.* New York: International Universities Press.

Lidz, T., Fleck, S., & Corneilson, A. (1971). *Schizophrenia and the family* (2nd ed.). New York: International Universities Press.

Loranger, A. W., Susman, V. L., Oldham, J. M., & Russakoff, L. M. (1987). The personality disorder examination: A preliminary report. *Journal of Personality Disorders, 1*(1), 1–13.

Lyons, R. K., Connell, D., Zoll, D., & Stahl, J. (1987). Infants at risk: Relations among infant maltreatment, maternal behavior and infant attachment behavior. *Developmental Psychology, 23,* 223–232.

MacMillan, J. F., Gold, A., Crow, T. J., Johnson, A. L., & Johnstone, E. C. (1986). The Northwick Park study of first episodes of schizophrenia: IV. Expressed emotion and relapse. *British Journal of Psychiatry, 148,* 133–143.

Mahler, M., Pine, F., & Bergman, A. (1975). *The psychological birth of the human infant.* New York: Basic Books.

Main, M., & Cassidy, J. (1988). Categories of response with the parent at age six: Predicted from infant attachment classifications and stable over a one-month period. *Developmental Psychology, 24,* 415–426.

Main, M., & Goldwyn, R. (1984). Predicting rejection of her infant from mother's representation of her own experience: Implications for abused-abusing intergenerational cycle. *Child Abuse and Neglect, 8,* 208–217.

Main, M., & Goldwyn, R. (in press). Interview-based adult attachment classifications: Related to infant-mother and infant-father attachment. *Developmental Psychology*.

Main, M., & Hesse, E. (1990). Parents' unresolved traumatic experiences are related to infant disorganized attachment status: Is frightened and/or frightening parental behavior the linking mechanism? In M. T. Greenberg, D. Cicchetti, & E. M. Cummings (Eds.), *Attachment in the preschool years* (pp. 161–185). Chicago: University of Chicago Press.

Main, M., Kaplan, N., & Cassidy, J. (1985). Security in infancy, childhood and adulthood: A move to the level of representation. In I. Bretherton, & E. Waters (Eds.), Growing points of attachment: Theory and research. *Monographs of the Society for Research in Child Development, 50*(1–2, Serial No. 209), 66–104.

Main, M., & Solomon, J. (1986). Discovery of a new, insecure-disorganized/disoriented attachment pattern. In T. B. Brazelton & M. Yogman (Eds)., *Affective development in infancy* (pp. 95–124). Norwood, N.J.: Ablex.

Main, M., & Solomon, J. (1990). Procedures for identifying infants disorganized/disoriented during the Ainsworth Strange Situation. In M. T. Greenberg, D. Cicchetti, & E. M. Cummings (Eds.), *Attachment in the preschool years* (pp. 121–161). Chicago: University of Chicago Press.

Main, M., & Stadtman, J. (1981). Infant responses to rejection of physical contact by the mother: Aggression, avoidance and conflict. *Journal of the American Academy of Child Psychiatry, 2,* 292–307.

Main, M., & Weston, D. (1981). The quality of the toddler's relationship to mother and father. *Child Development, 52,* 923–940.

Malestesta, C. Z., Culver, C., Tesman, J. R. G., Shephard, B. (1989). The development of emotional expression during the first two years of life. In I. Bretherton, & E. Waters (Eds.), Growing points of attachment: Theory and research. *Monographs of the Society for Research in Child Development, 54*(1–2, Serial No. 219).

McGlashan, T. H. (1986). Chestnut Lodge follow-up study, III: Long-term outcome of borderline personalities. *Archives of General Psychiatry, 43,* 20–30.

Miklowitz, D. J., Goldstein, M. J., & Falloon, I. R. H. (1983). Premorbid and symptomatic characteristics of schizophrenics from families with high and low levels of expressed emotion. *Journal of Abnormal Psychology, 92,* 359–367.

Miklowitz, D. J., Goldstein, M. J., Falloon, I. R. H., & Doane, J. A. (1984). Interactional correlates of expressed emotion in the families of schizophrenics. *British Journal of Psychiatry, 144,* 482–487.

Miklowitz, D. J., Goldstein, M. J., Nuechterlein, K. M. (1987). The family and the course of recent-onset mania. In K. Hahlweg & M. J. Goldstein (Eds.), *Understanding major mental disorder: The contribution of family interaction research* (pp. 195–211). New York: Family Process Press.

Miklowitz, D. J., Goldstein, M. J., Nuechterlein, K. H., Snyder, K. S., & Mintz, J. (1988). Family factors and the course of bipolar affective disorder. *Archives of General Psychiatry, 45,* 225–231.

Mintz, L., Liberman, R. P., Miklowitz, D. J., & Mintz, J. (1987). Expressed emotion: A call for partnership among relatives, patients, and professionals. *Schizophrenia Bulletin, 13*(2), 227–235.

Miyake, K., Chen, S., & Campos, J. J. (1985). Infant temperament, mother's mode of interaction, and attachment in Japan: An interim report. In I. Bretherton & E. Waters (Eds.), Growing points of attachment: Theory and research. *Monographs of the Society for Research in Child Development, 50*(1–2, Serial No. 209), 276–297.

Olsen, D. H., Sprenkle, D. H., & Russell, C. (1979). Circumplex model of marital and family systems. I. Cohesion and adaptability dimensions, family types and clinical applications. *Family Process, 18*, 3–15.

Orvaschel, H., & Puig-Antich, J. (1987). A schedule for affective disorders and schizophrenia for school-age children. Epidemiologic version, kiddie-SADS-E. Philadelphia: Western Psychiatric Institute.

Overall, J. E., & Gorham, D. R. (1962). The Brief Psychiatric Rating Scale (BPRS). *Psychological Reports, 10*, 799–812.

Palazzoli, M. S. (1992). Identifying the various recurring processes in the family that lead to schizophrenia in an offspring. In J. K. Zeig (Ed.), *The evolution of psychotherapy* (pp. 66–73). New York: Brunner/Mazel.

Parker, G. (1979). Parental characteristics in relation to depressive disorders. *British Journal of Psychiatry, 134*, 138–147.

Parker, G. (1981). Parental reports of depressives: An investigation of several explanations. *Journal of Affective Disorders, 3*, 131–140.

Parker, G. (1983). Parental 'affectionless control' as an antecedent to adult depression: A risk factor delineated. *Archives of General Psychiatry, 40*, 956–960.

Parker, G., Fairley, M., Greenwood, J., Jurd, A., & Splove, D. (1982). Parental representations of schizophrenics and their association with onset and course of schizophrenia. *British Journal of Psychiatry, 141*, 575–581.

Parker, G., & Johnson, P. (1987). Parenting and schizophrenia: An Australian study of expressed emotion. *Australian and New Zealand Journal of Psychiatry, 21*(1), 60–66.

Parker, G., Johnston, P., & Hayward, L. (1988). Parental "expressed emotion" as a predictor of schizophrenic relapse. *Archives of General Psychiatry, 45*, 806–813.

Parker, G., Tuppling, H., & Braun, L. B. (1979). A parental bonding instrument. *British Journal of Medical Psychology, 52*, 1–10.

Pine, F. (1989). Motivation, personality organization, and the four psychologies of psychoanalysis. *Journal of the American Psychoanalytic Association, 37*, 31–64.

Platt, S., Weyman, A., Hirsch, S., & Hewett, S. (1980). The Social Behavior Assessment Schedule (SBAS): Rationale, contents, scoring and reliability of a new interview schedule. *Social Psychiatry, 15*, 43–55.

Plutchik, R., & Kellerman, H. (Eds.). (1983). *Emotion: Theory, research and experience: Vol. 2 . Emotions in early development.* New York: Academic Press.

Plutchik, R. (Ed.). (1980). *Emotions: A psychoevolutionary synthesis.* New York: Harper & Row.

Reiss, D. (1989). The represented and practicing family: Contrasting visions of family continuity. In A. Sameroff & R. Emde (Eds.), *Relationship disturbances in early childhood: A developmental approach* (pp. 191–220). New York: Basic Books.

Reiss, D., Costell, R., Jones, C., & Berkman, H. (1980). The family meets the hospital: A laboratory forecast of the encounter. *Archives of General Psychiatry, 34,* 141–154.

Reiss, D., Gonzalez, S., & Kramer, N. (1986). Family process, chronic illness and death: On the weakness of strong bonds. *Archives of General Psychiatry, 43,* 795–804.

Ricks, M. H. (1985). The social transmission of parental behavior: Attachment across generations. In I. Bretherton & E. Waters (Eds.), Growing points in attachment: Theory and research. *Monographs of the Society for Research in Child Development, 49*(6, Serial No. 209), 211–227.

Rosenstein, D. S., & Horowitz, H. A. (1993, March). *Working models of attachment in psychiatrically hospitalized adolescents: Relation to psychopathology and personality.* Paper presented at the biennial meeting of the Society for Research in Child Development, New Orleans.

Sagi, A., Lamb, M. E., Lewkowitz, K. S., Shoham, R., Dvir, R, & Estes, D. (1985). Security of infant-mother, -father, and -metapelet attachments among kibbutz-reared Israeli children. In I. Bretherton, & E. Water (Eds.), Growing points of attachment theory and research. *Monographs of the Society for Research in Child Development, 50*(1–2, Serial No. 209), 257–275.

Sagi, A., Mayseless, O., Aviezer, O., Donnell, F., Harel, Y., Joels, T., & Tuvia, M. (1990, April). Development of mother-infant attachment in traditional and nontraditional kibbutzim. In N. Fox (Chair), *Attachment measured by the strange situation: New directions.* Symposium conducted at the International Conference on Infant Studies, Montreal, Canada.

Sandler, J., & Sandler, A. M. (1978). On the development of object relations and affects. *International Journal of Psychoanalysis, 59,* 285–296.

Schafer, R. (1980). Narration in the psychoanalytic dialogue. *Critical Inquiry, 7,* 29–53.

Scharff, D. E., & Scharff, J. S. (1987). *Object relations family therapy.* New Jersey: Jason Aronson.

Shengold, L. (1989). *Soul murder: The effects of childhood abuse and deprivation.* New Haven: Yale University Press.

Sherman, M. H. (1990). Family narratives: Internal representations of family relationships and affective themes. *Infant Mental Health Journal, 11*(3), 253–258.

Singer, M., & Wynne, L. (1963). Differentiating characteristics of parents of childhood schizophrenics, childhood neurotics, and young adult schizophrenics. *American Journal of Psychiatry, 120,* 234–243.

Singer, M., & Wynne, L. (1965). Thought disorder and family relations of schizophrenics. IV. Results and implications. *Archives of General Psychiatry, 12,* 201–212.

Slade, A. (1993, March 27). Defense, affect regulation, and attachment. Paper presented at the biennial meetings of the Society for Research in Child Development, New Orleans, LA.

Slade, A., & Aber, L. J. (1986, April). *The internal experience of parenting tod-*

dlers: Towards an analysis of individual and developmental differences. Paper presented at the International Conference on Infant Studies, Los Angeles.

Slade, A., & Aber, L. J. (1992). Attachment, drives and development: Conflicts and convergences in theory. In J. Barron, M. Eagle, & D. Wolitsky (Eds.), *Interface of psychoanalysis and psychology* (pp. 154–185). Washington, D.C.: APA Publications.

Slade, A., Director, L., Grunebaum, L., Huganir, L., & Reeves, M.. (1991, April). *Representational and behavioral correlates of prebirth maternal attachment.* Paper presented at the biennial meeting of the Society for Research in Child Development, Seattle, WA.

Slipp, S. (1984). *Object relations: A dynamic bridge between individual and family treatment.* New York: Jason Aronson.

Spence, D. P. (1976). Clinical interpretation: Some comments on the nature of evidence. *Psychoanalysis and Contemporary Science, 5,* 367–388.

Sperling, M. B., & Lyons, L. (1994). Representations of attachment and psychotherapeutic change. In M. B. Sperling & W. H. Berman (Eds.), *Attachment in adults: Clinical and developmental perspectives* (pp. 331–347). New York: Guilford.

Sperling, M., Sharp, J. L., & Fishler, P. H. (1991). On the nature of attachment in a borderline population: A preliminary investigation. *Psychological Reports, 68,* 543–546.

Spitzer, R. L., & Williams, J. B. W. (1985). *Structured Clinical Interview for DSM-III-R—patient version (SCID-P, 5/86).* New York: New York State Psychiatric Institute, Biometrics Research Department.

Sroufe, L. A. (1979). The coherence of individual development. *American Psychologist, 34,* 834–841.

Sroufe, L. A. (1983). Infant-caregiver attachment and patterns of adaptation in preschool: The roots of maladaptations and competence. In M. Permutter (Ed.), *Minnesota symposium in child psychology* (Vol. 16, 41–83). Hillsdale, NJ: Erlbaum.

Sroufe, L. A., Schork, E., Frosso, M., Lawroski, N., & LaFreniere, P. (1984). The role of affect in social competence. In C. Izard, J. Kagan, & R. Zajonc (Eds.), *Emotions, cognitions, and behavior* (pp. 289–319). New York: Cambridge University Press.

Stein, Ruth. (1991). *Psychoanalytic theories of affect.* New York: Praeger.

Steinglass, P., Bennett, L. A., Wolin, S. J., & Reiss, D. (1987). *The alcoholic family.* New York: Basic Books.

Stern, D. N. (1985a). Affective attunement. In J. D. Call, E. Galenson, & R. L. Tyson (Eds.), *Frontiers of infant psychiatry* (Vol. 2, pp. 3–14). New York: Basic Books.

Stern, D. N. (1985b). *The interpersonal world of the infant.* New York: Basic Books.

Stern, D. N. (1988). The dialectic between the "interpersonal" and the "intrapsychic": With particular emphasis on the role of memory and representation. *Psychoanalytic Inquiry, 8,* 503–512.

Stern, D. N. (1989). The representation of relational patterns: Some developmental considerations. In A. Someroff & R. N. Emde (Eds.), *Relationship disorders in early childhood* (pp. 52–69). New York: Basic Books.

Stern, D. N. (1990). *Diary of a baby.* New York: Basic Books.

Stern-Bruschweiler, N., & Stern, D. N. (1989). A model for conceptualizing the role of the mother's representational world in various mother-infant therapies. *Infant Mental Health Journal, 10,* 142–156.

Strachan, A. M., Leff, J. P., Goldstein, M. J., Doane, J. A., & Burrt, (1986). Emotional attitudes and direct communication in the families of schizophrenics: A cross-national replication. *British Journal of Psychiatry, 149,* 279–287.

Stierlin, H. (1974). *Separating parents and adolescents: A perspective on running away, schizophrenia, and waywardness.* New York: Quadrangle.

Stierlin, H. (1977). *Psychoanalysis and family therapy.* New York: Jason Aronson.

Strodtbeck, F. L. (1954). The family as a three-person group. *American Sociological Review, 19,* 23–29.

Szmulkler, G. I., Berkowitz, R., Eisler, I., Leff, J., & Dare, C. (1987). Expressed emotion in individual and family settings: A comparative study. *British Journal of Psychiatry, 152,* 174–178.

Tarrier, N., Barrowclough, C., Vaughn, C. E., Bamrah, J. S., Porceddu, K., Watts, S., & Freeman, H. (1988). The community management of schizophrenia: A controlled trial of a behavioral intervention with families to reduce relapse. *British Journal of Psychiatry, 153,* 532–542.

Terkelsen, K. E. (1984). Response. *Family Process, 23,* 425– 428.

Thompson, W. D., Kidd, J. R., & Weissman, M. M. (1980). A procedure for the efficient collection and processing of pedigree data suitable for genetic analysis. *Journal of Psychiatry Research, 15,* 291–303.

Thompson, W. D., Orvaschel, H., Prusoff, B. A., & Kidd, K. K. (1982). An evaluation of the family history method for ascertaining psychiatric disorders. *Archives of General Psychiatry, 39,* 53–58.

Tienari, P., Sorri, A., Lahti, I., Naarala, M., Moring, J., & Wahlberg, K. E. (1989). The Finnish adoptive family study of schizophrenia: Possible joint effects of genetic vulnerability and family environment. *British Journal of Psychiatry, 155* (Suppl. 5), 29–32.

Tienari, P., Sorri, A., Lahti, I., Naarala, M., Wahlberg, K. E., Ronkko, T., Pohjola, J., & Moring, J. (1985). The Finnish adoptive family study of schizophrenia. *Yale Journal of Biology and Medicine, 58,* 227–237.

Valone, K., Norton, J., Goldstein, M. J., & Doane, J. A. (1983). Parental expressed emotion and affective style in an adolescent sample at risk for schizophrenia-spectrum disorders. *Journal of Abnormal Psychology, 2,* 399–407.

Vaughn, C. E. (1989). Annotation: Expressed emotion in family relationships. *Journal of Child Psychology and Psychiatry, 30*(1), 13–22.

Vaughn, C. E., & Leff, J. P. (1976a). The influence of family and social factors on the course of psychiatric illness. *British Journal of Psychiatry, 129,* 125–137.

Vaughn, C. E., & Leff, J. P. (1976b). The measurement of expressed emotion in the families of psychiatric patients. *British Journal of Social and Clinical Psychology, 15*(2), 157–165.

Vaughn, C. E., Snyder, K. S., Jones, S., Freeman, W., Falloon, I. R. H., & Lieberman, R. P. (1984). Family factors in schizophrenic relapse: Replication in California of British research on expressed emotion. *Archives of General Psychiatry, 41,* 1169–1177.

Waters, E., Wippman, J., & Sroufe, L. A. (1979). Attachment, positive affect, and competence in the peer group: Two studies in construct validation. *Child Development, 50,* 821–829.

Weissman, M. M., Gammon, G. D., Merikangas, K. R., Warner, V., Prusoff, B. A., & Shlomoskas, D. (1987). Children of depressed parents. Increased psychopathology and early onset of major depression. *Archives of General Psychiatry, 44,* 847–853.

Winnicott, D. W. (1960). The theory of the parent-infant relationship. *International Journal of Psychoanalysis, 41,* 585–595.

Wynne, L. (1984). The epigenesis of relational systems: A model for understanding family development. *Family Process, 23*(3), 297–318.

Wynne, L., Singer, M., Bartko, J., & Toohey, M. (1977). Schizophrenics and their families: Recent research on parental communication. In J. M. Tanner (Ed.), *Developments in psychiatric research* (pp. 254–286). London: Hodder & Stoughton.

Zeanah, C., Benoit, D., Hirshberg, L., Barton, M., & Regan, C. (1991, October). *Classifying mothers' representations of their infants: Results from structured interviews.* Paper presented at the annual meeting of the American Academy of Child and Adolescent Psychiatry, San Francisco.

Zeanah, C. H., & Zeanah, P. (1989). Intergenerational transmission of maltreatment: Insights from attachment theory and research. *Psychiatry, 52,* 177–196.

Index